**Three Italian Novelists
Moravia, Pavese, Vittorini**

Three Italian Novelists

Moravia, Pavese, Vittorini

by Donald Heiney

Ann Arbor
The University of Michigan Press

Acknowledgments

Gratitude is due to a number of people who helped with the writing of this book: first of all Elio Vittorini and Alberto Moravia, who were generous with their letters, comments, and advice; Italo Calvino, who provided material from his own resources and from those of Giulio Einaudi Editore; Professors Sergio Perosa, Sergio Pacifici, Giose Rimanelli, and Federico Mancini; Erich Linder of the Agenzia Letteraria Internazionale; Giansiro Ferrata; Miss Cipriana Scelba; and especially Fernanda Pivano, who contributed personal recollections of Pavese that only she could offer.

Assistance for the research that went into this book was supplied by the American Council of Learned Societies and the Humanities Research Institute of the University of California.

Excerpts from this book, in modified form, have appeared in *Contemporary Literature* (Autumn, 1968).

All translations in the text are my own. As a check, however, reference has often been made to the standard translations in English, published chiefly by Farrar, Straus, & Giroux in the case of Moravia, by this publisher and by Noonday Press in the case of Pavese, and by New Directions and Penguin Books in the case of Vittorini.

Declarations and Disclaimers

A great deal has already been written about Moravia, Pavese, and Vittorini. The material already in print, in English alone, ranges from Leslie Fiedler's pioneering article "Introducing Cesare Pavese" (*Kenyon Review*, 16:4) to R.W.B. Lewis' perceptive chapter on Moravia in *The Picaresque Saint* (1959). But these three novelists have not yet been treated at length, in a serious and critical way, and on their own terms; that is, regarding their fiction as fiction and not as a source of social, sexual, or philosophical attitudes or some kind of index to what is happening in Italian society. This book proposes to investigate how these writers work as craftsmen—how they relate to their métier not as political thinkers or anti-fascists or psychologists but as artists. In practice it was not possible to leave out the politics or the rest of it. But the center of the book has remained the creative act by which the novel itself is made: the difficult process of creating a reality out of the raw and unformed material of language.

One of the premises of this study is that the work of any writer worth taking seriously is a developing process—that he learns as he writes and applies what he learns in each new succeeding work. Biographical criticism is out of fashion at the moment, as well it should be, after all the books, and university courses, of a generation ago in which the study of literature was very largely distracted into gossip about the lives of authors. Yet novels do not write themselves; they are written by human beings who have personalities and idiosyncracies, who change as they grow older, who learn from their mistakes and are hardened by their vicissitudes. Another methodological axiom of this book is that it approaches literature from the viewpoint of the author as well as that of the critic or reader; instead of regarding the novel as a finished work of art it attempts to get inside the novelist's mind as he makes it. Why did he utilize one technical device and not another? Are his characters "based on" real people, and what exactly do we mean when we say this? To what extent can we regard a novel as a personal statement in the way that, for example, a sonnet of Keats is a personal statement? These are not the only questions that can be asked about a novel, but they are one way of bringing into focus certain aspects of the work itself. And to deal with such questions we first must know something of the conditions under which the author produced the work and his own emotional and aesthetic relation to it.

In spite of their obvious differences, these three novelists share sufficient qualities to make it worthwhile to consider them together. Above all they share a common respect, not so much for "the novel as an art form"—none of the three is very interested in form or formal questions—but for the novel as a serious and complex means of artistic expression. For them there is no traditional or received form of the novel; each new novel is a complicated mechanism to be simultaneously constructed and mastered. The work of all three has a certain repetitive tendency; the same themes, devices, techniques, recur in successive novels. But, especially in the cases of Pavese and Vittorini, this repetition is no mere coasting on momentum gained. Instead it is a constant and repeated effort to eliminate the imperfections that lie behind, an attempt to create a single novel that will bring to focus a lifetime of application to the craft of fiction. Naturally, the writer always thinks this novel is the one he is writing. But if he is an honest craftsman—and all three of the writers dealt with in this book are—he will recognize the flaws in his completed work and struggle again, like Sisyphus heaving away at a particularly exasperating and formless stone made of words, to write that one ideal novel that is still unexpressed inside him. Artistic creation is often compared with giving birth; it is comparably painful and comparably rewarding. But the mother is usually satisfied with her children, as ugly as they may be, whereas the novelist of the kind we are dealing with is not. His favorite child is not the one just born but the one he is pregnant with. It is out of this discontent, which some poets have had the temerity to call divine, that genuine works of art are made.

The three novelists of this book were young men in the early years of fascism; they emerged to consciousness in a society in which any honest creative impulse tended to be regarded with suspicion by the regime. The effect of totalitarianism on art is a more complex matter than it may seem on the surface. It is necessary to understand the political temper of Italy in the Thirties thoroughly, without oversimplifying it, in order to understand Moravia, Pavese, and Vittorini; and this is not merely because all three were anti-fascists, but because fascism was part of the air they breathed and would have influenced their styles and techniques even if they had never had difficulties with the censorship. Moravia was born in 1907, Pavese and Vittorini in 1908. Thus they grew up under the influence of the highly emotional patriotic rhetoric of the First World War, and they began to write just as this rhetoric was being taken over by fascism to be converted to a fake-Roman bombast for political purposes. Working almost entirely independently, they arrived at narrative techniques that are strikingly similar, chiefly because these techniques developed out of reaction against the same politically oriented rhetoric in the society around them. And this in spite of the fact that they belonged to markedly different social classes: Moravia a product of the bourgeois leisure class, Vittorini a self-educated worker, Pavese an intellectual. As novelists all three are concerned with the problem of vernacular style, that is with the problem of representing the sensations, feelings, and emotions of nonliterary characters through literary techniques. All three are intensely earnest but suspicious of fake-earnestness in literature. There is very little humor in their narrative, but there is irony, and it is an irony that is essentially antirhetorical.

All three of the writers dealt with here worked in forms other than that of the novel: poetry, criticism, the short story and the tale, diaries. But this book deals almost exclusively with their novelistic output, not only because this offers a critical unity that otherwise would be lacking but because the novel is the center of the work of all three and everything else is peripheral. For this reason I have been obliged to omit mention of some extremely interesting works, from Moravia's experiments in drama to Pavese's *Dialoghi con Leucò*. The shorter fiction is dealt with only to the extent that it illustrates the method or thematology of the novels. And there is brief mention of Pavese's poetry, especially the early verse of *Lavorare stanca*, because of the light it throws on his early development. The essays and criticism of all three authors are touched on only lightly, and I have omitted any discussion of Pavese's *Fuoco grande*, written in collaboration with Bianca Garufi, because it seems light and out of the stream of his main work.

A word about translation. All the excerpts are quoted in my own translations, for at least two reasons. The first is that any carefully written novel is a network of nuances; a translator can hope to communicate some of these nuances and not others, and each critic must emphasize those nuances, connotations, and suggestions that are important to his particular treatment of the work. The second is that in some cases these authors have been wretchedly translated. There is no doubt that, in the case of Pavese especially, the thinness of his reputation in the English-speaking world is due at least in part to the difficulty of translating him and the failure of most translators to do justice to his work. Translation is terribly hard work and rather badly paid, and in order to translate a novel adequately it is necessary for the translator not only to be an expert linguist, but to have something like a novelist's talent in his own right. Considering these difficulties it is surprising, perhaps, that most translations are as good as they are, but we are entitled at least to hope that in some cases they will be done better. Most of the novels dealt with in this book involve stylistic idiosyncracies that present a particular challenge to the translator. Perhaps what I have written will achieve the secondary effect of inspiring somebody to translate them a little better. But even if this does not happen, if someone reads the work of Moravia, Pavese, and Vittorini with a little more understanding, this book will have fulfilled its primary purpose.

Contents

The business of criticism in the matter of fiction seems clear, at any rate. There is nothing more that can usefully be said about a novel until we have fastened upon the question of its making and explored it to some purpose. In all our talk about novels we are hampered and held up by our unfamiliarity with what is called their technical aspect.

—Percy Lubbock, *The Craft of Fiction*

Alberto Moravia

Alberto Moravia was born Alberto Pincherle in Rome in 1907, the child of well-to-do Jewish parents. During much of his childhood and youth he was in bad health; stricken with bone tuberculosis at the age of nine, he spent several years bedridden or in sanatoriums and suffered from the effects of the disease until he was twenty-five. After several immature experiments in fiction, he began to write his first novel, *Gli indifferenti*, at Bressanone in 1925, when he was only eighteen. When this novel was published in 1929 it brought him immediate fame, but also provoked the suspicion of the fascist censors. The books that followed were increasingly harassed by the censors until, in 1941, he was forbidden to publish at all or even to write for newspapers. In this same year he married the novelist Elsa Morante, from whom he was later separated. In the fall of 1943, when Rome was occupied by the Nazis, he was forced to flee to the mountains south of the city to avoid arrest. Returning to Rome after the Liberation the following year, he resumed his writing career and soon established himself as one of the most prominent Italian writers of the postwar period, certainly the best-known outside of Italy. Both before and after the war he worked frequently in the cinema, and several of his novels were made into films. His politics in the postwar period were consistently leftist but independent. In addition to *Gli indifferenti* his novels include *Le ambizioni sbagliate* (1935), *La mascherata* (1941), *La romana* (1947), *Il conformista* (1951), *Il disprezzo* (1954), *La ciociara* (1957), *La noia* (1960), and *L'attenzione* (1965). He has also published several volumes of short fiction and a book of essays, *L'uomo come fine e altri saggi* (1964). In 1953, with Alberto Carocci, he founded the political-literary review *Nuovi Argomenti*. Except for frequent travels, and the interlude of his wartime exile, he has lived all of his life in Rome.

The Masked Voyeur

The first important question to be considered in dealing with Moravia is the matter of his pseudonym. There are a number of reasons for writers to publish under names that are not their own. In Moravia's case there was respect for a family which might be shocked by his scabrous themes, the well-known Jewishness of the name Pincherle, the existence of a professor of religious history who published under the name Alberto Pincherle, and the possibility of fascist censorship. Any one of these motives would be sufficient in itself, yet all of them taken together are perhaps only a rationalization or externalizing of something that lies deeper. Jean Starobinski has remarked, apropos of Stendhal, that writers who use pseudonyms are characterized by an ambivalence toward the flesh and a rejection of their own bodies—thus the invention of the second and bodiless identity—and this frequently leads to an ambiguity or tension in their attitude toward sensory experience.[1] This is a fair description of both Stendhal and Moravia, and the hypothesis can be applied to a number of other European writers who have used pseudonyms: Gorki, Svevo, Silone, Pierre Loti. There are other significant parallels between Moravia and Stendhal. Both rejected their family background, or at least the bourgeois part of it. Both developed as writers in a political atmosphere that stifled their talents and drove them into a kind of inner emigration: Stendhal under the Restoration, Moravia under fascism. And as novelistic technicians both are fascinated with masks or personae: they conceal their identities on the surface while revealing them in disguised forms, their work is a complex web of autobiography and fiction in which the identity of the writer reappears unexpectedly, in different social or political circumstances or even with altered sex. Mosca in *La Chartreuse de Parme*, a cynical minister in a sinister police state, is

3

one of the more startling of these Stendhalian masks. As for Moravia, he appears in disguise in practically every one of his novels, including *Il conformista* in which the protagonist is a fascist spy. Stendhal kept a diary in code and surrounded himself with an elaborate and completely unnecessary clandestine apparatus; both Stendhal and Moravia are reticent about the details of their private lives, although these lives are characterized chiefly by their banality. Or perhaps it is precisely because of this banality, this dissatisfaction with their real and concrete identities and the limitations placed on them by a real society, that both writers are driven to masquerade. For Stendhal and Moravia the function of art is not to reproduce reality but to transcend reality through the creation of conjectural or hypothetical modes of existence, in other words to invent masked balls in which we believe more strongly than we do in real life. Naturally the disguises in a masquerade bear some relation, even though a devious one, to reality; otherwise we would not be interested in them. The better ones are parodies, or distorted projections, of the true identities of their wearers.

Moravia is ordinarily considered a specialist in sex, or the psychology of sex. Like many truisms this is true on the surface and rather profoundly wrong underneath. There is no doubt that, taken superficially, his work consists very largely of analysis of the human sexual impulse. But Moravia is primarily and fundamentally an artist; if there is any sense in which he himself considers himself a specialist it is as a specialist in fiction. He relates to his craft in a highly personal and serious way, to the point where this craft is the most important aspect of existence for him. Other aspects, like politics, sex, or sensory experience in general, are important only insofar as they relate to this craft. To classify him as a specialist in sex is comparable to saying that Melville is a specialist in whales, or that Dostoevski is a specialist in crime. Sex for Moravia, like the whale for Melville, is only a kind of metaphor that leads him to the larger and more fundamental problems of human existence. Naturally these two writers, and Dostoevski too, may differ on what the fundamental problems are, but they resemble each other in the way they convert these problems to the concrete matter of their narrative. This relation between the concrete and the abstract lies at the heart of any serious analysis of modern fiction.

Fiction has always involved sex from the time of its beginning; this is why novels were forbidden to young ladies in the eighteenth century. The reason for this is partly that fiction is built around conflict, and sexual relations provide an abundant supply of conflicts and problems. But these are problems—of will, of altruism and egotism, of communication and misunderstanding—that would undoubtedly exist even if people had no sex lives and had been created without sexual natures. Sex simply provides a set of experiences through which we can externalize and come to grips with these problems in a concrete way. The sexual encounter is a microcosm of all human relations, and this is why it is so useful to novelists—why love plays an even larger part in the history of literature than it does in life. Furthermore, when we examine the treatment of love in a literary work this invariably leads us to an understanding of what the author thinks about broader and more general matters. In *Le Père Goriot*, for example, love is simply a mechanism for achieving social success, the process that Balzac was really interested in. And in Choderlos de Laclos love is a kind of objective correlative for the struggle of human wills. If the characters in *Les liaisons dangereuses* had been incapable of love they would have turned to some other kind of contest of wills, for example war, or court intrigue. And yet the surface detail of these writers, the mechanism and technique of love in a particular society, is authentic and complete in itself. This is exactly the case with Moravia; love is simultaneously a subject of interest in itself and a metaphor for something else. If this "something else" in any writer is examined it invariably turns out to be the structural center of his work, as well as the center of his interest as an individual.

In his treatment of sexual relations Moravia belongs essentially in the camp of Choderlos de Laclos. Apart from whatever personal interest he may have in the subject, it is useful to him artistically because in a sexual encounter the conflict of human egos is seen more simply, and more vividly, than in other more abstract modes of human activity like politics or business. Sex for his protagonists is never an end in itself; instead it is an expression of will, a means to power. This is the key to the puzzle of why they seem to derive so little pleasure from it, a phenomenon that has often struck Moravia's readers. The goal of sex is not pleasure, or reproduction; it is dominance over others. And it is only in this relation to others that the individual can establish an identity, can be somebody, even to himself. This is the sense in which Moravia is a highly social writer; it is also the sense in which, in the general meaning of the term, he can be considered an existentialist. At the same time Moravia is not a philosopher and he is not really even a novelist of ideas. His way of looking at things is not a philosophical attitude and it is something more than a theme as this term is ordinarily used; it is a kind of fundamental matrix around which all his work is built. The individual themes, the characters and their situation, the novelistic devices, may vary from book to book, but the matrix is always there underneath. It is ubiquitous in his work because it is a fundamental part of his personality, and Moravia is a writer whose personality is involved with his work to the point where the two are virtually synonymous.

In order to clarify how this came about it is necessary to go very far back in Moravia's work, in fact beyond his work to his childhood and formative years. He came from a family that was in many ways typical of the Roman bourgeoisie of the turn of the century. It was this class that provided the characters for his first two novels, *Gli indifferenti* and *Le ambizioni sbagliate,* and in fact a high proportion of the heroes in all his work. It was a class financially secure, relatively cultured and conscious of its cultural superiority, decadent out of indolence rather than out of perversion, anxious to defend its privileges or better yet to find someone else to defend them: in short the social class that made fascism possible. If there was any way in which Moravia himself departed from the norm it was that he had Jewish blood. But it was not this that provided the initial impulse that made him into a writer; instead it was illness. He was an invalid when he began to write *Gli indifferenti* at Bressanone in 1925, and the mentality of the invalid pervades his work from beginning to end, even the fiction written after he himself had regained his health. This is the true source of the indecision or Hamletism of his characters, the curious Moravian disease of the will that frequently takes sexual forms.

There are at least two qualities to the life of an invalid that are often reflected in the work of writers who are invalids or semi-invalids, for example Proust and Chekhov. The first is that the invalid's life is almost entirely passive. He is unable to do things for himself, and instead things are done to him: he is fed, his clothing is changed, his excretory and hygienic needs are taken care of by other hands. The second is that, especially in the convalescent phase, he becomes abnormally and even pathologically aware of physical sensation. Things that escape the ordinary person—the buzzing of a fly, the pattern of shadows on a ceiling, the pulsing of blood in his own ears—assume an extraordinary significance for him, and this condition is enhanced by the boredom of his surroundings and the hypersensitivity that follows on the experience of pain. These two qualities —passiveness and hypersensitivity—are strikingly reflected in *Gli indifferenti* and especially in the character of Michele, a youth about the age of Moravia himself when he began the novel. Yet in spite of the obvious parallels Michele is not Moravia; the autobiographical fallacy is always a trap in the case of a writer whose work is so obviously personal. The difference is a small but important one: Moravia is a Michele who has solved the problem of action by becoming an artist. He retains for his own use those parts of Michele's character that are useful to his craft as a writer: a keenness of observation, a hypersensitivity of feeling, an anonymity easily converted into a measured aesthetic detachment from his characters and their emotions. Since it is unnecessary for Moravia-the-artist to act, only to write, he is in no danger of falling into the kind of blunders that Michele makes in the practical world. It is true that writing is a kind of action, but it is an action in which mistakes can be prevented through leisurely and considered reflection. Best of all, the writer as observer is allowed privileges denied to the ordinary person; he can pass through walls, see under clothing, penetrate to the innermost secrets of his characters' lives. This privilege of observation leads him to a special kind of Stendhalian irony, the irony of the watcher who looks on secretly as others strive, love, hate, bungle, and make mistakes. This conversion of self to ironic spectator is a fundamental part of Moravia's nature as a writer. Who is he? He conceals his identity. What is he doing? He is watching others.

Especially in Moravia's later work, that published after 1947, this guiding matrix often takes the form of a stylized conflict. The typical protagonist is passive, unconfident, and cerebral; he tends to overanalyze his problem, often very shrewdly, instead of doing something practical or concrete about it. What he wants is near at hand—frequently, as in *L'amore coniugale* and *Il disprezzo*, it is his own wife—but for some reason he is unable to reach out and take it. While he is reflecting on this problem another character, one who acts rather than thinks, comes along and seizes the object of his desire from under his very nose. Moravia's recurring adjective for this antagonist is *prepotente*, literally overbearing or arrogant, but in his private vocabulary carrying with it a special meaning of instinctive, masterful, or virile. The "impotent" protagonist (and the term should not be taken only in its narrow sexual sense) is typically an intellectual or at least a person of a certain culture. The prepotent antagonist is frequently of the lower class, often an artisan or worker who does something with his hands. Some typical protagonists are Michele in *Gli indifferenti*, the narrator Silvio in *L'amore coniugale*, Dino in *La noia*, and Francesco in *L'attenzione*. Their respective antagonists are the family friend Leo, the barber Antonio, the virile painter Balestrieri, and the Santoro who seduces and finally marries Francesco's daughter. Not all of these antagonists are lower class, in fact Santoro is a student; but they are all distinguished by their confident and instinctive dominance in physical matters, especially sexual. In addition, Leo is by profession a financial speculator; money is always an analogue of sexual power in Moravia. The name Santoro, in fact, can be broken down either as "San Toro," holy bull, or "Sant'Oro," holy gold. These clues are so obvious that often Moravia seems to be joking with his reader.

In Moravia's fiction, then, the basic premise is the interaction of the individual human will with its environment, including other human beings, and this conflict is characteristically presented in sexual terms. But underlying the problem of will is the problem of communication. Before we can love other people, or do anything else to them, we must know them. Or to be more precise it is the other way around: by loving other human beings or relating to them in some other physical way, and only in such ways, can we come to know them. The Moravian hero is isolated within his own skin, estranged from other men and from the world around him, and in order to comprehend the external world he must establish some physical contact with it. The normal way in which we touch other human beings is through love; unless we are bullies or pugilists, in which case we strike other people forcibly and even destroy them and in this way arrive at some kind of understanding of them. (The understanding is shared by the victim; in fact with his hypersensitivity and his obsession for analysis the victim is far better qualified to comprehend the situation than his antagonist). But it is not only other human beings we seek to relate to and understand; it is the whole physical universe. Moravia's heroes often suffer from a loss of contact with the physical world and concrete experience; after their sexual obsessions, in fact, this is the main preoccupation of the heroes of *La noia* and *L'attenzione*. This kind of failure to relate to or comprehend anything outside the ego, the condition that has come to be called alienation in the jargon of modern intellectualism, has its political correlative as well. For Moravia the ultimate political sin is egotism or a failure to comprehend or take into account the political needs of others; it is this characteristic that dominates the bourgeois mentality that made fascism possible. In these philosophical and political implications of his work Moravia shares the tendencies of Kafka, Malraux, Camus, and the whole existentialist movement in modern fiction. It was above all Camus who, struggling to reconcile ethics with metaphysics, finally came to grips with the "absurd" and the absolute necessity for the individual of some kind of revolt against annihilation by an immense and indifferent universe. Moravia has no pretensions to a metaphysics; as a thinker he is very well aware of his limitations and confines himself to operating

confidently and lucidly within them. But, with due allowance for the
difference in terminology, he deals with the same conflicts as Camus
and regards them in much the same ethical light. To act or not to
act? How to establish contact with one's fellowman, regain the lost
intimacy with the earth? Meursault in *L'étranger* and Clamence in
La chute are the secret brothers of the Moravian hero.

I have already suggested that for the artist the problem of action
is somewhat different than for the ordinary man. This is true in an
even more fundamental way of the problem of alienation. It goes
without saying that art is a means of self-expression or communication with one's fellow human beings, somewhat more complex in its
effects than ordinary language. But it may be a great deal more. Perhaps a third of Moravia's heroes are artists, would-be artists, or
dilettantes with vague artistic aspirations, and they all more or less
consciously regard art as a means of bringing order into an otherwise absurd existence. If they succeed as artists they define themselves existentially as human beings; if they fail as artists—which is
more commonly the case—they are unable to believe in their own
identities or in the importance or existence of the physical world
around them. "With *Gli indifferenti*," Moravia recalled of his first
novel, "I felt for the first time in my life that I was putting my feet
on solid ground. All at once I had the sensation of passing from the
stage of good intentions to that of spontaneity. I hope all those who
want to write will have this important experience at least once in
their lives. It is the transition from the desperate métier of literature
to literary expression as a means of knowledge."[2] In the original
"knowledge" is *conoscenza,* acquaintance: not information or wisdom
but the knowing of one's self and the objects of one's daily existence.
For Moravia this novel was the transition from the hypersensitive
passivity of the sickroom to the positive act of creation, the act by
which the individual imposes his will on the environment in order to
modify it or even create an environment that was not there before:
the passage from impotence to mastery. "Knowledge," in the Old
Testament and elsewhere, is a euphemism for the sexual act. To
create as the artist creates—to bring into existence creatures that
were not there before through a secret and mysterious intimacy with
the phenomena of physical experience—is perhaps only an infinitely
more complicated version of the same kind of knowledge.

The association of sexual experience with artistic creation is, of
course, one of the banalities of psychoanalytic criticism. It is often
pointed out that insofar as Moravia is a novelist of ideas Freud and
Marx are the two poles of his thought. But it is not likely that he
owes these elements in his work to any specific encounter with

psychoanalytic literature or Marxist theory. Instead, like many artists, he simply absorbed these ideas because they were in the air at the time when he began to write, or because he already felt them inside himself and Freud and Marx merely provided him with a vocabulary or apparatus to deal with them. "When I wrote *Gli indifferenti* I knew nothing of Freud, I read psychoanalytic texts only later, and then they were mainly American texts. Freud himself I skimmed rather than read, I understood he was an important scientist but I found him rather boring. At the same time I agree that his vindication of the importance of sex is a basic one, and his psychological discoveries are the work of a fundamentally revolutionary genius."[3] The key word here is "revolutionary"—for Moravia always synonymous with clear-sighted, progressive, or correct. But his Marxism is like his Freudianism, a system from which he has borrowed certain elements to use them in a highly personal and idiosyncratic way. For him Marxism performs an important function, quite important enough to justify itself, in explaining the basic malfunction of prerevolutionary society: a malfunction due not so much to economic causes in the narrow sense as to the historical obsolescence, and consequently the moral and cultural degeneracy of the capitalistic class. Moravia develops these historical theories at some length in his 1960 introduction to Manzoni's *I promessi sposi*. The bourgeoisie once, in its time, was a revolutionary class. It then reached its peak of stability or predominance in the early nineteenth century, the epoch of Manzoni. Manzoni's novel, in fact, is "Catholic realism" in exactly the same sense that the work of modern Soviet novelists is "socialist realism," and subject to the same limitations. (For Moravia, an Italian living in a country dominated by a Catholic political party, capitalism is practically synonymous with Catholicism.) By 1930 the failure of this whole Christian-bourgeois system to organize any effective resistance to fascism demonstrated its fundamental senility, if there was any need of proof. Fascism was a logical, even inevitable, outgrowth of Christianity: "We are all Christians, even Hitler was a Christian."[4]

Thus Marxism provided Moravia with an explanation of the decadence of his own social class, but its function in his system of thought was a purely negative one; it offered no positive alternative or antidote that he felt obliged to accept. In the same period that he was criticizing Manzoni for his "Catholic realism" he attacked the Marxist concept of art as a mere "superstructure" left behind by society on its way toward more important political and social goals and condemned the political management of art in the Soviet Union. "The Marxists want a completely social art, with no unessentials or

evasions of any kind. The girl who loves the worker because he has
surpassed his 'norm' of work is a good example. And perhaps they
will succeed in this aim. But on that day they will discover that the
'norm' has assumed an erotic quality. It is nature that reigns in art,
not society."[5] In Moravia's fiction art takes precedence, influencing
the novelist's attitude toward his characters and implicitly diagnos-
ing their society without offering any particular cure for the malady.
With the possible exception of Michele in *La ciociara* there is not a
single Marxist or socialist hero in Moravia. Michele is a shopkeeper's
son who has gone to the university and become an anti-fascist intellectual, and his function in the novel is that of a raisonneur rather
than a true hero or protagonist. Probably all or most of what he says
can be taken as Moravia's own opinion. But except for his anticlericalism there is very little that can be associated with Marxism
in what he says to the others. Instead he is an old-fashioned idealist
and altruist, above all concerned with the question of responsibility.
Among the small shopkeepers and peasants hiding in the mountains
he is the only one who sees the true cause of the war: that evil produces evil in return, that foreigners are killing and destroying in
Italy because Italians killed and destroyed in Abyssinia. "What is
done to me today will be done to you tomorrow."

In short, Michele says nothing to indicate that he believes
socialism or any other political system could cure the selfishness or
moral rottenness he sees about him. But he does believe we are
responsible for our acts, and he believes that passiveness itself can
be an act, the kind of hypocritical and unrealistic act known in the
existentialist vocabulary as bad faith. When Moravia's work is viewed
in retrospect it is clear that from the time of *Gli indifferenti* in 1929
he has been preoccupied with a single problem: the human will in its
relation to other wills, and the moral consequences of the act of will
or failure to act. If there is a system of ethics implied in his fiction
it is simply that the successful characters, those who fulfill themselves
or achieve some kind of satisfaction, are those who succeed in expressing their wills through some kind of positive act: sexual,
artistic, political, or even criminal. Those who fail are those who in
some way are unable to bring the will to bear, who analyze instead
of acting, who allow things to be done to them: the impotent, the
passive, the conformist. The prepotent are not always admirable; in
fact they frequently represent brute and unthinking force. And the
Moravian antihero often wins the reader's sympathy through the
very intelligence with which he analyzes his own impotence. But in
order to oppose the human condition it is not enough merely to comprehend it, in other words to think. In addition it is necessary to

come to grips with the problem of action in some such way that the external world is altered, if possible for the better, by your act. For Moravia himself this engagement is primarily the act of artistic creation. For his characters it may be sexual, or grossly physical in some other way, but the important thing is that each human being must define himself through an act that comes out of him and is consistent with the identity he has willfully and voluntarily chosen. Even the brutish Sonzogno in *La romana*, who throws people downstairs, is superior to the Marcello of *Il conformista*, who does what he imagines other people expect of him.

The Stories as Models of the Novels

Moravia began to write short fiction as early as the period of *Gli indifferenti;* his first story, "Cortigiana stanca," dates from 1927. Although the novel remained his primary concern and the important steps in his development are invariably marked by novels, this interest in short fiction continued throughout his career. By 1967 he had published thirteen volumes of stories, tales, and novelettes, although the 1956 *Racconti* duplicates some of the stories in the earlier volumes. This material falls into three fairly well-defined categories. First there are the "Roman tales" written for the *Corriere della Sera* and later collected in *Racconti romani* (1954) and *Nuovi racconti romani* (1959).* Practically all of these are told in the first person by lower-class narrators, and for the most part they are short and slight. Next there are the full-scale short stories collected in the 1956 *Racconti* and the 1963 volume *L'automa.*† These are a good deal more solid in technique, and they include some of Moravia's most skillful and characteristic work. Finally there are the novelettes or short novels: *L'amore coniugale, Agostino, La disubbidienza,* and a few others.‡ (*La mascherata* is included in the 1964 *Romanzi brevi,* but in length and intricacy it is really a full-scale short novel.) The note that emerges from this mass of material is first of all that the short fiction is an integral part of Moravia's work; the themes, the character types, the recurring situations are those of his major novels.

---

* Translated as *Roman Tales* (Farrar, Straus & Giroux, 1956) and *More Roman Tales* (Farrar, Straus & Giroux, 1964).

† Most of the stories in this first volume ("Tales") have not been translated. The second, literally "The Automaton," is published in English as *The Fetish and Other Stories* (Farrar, Straus & Giroux, 1964).

‡ The first appears in English as *Conjugal Love* (Farrar, Straus & Young, 1951), and the other two are collected as *Two Adolescents* (Farrar, Straus, 1950).

Often, in fact, the stories seem to serve as preliminary treatments or sketches of ideas that were later converted to novelistic form; one, "La ciociara," even has the same title as a later novel. A good many of them deal in some way with art and artistic creativity and associate this with mastery or impotence in sex: the theme of *La noia*. In addition to their intrinsic interest, therefore, the stories are valuable in another way: they present the elements of Moravia's major novels in simplified or diagrammatic form, like specimens in a laboratory demonstration. A reader who knew nothing but the short fiction would lack a sense of Moravia's true stature as a writer, but he would have a fairly balanced view of the themes and characteristics of his work.

One story dating from 1930, "Inverno di malato,"* is indispensable in understanding the relation between sickness and love, a theme that plays a fundamental part in Moravia's work as it does in Proust's. The setting and situation are directly autobiographical: a sanatorium in the Alps, probably at Cortina d'Ampezzo; an adolescent protagonist ill of some unspecified wasting disease. The basic framework of the story, in fact, resembles that of Mann's *Zauberberg*. The difference is that for Mann the sanatorium is a more or less synthetic setting for an intricate philosophical allegory, whereas for Moravia it is the reflection of a powerful personal experience, perhaps the crucial experience of his life. Naturally *Der Zauberberg* is a major work and "Inverno di malato" is not; it would be fairer to set it alongside "Tristan," a story that Mann used, as Moravia often did, as a preliminary study for a later novel. If the two are compared Mann's story is richer in incident, more grotesque, a good deal more ironic; Moravia's is more analytical and seems to take itself more seriously. The central device is the same: the conflict of two archetypal male figures turns around their relation to a third female character. Moravia's hero Girolamo is a sensitive adolescent with a bourgeois background, although his family is no longer as rich as it once was. His antagonist Brambilla is a vigorous, confident, and somewhat vulgar commercial traveler—the son, as he frequently boasts, of an uneducated stonemason. There are only two other characters, the sturdy Austrian attendant Joseph and the fourteen-year-old English girl Polly. Except for Joseph all the characters are bedridden invalids, although Brambilla is in the last stages of convalescence. In the early part of the story Brambilla taunts Girolamo about his innocence and his bourgeois background. Brambilla him-

* Available in English as "A Sick Boy's Winter," in Ben Johnson, ed., *Stories of Modern Italy* (Modern Library, 1960).

self is full of stories about women, and the impressionable Girolamo associates this coarse virility with life, health, mastery of the physical world; Brambilla becomes for him "the ideal type he ought to make every effort to resemble."[6] Driven more by Brambilla's taunts than by desire, he attempts to make love to the innocent Polly and succeeds up to a point. But this does not have the effect he expects. Polly, who is ill of a disease of the spine, takes a turn for the worse and for a time is in danger of dying, and Girolamo's health, too, deteriorates under the influence of love. Worst of all, his action fails to win him the respect of Brambilla; in fact Brambilla treats the seduction as a typical example of bourgeois perversion and tells him he ought to be ashamed of himself. Brambilla, cured, leaves the sanatorium, and Girolamo is left alone with his thoughts. He concludes that Brambilla is right in considering him corrupt. In spite of their vulgarity Brambilla's adventures with women were normal in a straightforward and animal-like way, whereas in his own relations with Polly he senses something "illicit, triste, and confused."[7]

The real point of this story is the contrast of the two male characters; the thin plot is only an excuse for this demonstration. Girolamo is particularly interesting in that he represents a link between Moravia the author and the typical Moravian hero of the later fiction. In this story Moravia's own adolescent experience is only partly assimilated to fiction; the temperament of the hero, "habituated to regard illness as a normal state, a breathable atmosphere,"[8] is for all practical purposes that of Moravia himself. But Moravia's experience of sickness, infinitely complicated like all experiences extending over a period of time, has been simplified into a tight and economical framework in which everything not pertaining to the theme has been deleted. This story was originally published in the review *Pegaso* in 1930, about a year after *Gli indifferenti*. But thematically Girolamo antedates the Michele of Moravia's first novel; he represents the autobiographical persona in a less complete state of conversion to fiction. In Girolamo the sickness that prevents action is real and physical; in Michele it is sublimated into an intangible paralysis of the will. The relation between Girolamo and Brambilla is a preliminary version of the Michele-Leo relation in *Gli indifferenti*: impotent intelligence confronted by crude vitality. But in the novel this relation—like the matter of the hero's sickness —has been projected one step farther into fiction; the hero is harder and more sarcastic, his antagonist is more sophisticated, more complex, by no means lacking in intelligence. Brambilla is a puppet; Leo in *Gli indifferenti* is a fully rounded character who succeeds in winning, at least to some degree, the sympathy of the reader.

Perhaps the most intriguing of the four characters of the story is the one who is seen only indirectly: the girl Polly. At first she seems innocence personified: taciturn, shy, held by her illness in a kind of retarded babyhood. When Girolamo comes to see her she plays with a doll; the sarcastic Brambilla refers to her room as the "kindergarten." But her face is flushed, "perhaps because of the heat of the room,"[9] and there is something sly, complacent, and knowing about her from the beginning. After Girolamo's fumbling "seduction," which he begins by assuring her kissing is very pleasant, she is unexpectedly placid and satisfied with herself, and he concludes, "She knows more about it than I do."[10] The adventure hardly progresses beyond a kiss; at one point he takes her arm and puts it around his neck, and it hangs there, inert and motionless. This affair is a model in miniature of the Moravian sexual relationship. Polly is an embryonic version of the enigmatic, sensual, and yet unattainable heroines of the later novels—far more than the Carla of *Gli indifferenti*, who is almost totally passive and is really only a feminine copy of Michele. It may be significant that Moravia was reading Dostoevski about this time; Polly is a cousin of that child-monster Svidrigailov finds whimpering in a tavern and who turns into a witch under his very eyes.

The diffident adolescent hero is portrayed again in two long stories or novellas that rank among Moravia's best work: "Agostino" (1945) and "La disubbidienza" (1948).* "Agostino" is set for the most part at a seaside resort. It deals with a typical Oedipal situation: there is no father in sight, the boy is subconsciously attracted to his young and pretty mother, and his attempts to explore the sexual world outside his family lead only to confusion and frustration. For Agostino this outside world is represented by the strange six-fingered beachcomber, Saro, and the band of urchins who follow him, a circle held together by vague homosexual implications. Saro is a crafty and grotesque monster of epic proportions, and the scenes in which he embarks with the boys in a sailboat are a kind of perverse parody of Homer: "Saro took the mast with the six fingers of his right hand, and then with the six fingers of the left he raised it and planted it in a hole in the midships thwart. Then he mounted into the boat, fastened the top of the sail, and made the cord fly; the sail rose to the top of the mast."[11] And a little later, as the boat is being rolled into the water with the help of the Negro boy Homs: "The boat slid on the rollers and advanced over the sand. As soon as the

---

* Published together in English as *Two Adolescents* (Farrar, Straus, 1950). The second story, literally "Disobedience," is translated as "Luca."

after roller was free of the keel the Negro took it and held it in his arms, pressing it against his chest like a baby, and then, leaping over the sand as though in some new kind of ballet, ran to place it under the bow."[12] Several things are new here: the interest in the details of a mechanical operation, lacking in Moravia's rather abstract early work; the use of multiple images to describe a single phenomenon ("pressing it against his chest like a baby," "leaping . . . as though in some new kind of ballet"); and the creation of grotesque characters like Saro and Homs as projections of latent impulses or tendencies of the hero. "Agostino," published two years before *La romana,* is Moravia's first fiction in the new and more complex postwar style.

"La disubbidienza" is similar; the protagonist belongs to the same social class, has the same dispositions, gropes with the same problems. It even begins where "Agostino" ends, with a return from the seaside; in a sense it is a kind of sequel. But the Luca of "La disubbidienza" has a father, and his psychological predicament is somewhat more complex; his revolt against his parents has economic as well as sexual implications, and there is also a philosophical or epistemological thread in the story that is an important foreshadowing of the later novels. Agostino's unhappiness stems from his awakening sexual nature; Luca's sickness—he is physically ill at the beginning of the story—begins as an estrangement from the world of physical objects. In the evolution of Moravia's themes the two tales, written almost at the same time, are on the opposite sides of a kind of watershed. In his early work—in general that written before and during the war—the protagonists are sexually inadequate and suffer from a paralysis of the will, and this leads to a sense of alienation from the world they are unable to dominate. In the later postwar fiction the situation is increasingly the other way around: the hero is first alienated—that is, he is unable to grasp the meaning, or even believe in the existence, of the physical objects around him—and as a result of this he falls into the paralysis which takes sexual and other forms. It is precisely at the seaside resort with its rich profusion of sensory experience that Luca becomes aware of "this revolt of the objects and his own incapacity to love and dominate them."[13] On the trip home from the seaside he does a peculiar thing that is typical of Moravia's rather obvious symbolism: in the train station he leans against the locomotive and vomits on it. This incident is slightly more complex than it seems; he is revolting against the machine that has brought him unwillingly back to the city, but by implication he is also nauseated by this iron monster whose power and self-possession are a reproach to his own alienation from the sensory world. During this incident the engineer of the locomotive, who serves as a kind of analogue of his machine, is eating "with hearty appetite" a loaf of bread stuffed with an enormous spinach omelette.[14]

Feeling himself the enemy of this physical world, Luca takes the offensive and attacks it head-on. In rejecting any relation to the physical objects around him he also rejects the bourgeois and material values of his family; this is the "disobedience" of the title. The Mammon-worship of his parents is demonstrated in a scene that, in spite of its obviousness, is curiously effective. Coming unexpectedly into their bedroom one night, Luca finds them removing money and stocks from the wall behind a picture of the Madonna: the shrine before which the family prayers have been conducted for years is actually a safe. At first this discovery seems to make little impression on Luca. But later, when he is reproached for entering the bedroom without knocking, he feels an impulse to blurt out, "And you, why did you make me kneel down and pray all those years in front of your money?"[15] This is the beginning of his active revolt against the bourgeois world. Luca, in fact, is one of the few heroes of Moravia who reacts against his impotence or alienation in any effective way. First he gives away his stamp collection to another boy, then he sells his books and buries the money under a tree in the park. And in burying the money, he tells himself, he is in a certain sense burying himself, or at least that part of himself that was attached to the money: the bourgeois and external part of his identity he is determined to reject. Finally this crisis results in a genuine physical illness that brings him to the point of death. He is rescued by a middle-aged nurse who bathes and feeds him, encourages him to life, and finally, in a strange and curiously chaste scene, offers him physical love, a gift he accepts with "a tremor of veneration."[16] The nurse leaves the next day, but Luca feels no regret, only a gratitude for this initiation into love which brings with it a reconciliation with the world of things. The nurse is obviously of plebian origin; her health is the antithesis of the bourgeois morbidity of the parents. The three threads of the story—the sexual initiation, the theme of money and bourgeois materialism, and the philosophical problem of sensation—are woven into a narrative that is deceptively simple on the surface.

*L'amore coniugale,** a long narrative dating from 1949, even more clearly anticipates the novels of the Fifties. In form it falls somewhere between a story and a novel; it is included in an Italian volume called *L'amore coniugale e altri racconti,* but in thematic

* *Conjugal Love* (Farrar, Straus & Young, 1951).

complexity at least it is a true novel, closely resembling the later *Il disprezzo*. It is the first of the short novels to be narrated in the first person, and in this it reflects the lessons learned in the writing of *La romana* two years earlier. The hero and his situation are those of the later novels, especially *Il disprezzo* and *La noia:* an intellectual, a creative artist, unable to create because of his sexual inadequacy and unable to fulfill himself sexually because of his sterility as an artist. Or, to put the matter somewhat more precisely: an artist afflicted with a creative sterility which is simply another aspect of his loss of contact with the whole world of sensation including the sexual. Silvio, the narrator of *L'amore coniugale,* is a writer who moves with his wife to the country in order to write a novel called *L'amore coniugale,* in other words some kind of parallel to the story we are reading. But he gets nowhere and soon realizes that what he is writing is "a mass of vague sentences without concrete meaning."[17] He is suffering from the same malaise as Luca in "La disubbidienza," a failure to comprehend or grasp the existence of the external world. His wife, who is thoroughly at home in the physical world as most of Moravia's women are (she has the legs of a dancer and her customary stance is "provoking"), soon begins betraying him with the barber Antonio. The usual mythological apparatus of Moravia's later fiction is present here, although it is really less an apparatus than a set of half-playful suggestions: the wife's name is Leda, barbers cut off people's hair and hair is a symbol of virility, and the union of Leda and Antonio takes place on a threshing floor in the moonlight, in a kind of parody of a pagan ritual. This latter scene, in fact, is typical not only of Moravia's use of symbolism but of his rather self-conscious intricacy as an artist. It is Silvio himself who first suggests to Leda the idea of making love on the threshing floor, and in doing so he compares the haystacks to the dolmens of Brittany and then explains to her "something about the pagan rites that were celebrated in those prehistoric temples."[18] The reader has already guessed that it is the true pagans Leda and Antonio who will carry out this excellent idea. Antonio goes on to comment, rather naively, "I admit that certain literary reminiscences played a part in my desire, but so be it; I was a man of letters and it was proper that literature should be fused in me with the deepest and truest impulses."[19] Moravia seems to defend himself in advance against the charge of banal symbolism by wrapping his symbol in an elaborate apparatus of self-irony. The device is essentially Gidean: the writer-narrator (Silvio) pretends to understand everything, but the author and the reader understand a little more than he does. Moravia thus has all the psychological advantage of associating himself with Silvio and all the literary advantage of regarding him with detachment. When Silvio shows his book to Leda she comments, "You've idealized me too much." The final irony is that Silvio has written a bad book and that Moravia, quite innocently and without comment, offers us a good one.

The 1949 *L'amore coniugale* volume includes seven short stories that are among Moravia's best. In "Ritorno al mare"* the protagonist Lorenzo takes his wife to the beach in the hope of improving his physical relations with her. The sea in Moravia is a source of elemental strength, usually associated with the sexual, and a large proportion of his stories are set in the popular seaside resorts near Rome. At the beach Lorenzo encounters images of an energetic, even intimidating, violence: the vigor of the surf, the hot sun, the rubble of a restaurant smashed by Allied bombings. The usual Moravian attempt at love comes to nothing. His wife feels only contempt for him; as for the violence of the nature around them she says indifferently, "It isn't the first time I've seen the sea."[19] As a typical Moravian female she is in possession of the elemental forces without being obliged to intellectualize them or even being aware of them; it is the male who intellectualizes while the force itself slips from his grasp. A secondary reason for Lorenzo's impotence and his wife's scorn for him is that he has a fascist background. She has no specific objection to fascism and in fact is totally ignorant of politics. But she is contemptuous of failure, and it is amid the rubble of Allied bombing that the former fascist is most aware of his uselessness. Finally his wife disappears and he is walking along the beach, moved by a vague desire to "remind himself once more of that eternal movement, of that eternal clamor, before going back to the city. And then he wanted to do a thing that in the presence of his wife he wouldn't have had the courage to do: take off his shoes, roll up his pants and walk along the sea in the shallow fluid water, in the surge and flow of the waves."[20] Like his Anglo-Saxon equivalent Prufrock ("I shall wear the bottoms of my trousers rolled"), he ends by drowning. In Lorenzo's case the human voice that wakes him is his own, eternally verbalizing and analyzing while the moment of action slips irretrievably away. This story, incidentally, is narrated in the third person and probably dates from slightly earlier than *L'amore coniugale* itself.

Another story involving the sea in a somewhat more complex way is "Il negro e il vecchio dalla roncola,"† also included in the

* "Return to the Sea."
† "The Negro and the Old Man with the Bill-hook."

volume *L'amore coniugale.* The third-person technique, the setting and period, and even the basic situation are those of "Ritorno al mare," although the central characters in this case are not married. Cosimo, who hopes to make love to Cora, takes her to a deserted spot on the beach. A huge Negro soldier, evidently an American, comes along and menaces them with a knife, and Cora goes off quite placidly with him. Cosimo has the impression that he is watching "not a woman carried off by force . . . but two friends, two lovers, going for a walk together,"[21] and under his breath he begins to curse Cora. She is rescued not by Cosimo but by an old fisherman who comes out of the sea and talks quite calmly to the Negro, gesturing with his bill-hook in a way "more oratorical than menacing." Persuaded by this discourse, the Negro retreats down the beach. When Cora comes back to Cosimo he apologizes for his cowardice, but she says simply, "What could you do? He was a giant. I was afraid."[22]

Superficially this is a somewhat ironic narrative of a sexual fiasco. But Cosimo's real effort in this story is that of the protagonists of Moravia's major novels: to define himself as a human being, or more precisely to create an identity for himself through an act of will. This act would, in fact, *constitute* that identity, since for Moravia the nature of a human being is no more or less than the sum of his actions. That the act he plans is a sexual one is incidental; this is merely the working material of Moravia's fiction. It is immaterial, too, that Cosimo is unaware of the deeper implications of what is happening to him. If he were fully aware of the significance of what he is doing, in fact, this would be an evidence that his effort had succeeded. The proof of the existence of a valid identity is a self-knowledge of the powers that go along with the identity. Or, to put it the other way around, the proof that Cosimo has not yet established an identity is that he is unsure what he can and cannot do, and so ends by doing nothing. In this story he is confronted by three examples of people who have solved this problem, or for whom the problem does not exist. The Negro and the old fisherman are both *prepotenti,* but in different ways. The Negro's gross physical confidence is that of brute force, of desire. He knows what he wants and he knows how to get it, but he does not really understand why he wants it, or more important, who he is. The fisherman is also prepotent, both physically and morally. But he is also aware of the implications of what he is doing; this is apparent in the fact that he persuades "oratorically" rather than by force, even though both he and the Negro are aware he possesses the force to lend authority to his oratory. The Negro is *merely* a force, whereas the fisherman is a personality. Finally there is Cora: confident and intact in her female mindlessness. Like a typical Moravian heroine she is absolutely amoral; she behaves entirely out of impulse, and intellectual or ethical factors play no part in her decisions. She feels no obligation to return Cosimo's caresses, for example, even though she has accepted an invitation which she knew to be at least partly erotic in its motives. She goes off quite calmly with the Negro as soon as she sees it is necessary, and at the crucial moment she runs quite simply and instinctively to the fisherman for protection. She doesn't even reproach Cosimo afterward, because she intuitively understands and accepts the fact that both she and Cosimo are cowards: "What could you do? He was a giant. I was afraid." She was born, if not prepotent, at least invulnerable. She belongs with all of Moravia's heroines who accept men's caresses or reject them, remain faithful to their lovers or betray them, destroy those about them or become themselves victims: but always with the same Gioconda smile, slightly mocking.

In a third story in this volume, "Andare verso il popolo,"* the basic sexual situation is turned to political satire. Mario and Ornella are out for a drive in the country, and when their car runs out of water they have an argument about politics. Mario wants to ask the peasants for water, because "you can learn a lot of interesting things from them,"[23] but Ornella—instinctively and without citing any reasons—dislikes them. Mario's arguments prevail, and they go together to a lonely farmhouse. There they are robbed and stripped practically naked by the peasants, led by a placid old grandmother who explains that "robbing is ugly but dying of hunger is even uglier."[24] This story is in a sense Moravia's declaration of independence from the Party rhetoric, but it also implies a genuine sympathy for poverty and suffering, and a conviction that matters are not going to be improved without a radical change in the way society is organized. His postwar political position is accurately defined here: he is a revolutionary but an independent one, refusing to take an orthodox Party attitude either toward intellectual leftists or toward the allegedly angelic masses. The old woman is an extraordinary invention. "Cry, Signorina, cry," she tells Ornella almost joyfully. "I cried too when the Germans took my gold, I cried and then I felt better."[25] She prattles on this way throughout the story, praising Ornella's feet as she pulls off her stockings, refusing to take her dress because it is not modest for women to go around naked, even offering some of the

* Literally "going to the people." This phrase is a bit of Party jargon of the post-1945 period, when the leftist movement was considered to be excessively dominated by intellectuals.

boiled kid that is all the family has to eat. Her cynicism is candid and totally lacking in malice. She is by no means inhuman; she has simply been brought by suffering to a point of absolute clarity, a clarity that transcends both conventional ethics and Party dogma. Moravia wrote this story shortly after he returned from his long winter's stay with the peasants of the Ciociaria.

The title story of the 1963 volume *L'automa***** is a final demonstration of the intimate relation between Moravia's stories and his novels. It opens with a device that is a conventional part of Moravia's technique by this time: a symbolic incident that prefigures the main action. In an apartment in the expensive Parioli quarter of Rome the hero Guido plays with his American record player. Again and again it works perfectly. But once, curiously, the automatic arm fails to lower itself; instead it goes on moving "in what seemed a reflective way"[26] and drops down in the middle of the record, ruining it. There is no explanation, unless it is something like Lucretius' swerving atoms or Heisenberg's principle of uncertainty. Still puzzling over this, Guido sets out with his family for an excursion to Lake Albano. He is a model bourgeois husband; his wife tells him complacently, "I know that with you there can't be any surprises." With this remark she demonstrates that she knows Guido about as well as he knows his record player but no better. Shortly after she says this Guido has an "almost irresistible" temptation: he sees that if he drives straight ahead at a certain point the car will plunge three hundred meters down into the lake. The whole story is simply a framework for this moment of choice, the possibility of breaking once and for all out of the trap of conformity and automatic behavior. As a matter of fact he does not drive the car over the cliff. But this is not because he is "responsible" or because he is a good husband and father; his failure to act is simply another impotence, a failure of nerve. Guido is the model of all those Moravian heroes who ought to act and who vacillate instead, who ought to fulfill themselves as unique and creative individuals and end by conforming. As a categorical imperative suicide is not very admirable, but neither, in Moravia's view, is the idiotic automatism of the record player. This is the problem that oppresses the Dino of *La noia* and the Francesco of *L'attenzione:* it is called "boredom" in one novel and "inauthenticity" in the other, but the roots of the malady are the same. It is interesting to note that the English version of this volume, *The Fetish,* takes its title from another and much more superficial story about a husband who is jealous of a phallic-shaped piece of sculpture his wife keeps in the

* "The Automaton."

apartment; an instance of the way in which critics, translators, and others insist on emphasizing the sexual element in Moravia's work at the expense of the more fundamental themes. As a matter of fact the concept of automatism or estrangement dominates most of the forty-one stories of the book.

A Means of Knowledge

Moravia has described, with a certain irony, the conditions under which he wrote and published his first novel. Beginning at Bressanone in the autumn of 1925, he worked on it for three years. Meanwhile he had begun contributing to avant-garde reviews, among them Bontempelli's *900*. The *900* group made an agreement with Bontempelli that each of them would write a novel, but Moravia was the only one who ever finished his. "Then the editor of *900*, which was supposed to publish our novels, refused mine, after reading it, for the not very flattering reason that it was a 'cloud of words.' I took the novel to Milan, to the Alpes publishing house. Cesare Giardini, who was then the director of the firm, read it and accepted it immediately. Then presently I was asked to pay the costs. I paid 5000 lire; and the novel appeared in July 1929 with great success."[27]

This was *Gli indifferenti*,* the novel that, in an Italy already growing bored with official fascist art, was remarkable enough to win him an immediate literary reputation at the age of twenty-one. His second novel *Le ambizioni sbagliate* appeared in 1935, the third, *La mascherata*, in 1941. There is a certain tentative or exploratory quality to these three early books; technically they represent Moravia's search for a style which would correspond to, and fully express, the framework of reality or way of regarding experience that he was already working out in his own mind. In another sense it was the process of writing the novels that created the framework of reality—Moravia did not fully understand what he himself was, or how he related to the world around him, until he had defined himself as a novelist. This was what he meant when he said that in writing *Gli indifferenti* he felt for the first time he was putting his feet on solid ground, that it represented for him the discovery of "literary expression as a means of knowledge."

For a novel that played so important a part in the formation of its author, *Gli indifferenti* is extraordinarily lacking in autobiographical reference. None of its characters are semibedridden invalids with

---

* Translated as *The Time of Indifference* (Farrar, Straus & Young, 1953). The Italian is literally "the indifferent ones" or "those who are indifferent."

literary interests, as Moravia himself was when he wrote the novel. The action deals with domestic financial crises, social ambitions, and cynical sexual intrigues, with none of which had Moravia had very much experience. Moreover it appears that Moravia himself was not very interested in the social or thematic aspects of the novel and regarded it mainly as a technical exercise, a kind of self-taught apprentice work. He wrote in later years that he intended it as "nothing but a novel, that is a literary work written according to certain purely literary criteria."[28] Essentially the novel is a portrait of five persons and their rather complicated interrelations. In many respects it is a curiously sketchy and tentative work. There is relatively little action; a good part of the narrative is dialogue, and the rest consists of the inward reactions of the characters conveyed in a kind of modified stream-of-consciousness. The action covers only a few days, and most of the settings are luncheons, dinners, and other social events which give the opportunity for this combination of dialogue and analysis. The brief time span suggests a dramatic structure rather than the form of the conventional novel; and in fact Moravia has admitted that he set out to write "a tragedy in the form of a novel."[29] If he eventually abandoned or modified this idea it was because he discovered in the course of writing that tragedy was impossible in the milieu he had chosen, that his characters were incapable of tragic emotions or tragic actions. The sentence structure is repetitive and even monotonous. Probably the most remarkable aspect of the style is the punctuation. Moravia wrote the first draft of the novel "orally," composing each sentence aloud before transcribing it onto the page. As he did this he simply separated the sentences with white spaces or dashes, and later went through the manuscript distributing the punctuation more or less at random. The effects of this process survived into the final version, and the result is a kind of vague and sinuous style that manages to convey a sense of monotony without at the same time boring the reader. The mark commonly used to end a phrase or sentence is the ellipsis: "Ah fine really fine . . . then there's nothing more to say . . . everything's explained . . . evidently you like that kind of women . . ."[30] The impression left on the reader is a kind of vacuous formlessness that corresponds exactly to the mental state of the characters. When they are provoked by circumstances they invariably say the first thing that comes into their heads; they never foresee the consequences of their actions, nor are they capable of planning or influencing the events around them. Their minds drift passively from one trivial detail to another, exactly like their sentences. In this novel Moravia invents a "bourgeois" style corresponding to his view of the bourgeois mentality: passive, aimless, autistic, and profoundly and irretrievably corrupt.

In keeping with the "dramatic" structure, the framework of the action is relatively simple. The middleaged mother Mariagrazia is about to be abandoned by her lover, Leo. She hopes to marry her daughter Carla to Leo and thus save the family from financial disaster. But Leo—the one prepotent character among the five—is too astute to be maneuvered into this old-fashioned trap, and instead cynically seduces Carla as he has seduced the mother. Michele, the son of the family, sets out to avenge the dishonor of his sister, but fails in his attempt to kill Leo. Meanwhile he tries to recover his self-respect through an affair with Lisa, a family friend, but this only results in his further degradation. In the end Leo has reduced the whole family to abject submission: Carla sexually, the others financially and psychologically.

This is only the bare bones of the plot, and a very bad novel could be made from this outline. The interest of *Gli indifferenti* lies in the skill with which Moravia delineates the psychological state of his characters through the device of internal monologue, and the convincingness with which he portrays characters as different as the self-indulgent and sentimental mother, the inexperienced Carla, and the cynical and strong-willed Leo. The mother is one of the most disagreeable characters in fiction, and it is a tribute to Leo's self-discipline that he is able to stomach her long enough to divest her of her possessions and self-respect. (Moravia invariably calls her "the mother" rather than referring to her by her name; this was the period of the exaggerated respect for motherhood encouraged by fascism, when Grazia Deledda's *La madre* was widely read, and there is an element of sarcasm in the epithet.) Thinking of the economic ruin that faces her at the hands of Leo, she is seized by terror. "She had never wanted to know anything about the poor or even know them by name, she had preferred to ignore the existence of people who worked hard and lived squalid lives. 'They live better than we do,' she had always said; 'We have higher sensibilities and greater intelligence and so we suffer more than they do . . .' "[31] As her daughter is ruined sexually and her son becomes an abject parasite of Leo she notices nothing; she is totally preoccupied with her own self-pity and with her grotesque attempts to win back the affection of Leo. Her whining after a time grows physically irritating, and her self-indulgence is pathological. Considering the likelihood that Leo will abandon her once she has lost her money, she remarks, "Yes . . . even Christ was betrayed by his best friends."[32] The process of decline continues inevitably until Carla has been corrupted, Michele demoralized, and the family destroyed economically, all at Leo's hands. But the mother is scarcely aware of this and, even after Carla's seduction, looks forward brightly to her marriage to a wealthy young man in their circle. The novel ends with a masked ball, a metaphor of bourgeois concealment and hypocrisy that Moravia was later to use as the central image of a novel. " 'Remember,' the mother advises Carla, 'be . . . you know . . . nice with Pippo . . . I've been thinking about it . . . maybe he loves you . . . it's a good match.' " Carla tells her gravely not to worry. "Then the mother smiled satisfied: it occurred to her that her lover too might come to the ball, and she looked forward to a pleasant evening."[33]

Michele is somewhat more complex than either Carla or the mother. He has enough insight at least to be aware of his own impotence and to suffer from the consciousness of his predicament. When the mother comments apropos of an incompetent cook, "Without passion everything's lacking," Michele approves solemnly. "That's exactly it . . . without passion you can't do anything . . . for example, for all my efforts to slap Leo I've never succeeded . . . I lack the passion."[34] Remarks of this kind baffle the mother and she ends by concluding that Michele is frivolous, a particular irony when her own character is considered. Michele, in fact, is the first of a long line of Moravian heroes who are overwhelmed by the absurdity of their existence. Walking in the rain through the streets of Rome, he observes without comprehension the crowds of people hurrying toward some mysterious destination. "And I, where I am going? what am I? why don't I run, hurry like those people? why can't I be instinctive, sincere, why do I lack faith?"[35] The climax of his revolt against his own passivity is the scene in which he forces himself in a dreamlike state, something like Raskolnikov, to enter an arms shop and buy a revolver to kill Leo with. By this time the reader, whatever his opinions on homicide, sincerely hopes he will carry this out. But Michele neglects the essential detail, loading the revolver, and at the crucial moment all that results is a click. Leo treats him with the contempt he deserves, and at the end of the novel Michele attains at least some kind of fulfillment in perceiving the root of his problem: the connection between his passivity and his tendency to morbid self-analysis. "I didn't love Lisa . . . I didn't kill Leo . . . I've done nothing but think . . . and that was my mistake."[35] Michele, in fact, is not primarily a bourgeois like his mother; fundamentally he is an intellectual, and in Moravia's system of values at least this raises him a cut above the others. The others fail because they are egotistical, short-sighted, and materialistic; he fails because he thinks too much. With one exception he is the only character in the novel to understand himself and the processes going on around him.

The exception is, of course, Leo. This cynical egotist, seducer, and social parasite (he lives by trading on the stock market and buying apartments with the profits) is superficially the villain of the action, but like Milton's Satan he escapes from the author's ethical framework and ends as the most interesting character of the novel. In fact it is typical of Moravia's work that his "negative" or prepotent characters are more attractive than his ostensible protagonists, who are too passive and bland to be interesting for very long. Leo knows exactly what he wants and exactly how to get it, and he plans his tactics carefully to take advantage of his own strength and the weaknesses of others. He has weaknesses of his own, of which he is very well aware; in fact it is this understanding and acceptance of his own nature, including its imperfections, that chiefly sets him apart from the others. This realistic acceptance of himself is most evident in his relations with Carla. He sets out methodically to seduce Carla, not in order to prove any point to himself or anybody else, but to indulge the passion which he quite frankly recognizes in himself. To achieve this end he is ready to sacrifice even financial profit; although it would be good business to foreclose the mother's mortgage early in the novel, he refrains in order not to spoil things with Carla. Carla, on the other hand, is essentially a sentimentalist in spite of her superficial perversity and cynicism. As Leo makes the first moves toward seduction she tells herself resignedly, "He or another," yet after she has given herself to him she watches him sleeping and thinks, "How fine it would be if he woke up now and told me he loved me."[36] It is mainly out of weakness of will that she surrenders to Leo, but she is unable to admit this even to herself and instead convinces herself it is "to have a new life." This sarcastic allusion to the *Vita nuova* of Dante parallels the repeated use of *la madre* which, perhaps, comments tacitly on the idealized picture of motherhood in Grazia Deledda's novel. In both cases Moravia is attacking a literary tradition, and in both cases it is a sentimental one. To behave according to the formulas of medieval courtly love, as Carla does when she longs for Leo to say he loves her, is to regard human relations in a totally specious and unrealistic way and thus to condemn one's self to failure in the struggle of ego with others. It is typical of the bourgeois mentality, as Moravia sees it, that it simultaneously surrenders itself to perversity and attempts to cover up this perversity with a sentimental apparatus of idealism, frequently that of romantic love. And romantic love, in Italian culture, goes back through D'Annunzio and Tasso to Dante. At the same time it is not so much these classic figures of Italian literature he rejects as the cult made of them in the classroom, in the popular press, and in fascist rhetoric; it is to Grazia Deledda's readers, rather than to the author herself, that he says somewhat savagely, "Here's your typical bourgeois mother." This repudiation of literary sentimentalism is basic in Moravia's work, and is one of the attitudes he shares with Pavese and Vittorini.

Even Michele, for all his weakness, knows that a "new life" is not as simple as Carla imagines. The structural climax of the novel is the scene in which he fails in his effort to kill Leo and realizes that the defeat of the family has become total. He tells Carla that their mistake has been the failure to act sincerely: she has pretended to love Leo, he to hate him, but neither has been capable of true passion. And so, Carla concludes, since nothing is changed, it is better to "try nothing . . . and stay as we are." Michele's response is a final pitiful attempt to escape from self-deception and regard himself and the others around him realistically, in short to become a free human being in control of his own destiny. "But no . . . in order to live and change we must act sincerely . . . I believe you should leave this man you don't love . . . we'll sell the villa, we'll pay him, if anything is left over so much the better . . . we'll leave all these parties, these people, these places, these things that have become so boring . . . we'll go to live in a few rooms . . . it will be a new life . . ."[37] But almost immediately his conviction falters, he feels "indifferent and tired," and this last spasm of rebellion comes to nothing.

Leo is not addicted to deceiving himself and he is scarcely interested in deceiving others. He comes straight to the point and offers marriage to Carla—although not on the mother's original terms, involving financial support of the family. From Leo's standpoint the step would "regularize the situation" and make his enjoyment of Carla a little less precarious; from her point of view she can hardly hope for anything better, since she is now "discredited." Leo is the spiritual descendant not of Dante but of Machiavelli, a writer Moravia discusses with considerable sympathy in a 1950 essay. Everything Leo says is perfectly logical and also morally abominable, but since it is logical it is the best solution for everyone concerned under the circumstances. At the end, after the others have left, he regards his image in the mirror with a certain satisfaction. "Well, you're not so bad . . . Even married you'll still be the same Leo."[38] In one sense everyone will always be the same; in another sense the acceptance of one's own nature is the first step to the creation of an authentic personality. After this he goes to the ball, where the mother "smiles satisfied" at the thought that her lover will be there.

Pseudo-Dostoevski and Crypto-Stendhal

The emergence of Leo as a major character in *Gli indifferenti* was in a sense a technical accident. When Moravia began the novel he evidently associated himself with Michele, the character closest to himself in age and general attitude. But, because he wanted to permit himself access to the psychologies of the other characters as well, he chose a technique that switched from one consciousness to another and examined the motives and reactions of each character in turn. In this technical situation it was the personality of Leo that dominated the novel itself as it dominated in the action related by the novel. Only in a multiple point of view could this effect have been attained. At this stage in his development Moravia could hardly have written a convincing novel with the mature and cynical Leo as the central character, and if Leo had been seen only through the eyes of Michele the portrait would have lost a great deal of its effect. In this sense the switching point of view of *Gli indifferenti,* in spite of the difficulties it entailed, was a lucky invention and one that accounted for a great deal of the success of the novel. In short Moravia found himself confronted with a basic difficulty in technique and managed somehow to convert it to an asset.

In his next two novels this device of multiple point of view was carried a step farther, and the result was a partial failure. *Le ambizioni sbagliate** appeared in 1935 and passed practically unnoticed, by readers and critics alike. In large part this was due to the fact that the censors, after the clandestine enthusiasm created by *Gli indifferenti,* had forbidden the newspapers to review it. But there were intrinsic difficulties in the novel as well. *Le ambizioni sbagliate* is a closely packed work of over 450 pages, involving six major characters and a number of minor ones, and an action considerably more complicated than that of *Gli indifferenti.* After the somewhat limiting simplicity of his first novel Moravia set out deliberately to achieve richness through multiplication of scene, character, and situation. A number of years later, after he had passed this formative stage in his development, he called it "my most intentionally Dostoevskian novel."[38] This is an indispensable clue in understanding how the novel is made, even though it is Dostoevskian only in part, and the things it borrows from Dostoevski are not entirely those that make the Russian author important or interesting. One sense in

* Literally spoiled, or mistaken, ambitions. Translated both as *The Wheel of Fortune* (Viking, 1937) and *Mistaken Ambitions* (Farrar, Straus & Cudahay, 1955).

which it imitates Dostoevski is a purely mechanical one: each chapter consists of a "scene," limited to one room or place, in which characters are more or less contrivedly brought together and made to talk. Dostoevski derived this from Balzac and the French realists, who in turn were probably influenced by the French classic theatre. But in Dostoevski this device is merely a framework that serves to support the genuinely Dostoevskian part of the work: the strange, saintly and obsessed characterizations, the powerful visions of guilt and contrition, the unreal and yet vivid psychological mood. Moravia, at least in *Le ambizioni sbagliate,* lacks a characteristically Moravian world to oppose to this Dostoevskian world, and the result is a rather swollen novel full of Italians who give the impression they would like to behave like Dostoevsky characters but are not quite sure how it is done. *Le ambizioni sbagliate* illustrates the dictum that a novel stands or falls on its characters; it is successful exactly to the extent that these are successful, and it fails to the precise degree that they are contrived and unconvincing.

Structurally these characters are woven into a reasonably tight and ingenious intrigue. Maria Luisa, a wealthy society woman, is annoyed because her husband, Matteo, has a mistress, Andreina. Sofia, Matteo's sister, hopes to reconcile the couple, and in this she is assisted by her fiancé Pietro. But Pietro himself comes under the spell of Andreina and soon becomes her lover. On the periphery of this action the invalid Stefano, Maria Luisa's brother, offers cynical Nietzschean comments and is eventually revealed as the initial seducer of Andreina who started her on a life of vice. Except that it has more characters, this plot of lovers and jealousy is essentially comparable to the plot of *Gli indifferenti.* The difference is that, in contrast to the simplicity of the earlier novel, Moravia attempts to build in a complexity that frequently strikes the reader as spurious. The action covers a good deal more time, and there is more incident, although much of the incident is told about rather than seen. The chaste but proud and strong-willed Sofia goes to see Andreina in a scene reminiscent of the confrontation of Katerina Ivanovna and Grushenka in *The Brothers Karamazov,* with much the same result: in spite of her moral disadvantage the courtesan easily dominates the ingenue. Another effective scene, one in which Andreina again resembles Grushenka, is the one in which she reveals her criminal plan to Pietro. After the two have become lovers she begins hinting to him of some terrible secret that lies between them. Finally she asks if he will promise to do what she asks of him.

She did not turn her eyes from Pietro's, and, still watching him in her fixed and unflinching way, she moved her cold and restless hand over his breast. At this touch, under this glance, a strange trouble slowly invaded the soul of the young man. He felt horror, but along with horror an entranced wonder, an invincible and terrified curiosity to know more, to go to the end of the thing. "What do you want me to promise?" he could not help asking at last.

He felt Andreina's body move toward his own; then, lying next to him and embracing him tightly, she brought her pallid face with its fixed and frenzied eyes close to his. "Kill Maria Luisa!" she told him scarcely moving her lips, as though breathless.[39]

This scene perhaps resembles an old Theda Bara film more than *The Brothers Karamazov*. But the difficulties are not so much in the character or behavior of Andreina as in the reactions of Pietro to this behavior. Even though the incident is related from his point of view, the violent emotions of Pietro are never quite seen *en premier plan*. It is characteristic that at the climax of this scene he is referred to quite externally as *il giovane*, and thus the apprehension invades only "the soul of the young man" rather than that of the reader himself. In short there is a failure of empathy due to the author's failure to associate his own emotions sufficiently with those of the character, and this in turn is connected to the tendency of the point of view to switch rapidly from one character to another, sometimes even in the middle of a paragraph. The difficulties with the novel are not conceptual or psychological, or even thematic; they are simply technical.

Those parts of the novel that are most "Moravian" closely resemble *Gli indifferenti*. The character of Pietro is that of Michele in a later stage of development; where Michele is still troubled by his lack of sincerity, his inability to act spontaneously, Pietro has become auto-indoctrinated with bourgeois hypocrisy to the point where he actually believes he is an idealist. In his own view of himself he is sincere, altruistic, even naive. Yet he succeeds in the most complicated intrigues, leading him to conclude, "In actual fact the best shrewdness is not to be shrewd."[40] Pietro is too intelligent to be shrewd without knowing it; but he is also astute enough to keep this knowledge in a part of his mind where it will not interfere with his view of himself as a mysteriously lucky sheep among wolves. In this he is more complicated, probably, than any Moravian hero before Marcello of *Il conformista*.

Andreina is unsuccessful in her efforts to inspire this elegant self-deceiver to crime, and she receives only a blundering assistance from the servant Rosa. In the end she is obliged to murder Maria Luisa herself, justifying her act with rationalizations borrowed from

Crime and Punishment (" . . . killing Maria Luisa is no worse than killing the first dog you meet in the street. In fact it's not as bad, because the dog might attract people and be useful, whereas nobody likes Maria Luisa and she's useless even to herself").[41] The murder itself she carries out in a sudden access of violence, as it were unwilled and almost hypnotic. The scene is a powerful one, but awkward and lacking in verisimilitude; Moravia is not at his best in this kind of violent action. The reason for this lies in his concept of character; the point of his passive and overreflective heroes is that they are incapable of any resolute action, even a criminal one. It is interesting to compare this murder scene with the more typically Moravia dénouement of *Gli indifferenti*. Setting out to seize control of his destiny through a plan that is sound in theory, Michele flinches at the critical moment and ends by finding himself in the grip of forces over which he has no control. It is because Pietro too behaves in this way that he is a more authentic character than Andreina, even though a less vivid one. The Moravian touch is seen even in his minor actions: having come into possession of the stolen jewel box of Maria Luisa, he keeps the jewels in his pocket and throws the empty box from a bridge into the Tiber. This is a sound tactic, and in an ordinary novel—a novel of Simenon, for example—it would succeed. But the box lands in the mud at the riverside, and Pietro has to descend to the bank and wander around through the garbage and stagnant mud to find it. The whole business seems to him "symbolic and a bad omen," and he remembers that it was Andreina who got him involved with the jewels in the first place. He ends by reflecting that it is she, after all, who has made him behave "in a swinish manner" instead of his redeeming her as he had intended. It is in this lucid insight into his degradation that Pietro is a prototype of Moravia's postwar heroes.

*La mascherata** in 1941 represents an even further departure from the style and psychology of *Gli indifferenti*; it is technically Moravia's least "Moravian" novel. Disguises and masked identities play an essential thematic part in it. The very novel itself, in fact, is a disguise of the author; not only did he conceal what was essentially a comment on fascist Italy in an imaginary Latin-American setting, but he masked his authorship under a style which was not his own and which he used for no other novel before it or after. If *le style c'est l'homme*—and for a writer like Moravia it is—then for the purposes of this novel he quite literally assumed a fictitious identity. As

* Literally, "The Masquerade"; translated as *The Fancy Dress Party* (Farrar, Straus & Young, 1952).

a practical tactic the ruse was futile; after some vacillation *La mascherata* was suppressed by the censors, and Moravia was forbidden henceforth even to sign his name to newspaper articles. But for the purposes of a fancy-dress party it is not really necessary for anyone to believe in the disguise; it is enough if the mask itself is interesting, and if it reveals some novel or unexpected aspect of its wearer.

This *La mascherata* does; it reveals, for example, that the technical problems of *Le ambizioni sbagliate* were something Moravia was perfectly well aware of and which he was even willing to parody. The point of view is deliberately and exaggeratedly old-fashioned; the novel is narrated by a kind of invisible angel who hovers over the action, now and then sharing parcels of his omniscience with the reader, and frequently commenting on each character's ignorance of the motives of the others. "Thus Perro thought he was deceiving Sebastiano and Sebastiano thought he was deceiving Perro; but the only one who was really deceived was Saverio."[42] There are also ironic summaries of the history, social conditions, and national temperament of "a certain country on the other side of the ocean." This resembles *La Chartreuse de Parme* more than it does Dostoevski or any other classic author, and in fact the tone of the whole novel is Stendhalian. (Moravia himself has admitted, "When I wrote *La mascherata* I had somehow in mind the Stendhalian style, this is quite true."[43]) The central figure Sebastiano is a kind of ineffectual and diffident cousin of Fabrice; he attempts the same kind of amorous and political audacities as Stendhal's hero but usually bungles everything magnificently. Certain other characters can be roughly approximated to figures in the *Chartreuse:* the dictator Tereso is Prince Ernesto, Saverio resembles Ferrante Palla, and the chief of police Cinco is Mosca and Rassi rolled into one. As for the heroine Fausta, she resembles Clelia but only the corrupted and cynical Clelia of the end of Stendhal's novel. If we are not shown her progress from innocence to corruption it is partly because *La mascherata* is a less complex novel than Stendhal's and partly that Moravia does not really believe in female innocence, or at least that his male characters are so constituted that they seldom encounter this phenomenon. Yet Sebastiano, almost to the end, goes on looking for innocence in Fausta and for courage in himself. Nothing ever turns out quite as he expects, but it is to his credit that he regards these imperfections of his experience with a mild and intelligent irony. Sebastiano demonstrates the essential quality shared by the heroes of Moravia and Stendhal: their tendency to reflect quite calmly in the middle of highly emotional experience. Sebastiano's first amorous encounter with Fausta takes place after she loses her way during a walk (at least so he believes) and comes to his house to ask for directions. Since the once noble family is now impoverished, the house is empty except for a few sacks strewn around on the floor. Sebastiano, "afraid above all of being thought shy," fearfully puts his arm around her, expecting a slap or at least a rebuff of some kind. Instead he suddenly finds the lady lying in his arms with blank upturned eyes and parted lips. At this point the omniscient narrator comments, "It was brought home to Sebastiano at that moment how deeply his father had injured him by selling all the furniture,"[44] a most Stendhalian thought. Even Tereso for all his experience—he is a one-armed general who has fought many battles —shows the same mixture of naiveté and intelligence in matters of love; in the middle of his most excruciating passion for Fausta he sees quite clearly what a fool he is making of himself.

Once set in motion, these characters are woven into an implausible farrago involving a palace revolution—or rather a pseudo-revolution, since the whole thing is a hoax perpetrated by the chief of police, Cinco, for his own ends. This is one of the many "disguises" of the novel: a reactionary political maneuver is disguised as a revolt, just as Sebastiano is a Moravian character disguised as a Stendhalian hero and the novel itself is a political satire disguised as a Ruritanian romance. Sebastiano's half-brother Saverio, the key figure in the plot to assassinate Tereso, believes himself to be an idealist, an intellectual, and a revolutionary; in reality he is only a pawn of the reactionary police. Through his membership in a revolutionary party he experiences "a feeling of trusting surrender, of perilous security, as though you were gathered up in the arms of a giant and carried wherever the giant wishes, trusting utterly even though you knew not where you were carried,"[45] a fair description of the state of mind of certain Communist intellectuals under the fascist regime. But the party he belongs to is a fiction invented by a police agent, and he is the only member. Imagining himself a martyr, he is in reality only a victim. His mistake is the usual one of the intellectual who gets involved in politics: the confusing of verbal and idealistic constructions for the true realities of the situation. In his case the penalty is death; at the end of the novel he is in a car racing at full speed toward the cemetery, "with three mortal wounds in three different parts of his body."[46]

The unifying scene of the novel is the palace masquerade at which the assassination attempt takes place. Saverio and Sebastiano are provided with a bomb and disguised as footmen, in this costume gaining entry to the palace. Fausta is disguised as a chimney sweep in order to seduce Tereso, who for his part is wearing his general's uniform and pretending to be a dictator—which for the moment he is not, since he is at the absolute mercy of Fausta's whims. The epitome of this network of interlocking disguises is a scene in which Sebastiano in his footman's livery is obliged to make love to the fat and middle-aged Duchess. At this point the lover, disguised as footman, feigns another and even more spurious role as lover in order to escape detection in his role as footman. The deceptions operate at three levels: both he and the Duchess know he is not a lover in the sense he is pretending at this moment, he himself knows he is not a footman, and only the reader knows he is not an assassin but an ineffectual dreamer. Yet even in this scene his reaction to the predicament is a Stendhalian one. "For a moment he felt inclined to burst out laughing. It was thus, he thought, that Fate wished to cure him completely of the sweet illusion of love; after having revealed the treachery of Fausta it now piled jest on injury by offering him this turgid and repulsive caricature of amorous passion: the senile infatuation of the Duchess."[47] The novel is a tragedy for Saverio; for Sebastiano it begins as romance and ends as farce. Sebastiano is not only the most sympathetic character of the novel but the one closest to Moravia's own attitudes and temperament.

This perception of reality as travesty is a minor theme in Moravia's work, but it is a recognizable one that can be traced through his fiction from *Gli indifferenti* to the postwar novels. *Gli indifferenti* ends with a masked ball which is a travesty of the real lives of its characters, and the heroes of *La noia* and *L'attenzione* are preoccupied with the "inauthenticity" of the world around them. In the same way *La mascherata*, while not in the main stream of Moravia's development as a novelist, is an organic part of his work in ways that are somewhat more subtle than they appear at first examination. On the surface the tone of *La mascherata* was determined almost entirely by the exigencies of censorship. Under the surface it has an aesthetic—the aesthetic of parody—that elevates it considerably above the musical-comedy libretto it at first resembles. In this sense it bears the same relation to the genre of popular adventure-romance that Mann's *Felix Krull* does to the genre of rogue-memoirs on which it was modeled. The crucial question is: does the artist have a genuine awareness and control of the literary form he is using? Regarded in this way *La mascherata* is not a great novel but at least a competent one. But if it is approached through the character of Sebastiano, the key figure of the novel, it is revealed as a much more personal document than its form and style at first suggest. To the approximate degree that the fictional setting stands for fascist Italy—and this is true only in a limited sense—Sebastiano stands for Moravia himself. Like Moravia he has an ambivalent attitude toward the tyranny in which he finds himself living; in general he is profoundly bored except when he is with Fausta. "His boredom came from a complete skepticism about the fate of humanity as well as the fate of his own country. He had no political experience. He belonged to a generation rendered congenitally insensible, so to speak, by the recent violent upheavals. and he believed in nothing. Neither in the State nor in revolution, neither in freedom nor in authority. In this circumstance the majority of Sebastiano's contemporaries simply devoted themselves to their careers without scruples and without illusions. But in a few cases, as for example in Sebastiano's own, this skepticism led to dreaming, boredom, inertia, and dilettantism."[47] The polite term for this state of mind in contemporary Germany was "inner emigration." *La mascherata*, on the surface an escapist novel, thus contains his own auto-criticism of escapism as a reaction to tyranny. Sebastiano's dreamy eroticism, his elegant and complicated unhappiness, is a D'Annunzian aesthetic only lightly travestied, and his failure at the end is the failure of all dilettantism. But the activist Saverio comes to an even more terrible end, and his efforts to sacrifice himself for mankind are if anything more ineffectual. This farce is also profoundly pessimistic.

Going to the People

In the autumn of 1943 Moravia became aware that Rome was no longer safe for him; his name was on a list of antifascists marked for arrest. Shortly after the German occupation of Rome in September he tried to make his way to Naples, but found it was impossible to cross the Allied lines. Instead he spent nine months hiding with the peasants in the mountains near Fondi. After the breakout at Cassino in the spring he was liberated by the American Second Army and came back to Rome. Impatient to return to the normal working habits that had been denied him so long, first by the fascists and then by the conditions of his exile, he began writing immediately. But at first this impulse to write lacked a direction; he was disoriented by events and for a time seemed to hesitate among various modes and styles of fiction. It is a considerable tribute to his systematic working habits, in fact, that he was able to produce at all under the confused conditions of life in Rome in 1944. He first began writing about his experience in the mountains, and turned out several dozen pages of what was later to be *La ciociara* before abandoning it temporarily. Later in the year he published the satirical-surrealistic stories of *L'epidemia*. From this period also dates "Agostino," one of his finest tales. The major work he finally turned to, however, was the novel published in 1947 as *La romana*.*

Moravia thus spent a considerable time conceiving, planning, and writing this new novel, more than he had spent on any previous book except *Gli indifferenti*. And in fact *La romana* marks an important turning point in his development as a stylist. All his previous fiction, with the exception of a few scattered pages, had been written in the third person. *La romana* is told in the first person by a lower-class narrator, and the greater part of his subsequent work—the sole exceptions are the tale "La disubbidienza," *Il conformista,* and a few stories—is written in the first person. This was more than the matter of a mere stylistic device. At least Moravia himself considered it to be more, and even came to the conclusion that the problem of point of view lay at the heart of the problem of the modern novel. Essentially his choice of the first-person technique was a rejection of the omniscience of the realist-naturalist school, from Balzac through Flaubert to Zola, and represented in Italian literature especially by Manzoni. It was not only that this omniscience—the claim of the novelist to see into all hearts, understand all characters at once, permit or deny the reader the facts as he pleased—was presumptuous. It was also that this omniscience did not correspond to the psychological, or more precisely the epistemological, needs of the modern novel, which in their turn corresponded to a particular twentieth-century way of regarding the phenomenon of consciousness. The true function of the first person, according to Moravia, is "to indicate the lack of faith in an objective reality common to both writer and reader," while the effect of the objective or omniscient point of view is to reinforce or sustain this notion of objective reality. "The omniscience of the nineteenth-century novelist turned finally into a trick, a lifeless convention. Today we can no longer write 'He thought,' because we don't know with certainty what a third person is thinking from the moment there no longer exists a thought or a mode of thought common to all men. We can only write: 'I thought.'"[47] For the Anglo-Saxon reader a half-century after James and Joyce, this theorizing has a somewhat naive ring to it. The difference between "he" and "I" is after all only grammatical, and the third-person pronoun does not prevent the Joyce of *A Portrait of the Artist* from entering into psychological intimacy with his character. But the Italian novel had not been very much influ-

* Translated as *The Woman of Rome* (Farrar, Straus, 1949).

enced by the technical revolution represented by the generation of Joyce and Virginia Woolf; in the late Twenties, when Moravia began writing, it was still essentially a nineteenth-century form. Furthermore, Moravia's reasons for settling on the first person are somewhat more complicated than his own explanation would suggest. He seems gradually to have grasped that the main function of a novelistic style was to build a psychological rapport, a community of consciousness, between character and reader: in short the phenomenon of empathy. In novels like *Le ambizioni sbagliate* and *La mascherata,* where the point of view flits from one character to another, this empathy is built up on one page only to be demolished on the next by a switch to a new consciousness. "He thought . . . but little did he know what she thought. She, on the other hand . . ." In such a style the reader, bewildered by the task of empathizing with all characters at once, ends by believing in none. The characters become puppets seen only from the outside, and this is exactly what is not desired; above all Moravia wants to regard his characters from the inside.

Moravia's dissatisfaction with novelistic omniscience is connected to another of his theoretical tenets: the bankruptcy of *prosa d'arte* or the old-fashioned literary prose of Italian tradition. As long as the author—who is necessarily an intellectual, a person of a certain literary culture—permits himself the privilege of hovering over his characters, of viewing them and commenting on them from the outside—he will inevitably fall into a literary or "written" novelistic language. This problem is solved with one stroke if the novel becomes "spoken"—if it is narrated in the voice of a single character, if it confines itself to the rhythms, the stylistic idiosyncrasies, the limitations of that voice. This technique is most effective, at least in Moravia's opinion, if the narrator is a person without literary culture. *La romana* is told in the first person by a girl of the working class, and *La ciociara* is recounted by a semiliterate Trastevere shopkeeper. Both have been compared to *Moll Flanders,* and justly so; they are effective in exactly the same way as Defoe's novel and their technical limitations are the same. In actual fact the limitations are more theoretical than actual. When he deals with the problem in his criticism Moravia does not seem to grasp that in this kind of narrative recounted by a semiliterate character there is always a certain amount of artistic cheating. The important thing is not that the language should actually be that used by uneducated speakers but that it should give the aesthetic illusion of a proletarian style. In practice this is what happens in these two novels; they give the impression of authenticity without making direct use of Roman dialect in the manner, for example of Gadda's *Quer pasticciaccio brutto de via Merulana.*

Moravia's prewar heroines are seen mainly through the eyes of men and are always somewhat enigmatic. Adriana, the narrator of *La romana,* is the first woman in his fiction to be seen in the full intimacy and complexity of her motives; this is one of the immediate consequences of the new point of view. Outwardly she is a typical product of the Roman suburbs; her father was a railwayman and her widowed mother is a shirtmaker. Her culture is limited but she has an unmistakable intelligence, and particularly a clear and perceptive feminine insight; she tells her own story simply and yet with a considerable precision and eloquence. Whatever her limitations, she lacks the moral shabbiness of bourgeois heroines like the Carla of *Gli indifferenti.* She sees things clearly and realistically, and when she acts she does so out of a simple and direct impulse. Moreover she understands why she does things and acts in full knowledge of the implications of her behavior; here again she differs from Carla and practically all of Moravia's earlier protagonists. In characterization as well as in technique this novel marks a new turning in Moravia's development.

In structure *La romana* is simple to the point of the diagrammatic. In the early part of the novel Adriana is tacitly encouraged to become first a painter's model and then a prostitute by her mother, who is bitterly resentful of the poverty her own conventional marriage has brought her. Adriana thereupon becomes involved with five men in succession, each of whom represents a variety of male sexuality as well as a step in her own development or self-comprehension. Her influence on all these five men is evil; three of them die violently as a result of their involvement with her. But she herself is untouched; or more precisely, the effect of her profession on her is not evil but existential, causing her to examine her own nature and develop finally into a human being aware of her powers and limitations and fully in charge of her own destiny. If it had not been for the profession she entered half-unwittingly, under the pressure of her mother and others like her friend Gisella, she would undoubtedly have fallen into a typical petty-bourgeois marriage and lived out her life totally unconscious of the limitations of her existence. It is precisely the evil, the violence, and the cynicism she encounters as a prostitute that cause her to reexamine herself and the society around her and eventually come to grips with her own destiny, to make out of herself something that only she can make.

With a single exception the five men of the novel are more or less pawns or peripheral elements in this central drama of Adriana's self-emergence. Gino, her first lover, is a chauffeur whose ambitions are those of a typical flunky. He is impressed with the luxury of his employers' lives, and he imagines, somewhat naively, that he can get the same for himself by being "shrewd" (*furbo,* a favorite word in Moravia's vocabulary, and one he almost always uses ironically). Adriana herself says of him that his principal quality is a kind of fatuous and short-sighted astuteness. In his relations with her this astuteness consists of promising to marry her although he is already married—not a very original or ingenious trick. Astarita, the first man she accepts money from, is an agent of the political police: young, bald, yellow-faced, with large black eyes and an ironic mouth, an elegant dresser. His sexual nature is sado-masochistic. Adriana comments that he enjoys only what he can take by force, but when he finds himself in love with her he cringes before her and offers her anything she asks, even proposing to compromise his profession for her. We would not expect Moravia to admire a character who is not only a fascist policeman but a pervert, and he doesn't. But Astarita is presented with remarkable objectivity, and in one scene—the confrontation with Sonzogno in Adriana's room—he behaves impressively and even heroically. Moravia was to develop this sexual-pathological analysis of the fascist mentality with greater complexity in *Il conformista.*

Giacinti, a traveling salesman introduced to Adriana by her friend Gisella, is a kind of parody of the petty-bourgeois mentality, in his sexual behavior as well as his economic views. He knows the price of everything and is intent on getting his money's worth in any transaction. Except for this he is totally devoid of ethics or inhibitions. He is not embarrassed at making love in a taxi, and says of the driver, "I pay him to take me to my destination and not to concern himself with what happens in his taxi."[47] In the same way he considers that the duty of a prostitute is to please others for money. The gloomy Gisella doesn't know how to do this, Adriana does. Therefore in his scale of values Adriana is good, Gisella bad. No doubt there are people like Giacinti, but the characterization is so oversimplified that he becomes little more than a talking doll. Even his physical qualities are caricatural: when he is seated he seems normal except that his shoulders are very broad, but when he stands he is revealed as almost a dwarf. Moravia clearly has less sympathy for him than he has even for the fascist Astarita, who at least is a fairly complex character with something more than banal motivations.

Gino and Giacinti are studies of two kinds of *furberia* or astuteness, whereas Astarita and the "strong man" Sonzogno represent two kinds of prepotence. Astarita's power is political, Sonzogno's purely physical. But Astarita's authority is backed by physical force, while Sonzogno's power lacks any abstract or intellectual component; and this is his weakness. He murders twice in the course of the novel: in a moment of anger he smashes the skull of a goldsmith and receiver of stolen goods, and later he throws Astarita down a stairwell. In both cases he acts out of impulse and receives no gain from his crime. He is an automaton, a murdering machine: as soon as a given nerve is touched he reacts instantly and brutally, without feeling remorse for his act or even comprehending it. This kind of jack-in-the box is a type of character that interests Moravia, one he uses frequently in his stories. In physical appearance Sonzogno is characterized through the leitmotifs of the pulsing muscle in his jaw, his raincoat, and his close-clipped haircut. On the surface Adriana is terrified of him, but in the act of love she is thrilled by his unlimited and mindless strength. The fact that Sonzogno is probably the father of the child she carried at the end of the novel is one of those details in Moravia that seem significant, or just, even though the reason for the significance or justice is not immediately apparent.

The fifth member of this interlocking ring of males, the student Mino, is more complex and more fully portrayed than any of the others. As a clandestine political conspirator he is intellectually the opposite number of Astarita. In fact he is a kind of complement to Astarita in several ways. Astarita enjoys only what he can take by force; Mino is an idealist who believes force is evil and is ready to sacrifice himself for this principle. Astarita is both prepotent and astute. Mino is impotent in several senses, and he is the opposite of astute—the Italian is *fesso*, which may be superficially translated "foolish" but more precisely is used to refer to one who does not know his own interests or does not act to secure his own advantage. In this he resembles characters like Michele in *Gli indifferenti* or the "impotents" of some of the early stories. But there is an important difference: for the first time Moravia analyzes this impotence and discovers a metaphysical basis for it. Mino is an idealist and intellectual. He understands everything, but all his wisdom is out of books; he understands with his head. He lives in the intellectual or verbal world so completely, in fact, that he has lost contact with the concrete realities that are our only sources of basic and vivid experience. In a conversation with Adriana he explains to her that, although words are the sole reality of his life, he has come to the point where even words have no meaning; he could recite the Paternoster backwards or forwards and it would have exactly the same significance. "But not only words have that effect on me . . . things too . . . people . . . you're there opposite me, sitting on the arm of that chair, and you think I see you . . . but I don't see you because I don't understand you . . . even if I touched you I'd fail to understand you the same way . . ."[48] For this reason he does everything, including love, mechanically, "as though playing a part." This failure of contact with physical reality lies at the bottom of his character, and it is a key concept in Moravia's later novels. Adriana comments rather shrewdly—seeming to refer to Astarita, although she never mentions him—that it is probably this kind of incomprehension that causes cruelty in many people: "They try to regain contact with reality through the pain of others."[49] In Mino this metaphysical breakdown leads to a failure of political belief, the one realm in which he is totally committed. When he is arrested by the police he betrays his companions immediately, almost indifferently, not from cowardice but out of a "mysterious interruption of will."[50] Beginning abstractly as a political idealist, he has entered into certain physical relations with others in order to carry out his political principles. But he is unable to operate effectively in the physical realm, and so the political abstraction collapses along with the world of concrete sensation. First of all, Moravia suggests, we have to live in a world of things; if we learn to deal with this world effectively, to comprehend and manipulate it, then we have at least a chance for success in the more abstract realms of experience.

For Adriana this grasp on reality begins with sexual love, but it by no means ends there. She says of Mino, "If it's there, love for a person, you love not only your own lover but everybody else and everything, the way it happened to me; but if it isn't there, you love nothing and nobody, the way it was with him."[51] It takes her, however, a considerable time to work out this understanding of herself and others. When she first accepts money from Astarita she is bewildered by the "feeling of complicity and sensual understanding" this act entails. The crucial step in her development is her discovery of Gino's duplicity; she learns from Astarita that Gino is not only married but has a child, and Astarita furnishes her with the names of both. It is shortly after this that she makes the quite conscious decision to become a prostitute. "I thought that I liked love, and I liked money, and I liked the things you could get with money, and I said to myself that from now on, whenever I had the chance, I wouldn't refuse either love or money or the things you could get with money."[52] As soon as she has made this decision she becomes a different person, with far greater astuteness, inner strength, and self-control. Her first act of self-assertion is a crime: she steals a compact in the bedroom of Gino's employer. She steals on another occasion before the end of the novel, but in neither case for gain, instead to demonstrate her new character—to offer a practical and concrete proof of it—for herself and others. When Gino asks her why she took the compact she tells him, "I stole it not because I wanted it, or needed it, but because from now on I can steal *too*."[53] An even more marked evidence of her new character is the way in which she disposes of Gino shortly after she discovers his perfidy. She doesn't dismiss him immediately, with tears and hysterics, as a weaker woman might. Instead she arranges not to see him for a few days, then goes on making love with him as though nothing had happened. Then, in bed with him in the house of his employer, she quite coolly, "with a caressing voice," remarks, "And so, Gino . . . your wife is named Antonietta Partini."[54] That "caressing voice" is the mark of her new identity, her confidence in the power she has discovered in herself. Its hypocrisy is professional; from now on she will be able to make her voice, her body, her emotions do exactly as she wants in order to get the "money and the things that money can buy." This bombshell shatters Gino; for the rest of the novel he is unable to stand up to Adriana or anyone else. Adriana leaves him in bed and goes off to take a long and luxurious bath. "I smiled thinking of him, lost in the big double bed, with that news in the middle of his face like a slap. But I smiled without malice, the way you smile at something comic that has nothing to do with you, because, as I've said, I didn't hold anything against him and even, knowing him now for what he really was, felt a kind of affection for him."[54] Traditionally the whore in literature has a heart of gold; Moravia's has, or develops in the course of the novel, a will of iron.

At this point, about a third of the way through the novel, her battle to create an identity for herself is by no means won. All she has learned after her encounter with Gino is to understand and manipulate others, as she has previously been manipulated by them. It is still necessary for her to grasp the full implications of her pro-fession—to understand that what she is doing is evil even though she herself is not, that evil brings violence, pain, and death to human beings, and that she must accept her part of the responsibility for all this along with the "money and things money can buy" that her profession brings her. Now and then when she is alone in her room she sees her life with an icy clarity. "Sometimes I bring here a man I don't know, who has found me in the night. We struggle in each other's clutches like two enemies . . . then he gives me a piece of colored printed paper . . . the next day I exchange this paper for food, clothes, and other things."[55] Once she has become aware of the strangeness of all this she feels a bewilderment that even has its physical symptoms, making her shudder, making her flesh creep. "It seemed to me suddenly that the walls of the house, the city and even the world vanished and I found myself hanging in empty space, black and limitless; and not only that but hanging there with exactly these clothes, this name, this profession. A girl named Adriana hanging in nothing. It seemed to me that this nothing was a solemn, terrible, and incomprehensible thing."[56]

The life that Adriana has chosen brings little satisfaction to her, and it brings nothing but unhappiness, pain, and death to those around her. Once Mino's relation with her has demonstrated irrefutably to him that he is unable to love, or to feel anything for anyone, he commits suicide. Astarita dies at the hands of Sonzogno, and Sonzogno is killed by police bullets as he escapes over the rooftops. Gino is permanently demoralized by his encounter with Adriana; he knows now he will never be anything but a chauffeur, a negligible identity. This aura of evil that Adriana emanates—or more precisely, which is emanated by her way of life—is demonstrated quite obviously and physically by the change that takes place in her mother. It is the mother who first encourages Adriana to take up her way of life, and she even argues that it is more moral than the conventionally respectable life she herself has lived. Early in the novel, when Gino objects that Adriana's disrobing for painters is immoral, she answers with an angry outburst. "Ah, it's not moral . . . and what is moral then? Is it moral to slave the whole day long, wash dishes, sew, cook, iron, sweep, polish floors and then, at night, see your husband come home dead tired and fall into bed as soon as he's eaten, turn to the wall and fall asleep? That's moral, eh? Sacrifice yourself, never have a moment to breathe, grow old and ugly and then croak, that's moral, eh?"[57] If Moravia had stopped here the novel could be regarded as a typical Marxist comment on bourgeois marriage and prostitution; and certainly this picture of conventional lower-class marriage painted by the mother is worse even than the life Adriana leads. But the essential rottenness operates on the mother in an unexpected way. It is the prosperity of this new way of life that destroys her, in fact, and not its "evil" in any conventional sense. This prosperity, which the mother has always regarded as the only goal worth struggling for and the only ideal with any meaning, results only in a vulgar and tawdry *embourgeoisement*. "She had fattened but she had become neither prettier nor younger," Adriana comments. "It seemed to me that she carried instead of me, in her face and figure, the visible traces of our changed life; and I could never look at her without a painful feeling of remorse, compassion, and repugnance."[57] The mother performs an important technical or symbolic function. It would be unrealistic, and conventionally sentimental, for Adriana's way of life to destroy her body in the short course of the novel as it does, for example, in Zola's *Nana.* Instead, the flabbiness of the middle-aged widow serves as the emblem of the evil she herself has instigated.

In the early stages of the novel Adriana passively allows herself to be led into this life. But she eventually comes to realize that she is responsible for her acts and responsible for the misery and suffering these acts cause to others. And yet, she reflects, even after arriving at this understanding she goes on encountering strangers in the streets, bringing them to her room, and accepting from them the colored pieces of paper. It seems strange to her that her outward and inward lives have so little to do with each other, that they seem to take place in different universes with no communication between them. And this lack of communication is simply the gulf that separates every human being from the external world, that cuts him off from physical experience, from other human beings, from the universe in its final metaphysical sense. Through her love for Mino she arrives at a state of at least partial reconciliation with this nothingness. But she comes to understand finally that she will always be isolated, never able to communicate fully with others, always conscious of the incompatibility between what she says and does outwardly and what she feels in her innermost being.

> But I wasn't foolish enough to believe that I was the only one who had such violent and desperate thoughts. I knew it must happen to everybody, at least once a day, to feel his own life shrink to a point of anxiety, ineffable and absurd. It was just that, with them too, this knowledge didn't produce any visible effect. They left their houses, like me, and went around sincerely reciting their insincere roles. This thought confirmed me in the conviction that all men, without exception, are worthy of compassion for no other reason than because they live.[57]

This passage, somewhat too eloquent and too intellectually pretentious for the uneducated girl who speaks it, is one of those instances where Moravia's own voice patently breaks through the first-person narrative of the novel. Existence is "ineffable and absurd" for many people, but without a certain intellectual sophistication they are unlikely to realize it or at least to express it in these terms. This metaphysical humanism resembles that of Camus' *La peste,* which dates from the same year as Moravia's novel, and it also parallels the social and philosophical concepts Moravia expresses in his 1946 essay "L'uomo come fine."* Through the events of his daily life man is made aware of the imperfection of his world, and of his own limitations in dealing with this imperfection, and this leads him finally to a sense of the absurdity of his existence. But there is another step: the realization that this predicament is one he shares with all men, who are thus "worthy of compassion for no other reason than because they live." *La romana* is about sex, or prostitution, only in the most superficial and immediate sense. It might equally well have been given the title Malraux used for a novel which is superficially about Chinese politics: *La condition humaine*. But this is a title which might serve for any of Moravia's novels after the breakthrough into his mature period, marked ideologically by "L'uomo come fine" in 1946 and stylistically by *La romana* the following year.

Psychopathology and Fascism

In the years immediately following *La romana* Moravia devoted a good deal of his attention to short fiction, and some of the stories of this period, especially those in the volume *L'amore coniugale*, are among his best. It was four years before he published another novel, and *Il conformista†* in 1951 in some ways represents a reversion or setback in his technical development. It returns to the third-person narrative after the innovation of the first person in *La romana;* it was the last time he was to use this technique in a major novel. On the surface the protagonist seems to have little to recommend him to the reader's sympathy. Not only is he a fascist police agent but he is a perverse and rather spineless character, totally lacking in the hardness and self-assurance of the fascist agent Astarita in *La romana*. A novelist is under no obligation to make his characters attractive, but we must feel at least some empathy with the character through whose eyes the action is seen; if we do not the narrative lacks a sense of reality and becomes merely a mechanical recitation of events. When pressed by an interviewer on this point Moravia explained of Marcello, "He was a pitiable character—pitiable because a victim of circumstances," but also conceded, "I don't think it's possible to write a good novel around a negative personality."[58] Considering Moravia's own personal experience of fascism, this ambivalence in his attitude toward his protagonist inevitably resulted in a certain amount of unresolved tension in the novel itself.

* "Man as an End," included in the volume of the same title (Farrar, Straus & Giroux, 1965).

† *The Conformist* (Farrar, Straus & Young, 1951).

There are other technical difficulties. *Il conformista* is the only one of Moravia's novels not to observe a reasonable unity of time; a "prologue" takes place in Marcello's childhood in 1920, the middle part of the action during the Spanish Civil War, and the end in 1943. A large part of the novel is set in Paris, a city Moravia knew only as a visitor; these scenes lack the sense of authenticity of his Roman settings. For these reasons or others the critical reaction to the novel when it first appeared was largely negative. The period around 1950 seems to have been a time of crisis for the generation of Italian writers who developed under fascism; Pavese committed suicide in this year, and Vittorini in 1949 was struggling with the technical and ideological difficulties of *Le donne di Messina*. Moravia, as it happened, emerged from this struggle and went on writing. *Il conformista* can be read as a novel in its own right, in which case it has certain merits and certain weaknesses that are fairly obvious. At the same time it can be regarded as a document, and one of a certain interest, in this effort of a novelist to write his way through a period of technical and personal crisis and come out on the other side.

Il conformista is Moravia's most "political" novel. There is a political element, or an element of social criticism, in all his work, sometimes latent and sometimes more specific. In *La romana* there is an obvious effort to characterize the fascist mentality in the person of Astarita. In *Il conformista* the political question is elevated to the status of a major theme, although it is by no means the only theme of the novel. If we accept the suggestion of the title, in fact, the major theme is that of conformity: the extent to which an individual can, or ought to, model his personality and behavior on the values of the society around him. Moravia begins by presenting the child Marcello as a sadist and latent homosexual, to all appearances a deeply perverted personality. He chops the heads off the flowers in his family garden, then he slays lizards, then a cat, then—as he believes—a human being. When the young chauffeur Lino picks him up in the street he accepts a ride and even accompanies him to his room. But later, when Lino makes improper advances to him and then begs hysterically, "Kill me," Marcello fires a pistol at him and flees. This event determines the course of his whole life. Horrified by his deed, and more by the circumstances and motives underlying it, he spends the following years attempting to lose himself in the anonymity of the crowd, to become exactly like other people, to conform. Imagining that he is alone in possessing the impulses he has discovered in himself, he regards conformity as a mysterious achievement effortless for others but hedged about with infinite difficulties and complications for himself. In a fascist society the epitome of conformity is to be a fascist, and Marcello succeeds totally in this; he becomes an agent of the political secret service. His sexual development goes hand in hand with the social; determined to be "exactly like others," he selects for his fiancée Giulia, a girl of obvious and exuberant wholesomeness. In the middle of the novel these two sides of his life, in fact, are combined in an irony that approaches the grotesque. Marcello is assigned a particularly delicate task by his superiors: the assassination of the liberal Professor Quadri, a slight acquaintance of his who is now an emigré in Paris. Since the time for his marriage with Giulia is approaching anyhow, he decides to combine this assignment with his honeymoon. It is in conducting himself in this manner that he believes he is behaving "exactly like others."

The fact is that Marcello is most natural when he is following his innate impulses, even if these are "abnormal," and the most monstrous when he is trying the most strenuously to conform. Normality, which he regards as the state of the vast majority of mankind, is in reality only a fiction, a statistical abstraction. There are several other "abnormal" characters in the novel who accept their abnormality and somehow bring it into adjustment with the demands of practical life: the chauffeur Lino, the odd and goatlike Professor Quadri, his wife Lina who is a lesbian, an old British gentleman Marcello meets in a Paris park who is fond of young men. Marcello is instrumental in murdering two of these four people and attempts to murder a third, and this is a patently concrete equivalent of his urge to slay the abnormal in himself. But if he seems a monster in the end it is not because, as a child, he suffered from a latent tendency that afflicts a large proportion of adolescents; it is precisely because of his efforts to deny and obliterate this part of his nature by behaving as he imagines others expect of him. This point is made particularly by the contrast between Marcello and Giulia. On first appearance Giulia gives the impression of a healthy and uncomplicated animal. She comes from a typical middle-class home, she is "shapely . . . with a rather coarse, almost vulgar beauty, but fresh and solid,"[59] and she is girlishly enthusiastic about her imminent marriage. If there is anything to reproach in her it is that she is a little too frankly sensual; during her engagement she tells Marcello she is ready to give herself to him "right away" if he wants, and her kisses are so ardent as to be slightly embarrassing. Marcello is pleased by her and selects her as his fiancée because she seems to him the epitome of the normal; even the bad taste of the apartment she lives in is identical with the bad taste of all the other middle-class apartments in Rome. As a matter of fact he learns later that Giulia has had a middle-aged lover for several years, and even that she has been involved in an ambiguous relationship with another woman. But her healthy and elastic libido absorbs these experiences, even her discovery of the peculiarities of her husband and her encounter with the lesbian Lina later in the novel, and somehow converts them to normality. In fact her healthiness is so perfect that in the end there is something machinelike and slightly equivocal about it. In a world of more or less neurotic human beings who somehow come to terms with their neuroses, she seems far less "normal" than Marcello. Oreste del Buono, himself a keenly perceptive psychological novelist as well as a critic, has called her "inhuman."[60] Moravia is never as simple as he seems, and the character of Giulia is a good example of the subtlety, or at least of the ambiguity, of his method.

Seeking to recover from his encounter with Lino, Marcello embarks on his "normal" career as a secret agent. This leads him to complicity in the murder of Quadri, and to the rather involved psychological nexus that serves as the center of the novel. He has already killed—as he thinks—Lino, who symbolically represents the tendency to aberration in his own character. In helping to kill Quadri he is in effect suppressing the intellectual, reasonable, or humanitarian component in his personality, that is to say his own better nature. At the time of his encounter with Quadri in Rome, when he is still a student, he quite consciously regards Quadri as a representative of intellectual humanitarianism, the alternative to his own political choice. Quadri too is aware of this polarity in their relationship, and twice—in Rome and later in Paris—tries to persuade Marcello to obey his better nature and come over to the side of the men of good will. Instead—and perhaps partly to suppress the temptation this offer represents—he plays the part of Judas by pointing out Quadri to his murderers. As it happens, the circumstances are such that this also results in the death of Quadri's wife Lina. Lina is the other half of Lino, a ghost, or in the more precisely applicable French term, *revenant*. She has lesbian tendencies, she represents a threat to Marcello's normal existence (she tries to seduce his wife), and he himself is strongly attracted to her in spite of his intellectual repudiation of his feelings. The situation at this point is a complex web of paradoxes. Marcello has certain perverse tendencies, but in this he is "normal," since all men are more or less subject to such impulses at one time or another. Not comprehending this, he reacts by destroying his own intellectual, or better, nature. Lina too is "perverse." But she and Marcello might have made satisfactory mates, each finding in the other the equivalence and therefore the remedy of his own deviation. But this union cannot take place for several reasons. First, Marcello has already committed himself to a spurious "normality" by marrying Giulia. Second, he makes the same mistake with Lina he has earlier made with Lino, regarding her as a threat to his normality rather than a reflection of something that is already in his own nature. Finally, Lina herself quickly identifies him as a fascist agent and potential murderer of her husband, that is an embodiment of antihumanitarianism. Once this situation is established the violent deaths that follow are inevitable.

Marcello feels a certain remorse for these murders, even though Giulia—whose healthy digestion for crime and vice begins to appear slightly monstrous—does not. In the epilogue, which takes place in the turbulent September of 1943 as the fascist government collapses, he understands with a certain clarity that the danger now confronting himself and his family is the result of his previous choices—the result, in fact, of his impulse to gain security through conformity. Giulia regards the whole debacle as an accident. "I'm sure that those who gave you the orders will escape . . . and you who had nothing to do with it and only did your duty will be the one to suffer."[61] As they flee from Rome she, bourgeois to the end, clutches a crystal vase that she sentimentally associates with their happiness—"I'm fond of it first of all because it's pretty and also because it was you who gave it to me."[62] When the three of them—Marcello, Giulia, and their child—are killed by a strafing Allied plane it is at least a symmetrical end, although perhaps not quite as symmetrical as it might be. Conceivably it is not too much to ask that Marcello's death should be a direct consequence of the murder of Quadri and not merely a symbolic consequence. As a matter of fact that last part of the novel involves an even more implausible coincidence: on the eve of his departure from Rome, in the deserted park of the Villa Borghese, Marcello encounters Lino—not dead at all, now a middle-aged fairy in a black uniform, combing the park for "handsome boys like you." The resuscitated Lino performs a function that Moravia evidently considers important—he makes it clear to Marcello that his obsession with conformity has been unnecessary, telling him, "We all lose our innocence one way or another . . . it's normal." But this point has already been made anyhow, by the whole thematic tendency of the novel, and this unlikely apparition is the weakest point of the structure. Moravia is a good deal more skilled in delineating character than he is in contriving plot. This impulse to tie up the loose ends of a story even at the expense of plausibility was even more marked in his next novel, *Il disprezzo*.

In spite of these difficulties, some of them basic to the novel and some merely incidental, the final effect of *Il conformista* is powerful and convincing. The minor implausibilities like the reappearance of Lino are soon forgotten, and the reader is left with a strong impression of the character of Marcello: the perplexed intellectual, tormented and baffled by physical forces—both in himself and in the society around him—over which he has no control. Like the Astarita of *La romana* he is a latent sadist, an unloved lover, an incarnation of a forceful but deeply psychopathic element in fascism. But unlike Astarita he has a certain degree of insight into his own character and this pathological element of his relation to fascism. There is a side of him that resembles the Mino of *La romana:* the intellectual who perceives his predicament so clearly he can do nothing to extricate himself from it. On the most immediate level *Il conformista* is about politics. But the fascism of the novel is only an extension or perversion of certain aspects of bourgeois culture, just as Marcello's pathological conformity is only an exaggeration of the conformity that dominates all modern civilization. On a somewhat deeper level the novel deals with the problem of thought and action. We are recalled not only to *Hamlet* but to Yeats: why do the best in our time lack all conviction while the worst are full of passionate intensity? It is easy to see the passionate worst in Marcello; it requires a little more perception to see that he also has in him an element of this thoughtful but physically impotent best. In a less corrupt society, in classic Greece for example, he might have developed into a useful if unextraordinary individual, accepting his differences from other men and finding some means to turn them to advantage for himself and for his society. This is what Moravia means when he calls Marcello "pitiable because he was a victim of circumstances."

The Artist as Lover

In *Il disprezzo** in 1954 Moravia produced his first full-length treatment of a theme that was to dominate his work increasingly thereafter: the relation of art to sexuality. This relatively short novel —only a little over two hundred and fifty pages—also deals with the Proustian theme of the artistic mind that regards itself in the act of creation. But in Proust too the artistic problem is also a sexual one: the mind that observes itself in the artistic process is also the mind that observes itself in the act of love. Yet genuine art, like genuine love, is spontaneous or at least has a large spontaneous element; if it becomes excessively auto-analytical it loses its impetus and lapses

* Literally "contempt" or "scorn." Translated as *A Ghost at Noon* (Farrar, Straus, 1956).

into passivity. The question arises: is this true of *Il disprezzo* itself, the novel Moravia is writing in order to analyse the malady of auto-analysis? The issues raised by this novel extend far beyond the novel itself and penetrate to the heart of Moravia's own personal problem as an artist.

Like most of Moravia's passive artist-lovers, the Riccardo Molteni of *Il disprezzo* is not so much an artist as an *artiste manqué*. He would like to write for the serious theater, although so far he has shown no concrete evidence of talent as a dramatist. Meanwhile he makes his living as a film critic and later, as the novel proceeds, a scriptwriter for rather bad movies. He takes this latter job, although he does not really want it, for rather complicated reasons that are connected to his sex life. He is very much in love with his wife Emilia, whom he describes as "what is known as a homemaker" (*una donna di casa*), and he imagines that what she wants most of all is a fine and expensive apartment instead of the furnished room which is all he can afford as a journalist. Thus his career as a script-writer is a concession to what he takes for Emilia's wishes. This is a misconception, as the subsequent events demonstrate; but probably he would have been unable to make Emilia happy in any case. Even though *Il disprezzo* is told in the first person and Emilia is seen only through the eyes of Molteni, it is she herself who perceives all this most clearly—her husband's character, her own desires, and the im-possibility of Molteni's achieving any success either as a dramatist or as a scriptwriter. Emilia, who is shrewd and intuitive although she comes from an uneducated background, is not without resemblance to the Odette who fascinates and torments Swann in Proust's novel.

The plot of *Il disprezzo* baffles some readers and annoys others. Nothing very much happens for the first two-thirds of it, and it ends with what seems at first glance to be a flagrant *deus ex machina*. Molteni, having written one bad film in order to pay the first install-ment on his apartment, signs a contract to write another one, a retelling of the *Odyssey*. In this he is to collaborate with the German film writer Rheingold, who proposes to reinterpret Homer's story as a psychoanalytic drama. The producer Battista, on the other hand, wants a spectacular extravaganza along the line of the American biblical "epics." Molteni is not sure what he wants, but he sets out to tread a dubious path somewhere between Rheingold and Battista. It is at this point that his relations with his wife began to deteriorate. Emilia not only counters his embraces with a silent frigidity but tells him openly that she feels a "contempt" for him (*disprezzo*, the opposite of *prezzo*, value or price, is virtually untranslatable and perhaps expresses a particular Italian concept). The origin of this contempt is a mystery to Molteni, but it is hardly so either to Emilia or to the reader. The situation is well illustrated by an incident that takes place even before Molteni has begun work on the *Odyssey*. The four characters—Molteni, Emilia, Rheingold, and Battista—set out for Capri where the film is to be written, leaving from Rome in two cars. Battista is brassy, good-natured, and egocentric, one of the traditional Italian Don Juans sprinkled through Moravia's work. He suggests that Emilia accompany him in his powerful red custom-built car, leaving Molteni and Rheingold to follow in a small sedan. After some discussion Molteni accepts this arrangement, although Emilia is opposed to it. Molteni accepts because, as Battista points out, this will give him a chance to begin discussing the script with Rheingold. But he himself knows that he also wishes to avoid offending Battista, since Battista represents money, and money is necessary to buy the apartment which will make Emilia happy. In this he profoundly misunderstands his wife. Such a logic might operate in the case of a woman whose motivations were primarily mercenary, for example the Odette of Proust's novel. But Emilia is not Odette, in spite of the superficial resemblance. Her motivations are thoroughly sexual; that is to say her "homemaker's instinct" is only a part of a deep and fundamental feminity in her nature. Her real need is to play a genuine feminine role in relation to a man who plays a genuine and dominant masculine role. Her wish for an apartment is really only an instinct for a lair where she can greet her mate, feed him, and eventually be dominated by him sexually and psychologically. When Molteni thrusts her together with Battista under these ambiguous circumstances, therefore, it only increases her *disprezzo* for him and makes any genuine union between them even more difficult. There are other similar incidents in which the situation is demonstrated in this way, if anything a little too clearly. Only Molteni fails to see that his behavior is self-defeating—that his very efforts to please his wife only serve to alienate her totally and permanently from him.

Meanwhile the artistic side of the plot, the effort to write the film script, develops in parallel form. Molteni has a genuine artist's temperament, whatever the limitations of his talent as a dramatist. His basic impulse is to create something perfect and unique out of himself, a work of art that will be a genuine expression of his own identity. This a film script cannot be. Early in the novel there is a short dissertation on the métier of the scriptwriter that undoubtedly came out of Moravia's own experience. The burden of this discourse is that a film is basically a group undertaking, and that the scriptwriter is by no means the most important member of this group.

"The scriptwriter, therefore, is the man who remains always in the shadows; who pours out his best life's blood for the success of others; and who, although two-thirds of the fortune of the film depends on him, never sees his own name on the advertising posters where those of the director, the actors, and the producer are listed."[63] Furthermore he surrenders the most intimate part of himself to a relationship in which he has solely a mercenary interest; in short he is a kind of prostitute. Scriptwriting consists of "the marriage and fusing of one's own intelligence, one's own sensibility, one's own soul, with those of his collaborators; it means in short the creating, during the two or three months the writing lasts, of a spurious and artificial intimacy which has for its sole end the making of a film and therefore, in the last analysis . . . the making of money." At the end of the process the writers are hot and exasperated in their shirt-sleeves, "more sweaty and rumpled than if they had been made to rape a frigid and restive woman."[64] Again in a characteristic way Moravia links sex and artistic creation, metaphorically here, actually and concretely in Molteni's own life. Not only is his scriptwriting a "prostitution" in the economic sense, but it is a betrayal of his own masculinity, which ought to be expressed in a personal and genuine artistic creation; it is for this reason that Emilia instinctively feels contempt for him and rejects him sexually. His lack of manliness, his failure for example to defend Emilia against the overtures of Battista, is connected at its very root to this failure of authenticity as an artist. It would be difficult to say which came first, but one cannot exist without the other: he is not an artist because he is not a man, and he is not a man because he is not an artist. This is a foreshadowing of the more elaborate and complete treatment of this theme in *La noia*.

Rheingold, who at first glance seems incidental, plays an important part in this thematic structure. In the car on the way to Capri he explains his view of the film to Molteni. He proposes to throw away the superficial adventure story of Homer in order to get at the hidden Freudian drama underneath it. "Ulysses, in reality, is a man who is afraid to go home to his wife—we will see why later—and for this reason seeks in his subconscious to find obstacles to his return."[65] But it is precisely by failing to come home that Ulysses alienates Penelope, who has a deep need of being dominated by a vigorous male, and thus creates the basis of his own fear. This is Homer turned upside down, and Moravia, who is often sympathetic to Freudian theory, offers the psychoanalytic part of the novel with a certain detachment, more or less with a shrug. It is clear that, in Moravia's mind as in Molteni's, Rheingold is off on the wrong track in a heavy-handed and dogmatic way peculiar to the German temperament; he not only ignores the poetry that made the *Odyssey* a classic but falsifies—or at least complicates to the point of falsification—the character of its hero. But Rheingold is not a Homeric scholar; he is a Freudian dogmatist whose real purpose of the novel is to comment not on Homer but on Molteni's own predicament. In his interpretation of the *Odyssey* he is just as wrong as Battista, who wants to make it into a *kolossal* film in the American style. Battista makes films in a certain way because he has a *kolossal* view of life; for him everything is simple and vastly larger than it is in reality. Rheingold writes scripts in a certain way because he is an instinctive psychoanalyst; that is, he sees hidden meanings under the superficial events, even when the hidden meanings are perhaps not there. Even though Molteni rejects this psychoanalytic distortion of Homer, it is not difficult for him to recognize himself in Rheingold's characterization of Odysseus.

Molteni is far from unintelligent and sees many things quite clearly; everything in fact but the fundamental thing, the reasons for Emilia's *disprezzo*. In a later conversation with Rheingold he grasps the essence of the German's interpretation: Ulysses is a "civilized" man, Penelope a "primitive" woman. It is possible, whether or not it is desirable, to develop out of a primitive mentality into a civilized one. But how is it possible to reject one's civilization and revert to the primitive? This is to reject intelligence itself, the very lucid insight that creates awareness of the problem. The acquisition of intellectual clarity is irreversible; the world of simple and primitive instinct, once lost, is as difficult to retrieve as a lost innocence. Like most of Moravia's heroes Molteni has a Hamlet or Prufrock complex; he thinks too much. "It seemed to me that whether or not I was despicable, and I was convinced I wasn't, there still remained my intelligence, a quality that even Emilia recognized and that was my whole pride and justification. I was obliged to think, whatever the object of my thought might be; it was my duty to exercise my intelligence intrepidly in the face of whatever mystery. If I abandoned the exercise of my intelligence, I would be left with nothing but the discouraging sense of my alleged, even though not proved, despicableness."[66] All this is perfectly true, and by this time it is clear that Molteni's problem is insoluble. Once he has arrived at this degree of understanding—the limit of self-awareness he is to reach in the novel—all that remains is for the situation to work itself out to its inevitable catastrophe. This, unfortunately, is handled in a way that is somewhat less than satisfactory, or at least is the weakest link of the novel.

The study of a consciousness "sicklied o'er with the pale cast of thought" might end violently and tragically, like *Hamlet,* or futilely and without resolution, like "Prufrock." Moravia attempts a combination of these two dénouements and succeeds in achieving only a rather tenuous ambiguity. There is a final argument, or confrontation, in which the exasperated Emilia tells her husband he is "not a man." Then she leaves him, planning to go back to Rome with Battista in the producer's car. But later that day, going down to the beach to rent a boat, Molteni finds her waiting for him; she is contrite and evidently ready for a reconciliation. They go together in the boat to one of the grottoes that are the chief touristical attraction of Capri, and on the way she tells him, "I've always loved you . . . I shall always love you."[67] But when he reaches toward her in the dark cave she evaporates from his grasp like the ghost of Creusa eluding the embrace of Aeneas. Her appearance has been only a hallucination, and he has not even the satisfaction of Aeneas in knowing he has conversed with the authentic ghost of his wife. Later he learns that Emilia, returning to Rome with Battista, was killed that afternoon in an accident. But at the moment of her apparition on the beach she was still alive and her contempt for him was unchanged; it remained unchanged until her death. Like Molteni's other problems, the hallucination is totally inside his own head and there is nothing outside himself to blame it on.

Thus the novel is resolved through a *deus ex machina,* at least on the surface. There is nothing in Molteni's character, or in Emilia's either, that makes it inevitable their relations should end this way in a violent accident. Yet it can be argued that Emilia's death is in some sense meaningful or aesthetically plausible: it is necessary to her nature that she be loved, and even dominated, by a genuine male, and when Molteni is unable to satisfy this need he negates her fundamental identity and thus destroys her. It is unnatural for a woman of her temperament to live in such cold and contemptuous relations with her mate, and Emilia in fact is "not herself" for the major part of the novel. The manner of her death is a curious one. Battista, a violent driver, slams on the brakes of his car to avoid an oxcart, and the sleeping Emilia dies of a broken neck from the jolt. There is a slightly grotesque parallel in this to the basic theme of the novel; body and brain are mutually necessary to each other, and when the communication between them is severed life ceases. Even more intricate and ingenious justifications for this ending might be contrived. But in the final analysis the test of a plot resolution must be the reader's own subjective rejection or acceptance of it, and on these grounds *Il disprezzo* is the least satisfactory of Moravia's novels. The problem involved is basically a technical one that extends throughout his work: how to resolve the plot of a story in which the hero is fundamentally passive or impotent? In *Le ambizioni sbagliate* the dilemma is solved through a "Dostoevskian" murder which, freakish though it may be, is a plausible resultant of the characters and the intrigue in which they are involved. In *Il conformista* the catastrophic agent is the war, which is something more than a mere external and fortuitous event; the death of Marcello is at least indirectly a consequence of his pathological obsession with conformity. The strongest and most convincing resolution in the novels up to 1954 is that of *Gli indifferenti*; it is highly plausible, even necessary, that Michele should be driven to an act of violence, and it is also fitting that this act should come to nothing because he forgets to load the gun. To say that he "forgets" almost misses the point; it is his nature to point unloaded guns at strong men and be humiliated as a result. Some ending as fitting might have been devised for *Il disprezzo,* but it was not. Both Molteni and the reader are left uncertain as to precisely what happened, and Molteni concludes that the experiences and satisfactions that elude us in so baffling a way in reality can only be recaptured in the world of imagination. "It depended on me, and not on any dream or hallucination, to find her again and continue our earthly dialogue in a serene manner. Only in this way could she be released from me, freed from my sentiments, to bend over me like an image of consolation and beauty."[68] In the end he finds some limited consolation in writing the account of his relations with Emilia that constitutes the novel.

Thus the novel returns to the theme of art and the relation of the artist to his creation. Molteni knows that he is not Prince Hamlet nor was meant to be, neither is he the Odysseus who slew the suitors. But perhaps he can be Homer, or something like him. Of the three interpretations of the *Odyssey*—Battista's crude spectacular, Rheingold's riddle of neurosis, and his own—his was the best: a glimpse of a Homeric life unmarred by compromise, free from the taint of money, and exalted by simple heroism above the physiological and material. Homer too may have been despised by his wife, as we know for a fact that Socrates was. But he nevertheless wrote the *Odyssey,* and thus not only got the better of her but achieved an even greater satisfaction for himself than successful conjugal relations can bring. If there is any fault with this analogy it is that neither Molteni nor Moravia has produced such a heroic transformation of the events, but only the novel we are reading. In the end perhaps the most useful thing about *Il disprezzo* is that it illustrates the modern problem of the creative mind turning inward upon itself, the novel about a novelist writing a novel. In this regard at least it offers a perfectly clear and, in a sense, definitive statement. But Moravia was not yet done with the problem of the artist.

Another Mask: The Transvestite

Moravia's winter in the mountains in 1943-44 left a strong impression on him. For nine months he ate peasant food and slept in a stable and was in constant danger of his life from the German patrols who searched the hills looking for partisans. Up to this time he had been a person of fixed habits and had always been in frail health, and he was not used to discomfort. In later years, commenting on his childhood illness and on this winter in hiding, he remarked, "The things that form our character are those we are obliged to do, not those we do out of our own will."[69] When he returned to Rome he immediately began to write about this experience, but turned from it to work on the stories of *L'epidemia* and then on *La romana*. The idea needed more time to germinate. After *La romana* came *Il conformista*, in which he temporarily abandoned the first person, and then the somewhat unsatisfactory *Il disprezzo*. The novel based on the winter in the mountains, *La ciociara*,* did not appear until 1957.

Technically this novel represents an attempt to create a vernacular or dialectal style, or at least a style that would give the impression of vernacular while at the same time retaining the precision and flexibility of a literary language. In this it follows in the pattern of *La romana* and of the *Racconti romani*, practically all of which are recounted in the first person by lower-class narrators. The problem of vernacular style was one that greatly preoccupied Moravia in this period when he was also focusing and clarifying his political opinions. The use of dialect in literature, he contended, always corresponded to a "crisis of educated language"[70] and therefore to a serious fracture between the Italian ruling class and the genuine culture of the country. Moravia intended this primarily as a kind of Marxist interpretation of writers like Belli, Pasolini, and Gadda rather than a comment on his own work. In actual fact *La ciociara* is not written in dialect in this sense, instead in a language

* The Ciociaria is the mountainous country lying south of Rome, a region that furnishes a high proportion of Roman servants and small shopkeepers. For the urban Roman the term *ciociaro* is slightly humorous, implying some kind of rustic bumpkin attempting to apply his peasant shrewdness to city problems. The American edition appeared as *Two Women* (Farrar, Straus & Cudahy, 1958).

that simulates the rhythm and flavor of Roman speech while retaining an essentially literary diction and even permitting itself relatively sophisticated literary devices. Furthermore—and this is important in understanding the political substructure of the novel—*La ciociara* does not present an orthodox Marxist view of popular character. The lower-class characters are often sympathetic, but this is simply because they are made human and believable to the point where the reader associates himself strongly with them; their behavior under stress is not very admirable. The protagonist, Cesira, a Trastevere shopkeeper, turns to black-marketing during the war without a scruple of conscience, and comments on political events, "For me Mussolini or Badoglio or somebody else, what's the difference as long as the business goes on."[71] In a precise sense Cesira is petty bourgeois rather than proletarian, but Moravia's workers and peasants are not much better. In the matter of social classes he judges people not by political doctrines but by the way they rub up against him in his daily experience, and his experience of shopkeepers, mechanics, electricians, taxi drivers, and plumbers—especially during the war—was not always felicitous. The only really admirable character in *La ciociara,* in fact, is Michele, a bookish intellectual who is regarded by the others as an idiot.

The striking achievement of *La ciociara* is that the rather complicated action, the more or less subtle ethical concepts involved, and even the limitations of Cesira's petty-bourgeois mentality are conveyed in Cesira's own telling of the story. The interesting question, in fact, is why Moravia chose to relate events that had obviously made so strong an impression on him through a narrator so unlike himself: of the opposite sex, of a different social class, and of markedly different personal and political outlook. But it is typical of a certain kind of writer to conceal autobiographical material in this way, or to assimilate it to fictional characters to the point where the autobiographical element is detectable only with careful reading. Stendhal does this and so does Dostoevski, two of Moravia's models. In addition there are technical advantages in a female narrator: the events of 1943-44 obviously had a powerful emotional effect on Moravia, and the invention of Cesira enabled him to express these emotions in a way that might seem effeminate in a male character. Cesira's emotions are close to the surface and her thoughts flow from her naturally and ingenuously, like the thoughts of a child. This is especially useful when Moravia portrays her elation over the Liberation and her awe of the American army, emotions he undoubtedly felt himself but would not be likely to describe so candidly in his own voice.

Cesira tells her story quite frankly and intimately and without concealing her own mistakes, as she might tell it in secret to a friend. Her language is full of vernacular idioms and turns of speech, most of them untranslatable. She begins by quoting a popular song: "When the *ciociara* marries, there's one who gets the shoelace and one who gets the *ciocia*," a dialect term for the shoe worn by peasants. But she herself, she goes on to explain, gave herself to her husband shoelace and shoe, "because he was my husband and because he took me to Rome and I was happy to be going there and I didn't know it was exactly at Rome that misfortune was waiting for me."[72] This is typical of her wandering and rather inconsecutive way of speaking, as well as her frankness about her own motives. Her thoughts follow a natural stream of association, not because Moravia has read Joyce and Virginia Woolf but because he has a fine ear for speech patterns. Even though it stops short of dialect, the style manages to achieve not only the rhythm of the vernacular but the flavor and quality of the Roman mentality. "Quando cominciarono i bombardamenti a Napoli e nelle altre città, la gente veniva a dirmi: 'Scappiamo che qui ci ammazzano tutti;' e io rispondevo: 'A Roma non ci vengono, perché a Roma c'è il Papa.' "[73] In English this can be rendered only starkly and with the loss of most of the flavor: "When the bombings started in Naples and the other cities people came and said to me: 'Let's get out of here before they kill us all;' but I told them, 'They won't come to Rome, because in Rome there's the Pope.' " The essential quality of it is involved with the parataxis of *che* in place of *perché*, the repetition of *Roma* for emphasis or simply for rhythm, and especially the inverted syntax of the phrase *A Roma non ci vengono*, which suggests the confidence of the lower-class urban dweller in the superiority of his city: before the opponent can even begin to raise objections he is demolished with the word "Rome." Another characteristic Roman touch is Cesira's naive belief that the Pope will in some way protect her from all misfortune. And this in spite of the fact that, like most lower-class Romans, she is basically anticlerical and what religion she has is totally mechanical: get baptized, married, and buried in the Church, go to Mass once a year, and basta. Later in the novel, when she and her daughter are attacked by Moroccan soldiers in a church, her indignation is mainly that she had a right to sanctuary in such a place, not that the Moroccans have committed a sacrilege. "You see what war is, they don't even respect churches."[74]

Cesira has a typical shopkeeper mentality. This involves a number of admirable qualities: she is prudent, systematic, and frugal, and she is not inclined to bother in anybody else's business as long as she is left alone to conduct her own. Up to a point Moravia shares Dr. Johnson's opinion that people are seldom so innocently occupied as when they are making money. When Cesira hears of the Italian occupation of Yugoslavia she comments, "But what are we doing in that country? Can't we stay at home where we belong? They don't want to be under us and they're right, I tell you."[75] She is also, in her way, chaste; while her husband is alive she is faithful to him "shoelace and shoe," and after she is a widow she constantly rejects overtures from men. But this is simply because she regards promiscuity as bad for business. She tells one would-be suitor, "Those are things you ought to go and say to others . . . I'm a widow, I have the store, and I don't think of anything but the store . . ."[76] Like her sexual life, her politics is conditioned by avarice. "To the soldiers who came to the shop and said, we're winning here, we're going there, we're going to do this, we're going to do that, I said: to me it's fine as long as business goes well."[77] Like many uneducated people she clings doggedly to her one virtue, her economic astuteness, until it becomes an obsession. To every new situation, to every unfamiliar idea, she seems to say: I know what I know. And what she knows is money under the mattress.

After the prologue in Rome the action shifts to the mountains where Cesira and her daughter Rosetta take refuge in the troubled winter preceding the Liberation. There they encounter Michele, who is the diametric opposite of Cesira in practically every way and serves as the other ideological pole of the novel. The peasants and small shopkeepers in the mountains regard him as someone who is not quite right in the head but somehow not exactly stupid either. He is a phenomenon they have had very little experience with: an idealist. For this reason they treat him gently but patronizingly, as people do with small children, or as the characters in *The Idiot* do with Prince Myshkin. He reads them the story of Lazarus from the Gospel, stopping at one point in order to control his tears, even though he is a socialist and socialists are against the priests. Cesira is shrewd enough to see that he is "more like the priests than like other men."[78] Yet he baffles her completely on one occasion when he happens to see Rosetta nude. Secretly taking pride in her daughter's beauty, she expects him to show some reaction and "turn red or pale, according to his temperament." Instead he ignores Rosetta and reports the news he has come to tell: that the Russian offensive has opened in the East. When she reproaches him with not being like other men, he at first fails to understand her, and then explains simply, "For me those things don't exist."[79] Since Cesira has earlier said almost the same thing to the men who importuned her, she ought to understand him. But his chastity is determined by politics, or more precisely by idealism, whereas hers is determined by avarice.

Cesira is shrewd on the surface but basically naive about the larger forces that shape her existence and will eventually destroy her psychologically and morally. Michele is the opposite: he is foolish on the surface and wise underneath. Among the peasants and small shopkeepers in the mountains he is the only one to grasp the central truth of the situation: that Italians have no right to complain about the war, since they supported or passively accepted the fascism that made the war inevitable. "Until they lose everything they will understand nothing . . . they have got to lose everything and suffer and cry tears of blood . . . only then will they become mature."[80] It is not surprising that Cesira and the others fail at this point to understand his words. Fundamentally his position rests on a metaphysical or existential basis: we are all responsible for our acts, even for the consequences of our passivity, and the suffering we allow to be done to others will eventually become our own suffering. Essentially he is a prophetic figure in the Judeo-Christian tradition, and his end as a martyr is perfectly consistent with this role. When he offers himself passively to the retreating German troops and is eventually shot by them he does it explicitly in order that the others may be left alone and make their escape. But implicitly, or symbolically, he does it in order that his example will be remembered and later assume a special significance, which is after all the point of martyrdom.

Michele is removed from the action of the novel before the others have realized the full significance of what he has said and done. But what they fail to comprehend intellectually in his words they are forced to learn by experience. During the long winter the refugees, Cesira and Rosetta among them, look forward with a kind of messianic hope to the Liberation, which they imagine as a long line of American trucks carrying food and clothing. This reverie is at least temporarily confirmed in their first encounter with the Allied army: a column of armored vehicles filling the road from Naples to Rome, driven by gum-chewing Americans calling out friendly greetings. In the town of Fondi the two women find a great crowd of peasants and American troops, almost like a fair. But there is nothing to buy and nothing to be sold except "the hope of better days," and the peasants and refugees walk about aimlessly as though uncertain how this is bought. The Americans speak English and the Italians speak Italian, and neither side understands the other. Other Americans, standing on a balcony, throw candy and cigarettes to the Italians who scramble for them in the dust, not because they want them but because they sense this is what the Americans expect from them. Most of the houses in Fondi have been wrecked by the bombardments. All these details are drawn by Moravia from direct observation. Cesira shouts at an American, "Is this your Liberation? Die of hunger and go without a house as we did before, or worse?"[81]

Finally the two women are taken to a supply center and given some canned food; the immediate physical problems at least can be solved by an occupying army. But there is another and bitter side to the "Liberation" that Cesira has yet to learn. A few days later she and Rosetta are attacked and violated by Moroccan soldiers in a church. It is easy to accuse Moravia here of the most facile kind of sensationalism. But this scene is necessary for structural and psychological reasons inherent in the novel, in order to bring to a climax the process of wisdom through suffering in which Cesira is inexorably involved. War is more than "bad for business," she learns at last. It is impossible to go through a war and come out a virgin; war destroys not only economically but morally and spiritually, at the very deepest center of human nature. Even more than by the event itself she is impressed by Rosetta's reaction to the event. After the initial shock has worn off Rosetta quite simply accepts the world of violence and cynicism into which the war has thrust her. She rejects her mother's sympathy and quite openly begins going with men in return for nylons, fine underwear, and even money. She seems to mature overnight, but in a hard, cynical, and egotistic way. Her promiscuity is the skepticism and indifference of a whole generation of young Italians made bitter by the war. At the end of the novel Cesira knows the meaning of Michele's prophecy: "They will lose everything and suffer and cry tears of blood . . . only then will they become mature."

Michele is a curious and virtually unique figure in Moravia's fiction. In many ways—in his chastity, in his intellectual nature, in his ineffectualness in daily life—he resembles the "impotents" of the prewar tales or the intellectual antifascist Mino of *La romana*. But he differs from them in that he is to a much larger degree a positive character, a spokesman for Moravia's own opinions and even in a certain sense an active and effective participant in the action. Instead of retreating into the paralyzing and purely verbal intellectualism of most of Moravia's heroes, he believes what he says and acts directly and courageously in accordance with that belief. It is true that his action, regarded in terms of immediate effects, is largely futile. At first glance his intellectualism seems as ineffectual as, for example, that of Saverio in *La mascherata*, who is also annihilated by the logic of superior force. But before this happens he has succeeded in altering the events around him in another way; his influence on the action is not material but dialectic. When he serves as raisonneur it is to persuade not only the reader but also the other characters of the novel. Cesira, remembering the time when Michele read the story of Lazarus in the mountains, finally perceives the meaning in her own sufferings.

> Then those words of Michele had left me uncertain, but now I understood that Michele had been right, that for a time we too had been dead, Rosetta and I, dead to the compassion we owed to others and to ourselves. But our suffering had saved us at the last moment, and thus in a way the story of Lazarus was true for us too, because through our suffering we had finally come out of the war that closed us in its tomb of indifference and wickedness and taken up the path of our life again, a life that was perhaps a poor thing full of darkness and error but the only life we had to live, as Michele would probably have said if he had been with us.[82]

Naturally Michele in this incident influences only two people, but there are not very many people in the novel; every novel is a microcosm. And at this point it becomes clear that Michele is an autobiographical character in an even deeper way than Cesira is. For Michele in 1944 the important thing is not really to join the partisans and kill Germans. For those who are capable of it this is valid and admirable, but in the end it will not really change anything; the fate of Italy will be determined by the two enormous forces, the Allied army and the German, that are struggling for possession of the country. The important thing is to understand how the Italian people got in this predicament in the first place, to understand that fascism was a mistake that must be paid for now by every Italian through his own suffering, and if possible to help others to understand this too. In this way the novel contains two personae of the author: Cesira expresses the physical side of Moravia that suffered physically during the war, and Michele represents the intellectual side that sought to understand and resolve this suffering. Michele's curious physical passivity, his inability to convert his idealism into any effective concrete action, can only be understood as a projection of Moravia's own sedentary disposition. It would be, in fact, unfitting for a person of this disposition to express his idealism in concrete action; the function of an intellectual and artist is to deal with the problems around him in intellectual and artistic terms, rather than in a realm where he will be at an inherent disadvantage. The artist's engagement is with his own work, not with politics. Through this work he stands a chance of influencing events in his own way, through altering the opinions and finally the actions of others, as Michele influences the understanding of Cesira and

Rosetta. In this way a novel itself can be a form of activism far more effective in the long run than taking up arms or joining a political party. Moravia develops this concept of "engagement" at some length in his 1953 essay "Communism in Power and the Problem of Art."

At the same time it is always a mistake to regard a work of art in this way as a means to some kind of political or social end. Works of art created for such motives, like Malraux's *L'espoir,* are usually the worse for it. *La ciociara* is not primarily a didactic novel; it is the half-concealed and transmuted expression of a personal experience. But the real merit of the novel lies neither in its political content nor in the fact that it contains a concealed autobiographical element; it lies in the skill with which this personal experience has been converted to fiction. Cesira, who serves a double function as narrator and participant, is the most complex woman in Moravia's work and one of the few really believable female characters. In spite of her verbal and intellectual limitations she is a better storyteller than the Adriana of *La romana;* her maturity gives her a wisdom and an irony of expression lacking in the younger woman. Some scenes—the encounter with the American army, the confusion of the Liberation, the violence of the Moroccans—are among the most powerful in Moravia's fiction. There is enough action to save the novel from the rather monotonous passivity that hangs over most of the rest of his fiction from *Gli indifferenti* to *La noia* and *L'attenzione.* And in *La ciociara,* above all, the problem of point of view or narrative mode that dogged Moravia throughout his career is most successfully solved. Through a deceptively subtle literary sleight of hand the account of Cesira is made both eloquent and complex without losing its essential flavor of authenticity. Behind his heroine Moravia remains invisible, his temperament converted totally to the expression of his character.

Novel of Alienation

La noia* in 1960 attacks once more the problem of the artist. By this time the theme has assumed a considerable complexity; artistic creativity is connected not only to libido but to the metaphysical and ontological problems of the artist's relation to concrete reality. For the first time the nature of the parallel between art and sex is made explicit: in order to create a work of art it is first necessary to believe in the reality and meaningfulness of the external world. just as in order to love it is necessary to believe in the reality and meaningful-

---

* Literally "boredom," although "annoyance" is also implied. Translated as *The Empty Canvas* (Farrar, Straus, 1961).

ness of the beloved object. If, for some reason, the consciousness withdraws into autistic isolation so that the external world becomes unreal—a kind of cinematograph that can be observed but is not really solid—both love and art become impossible. It is obvious that the act of love cannot take place without a participation in the beloved object, a touching. In Moravia's view of things this is equally true of artistic creation.

As usual these aesthetic and erotic themes are paralleled by a political or pseudo-political subtheme. Dino, the narrator-protagonist of *La noia*, is a typical dilettante of the kind produced by the capitalistic leisure class. Born into wealth, he rejects the role expected of him by society and makes a spasmodic attempt to create an identity for himself. This identity, as he imagines it, will have two dominant features; he will be poor and he will be an artist. All this is involved as well with a personal revolt against his mother. He lacks a father (his father is an adventurer who abandons his family and spends his life wandering around the world) and his mother is a masculine and strongly assertive personality: the classic pattern for the production of an ineffectual male sexuality. In rejecting his mother Dino rejects his social class and also attempts to reject the passive and artificial sexual role the circumstances have prepared for him. But he finds it is not possible for a person in his social condition to be poor; he succeeds only in becoming a rich man pretending to be poor. And it is not as easy as he imagines to become an artist. It is not enough to live in a studio in Via Margutta and possess canvases, paints, brushes, and the other necessary materials. It is not really a question of talent. It is possible to be an untalented artist and yet a genuine artist, and in fact there is an example of this in the novel: Balestrieri, the painter who lives in the studio next to Dino's. For Dino the difficulty is the inability to believe in the reality of the simplest objects around him, for example a glass standing on a table. It is this condition, a condition of sensory impotence, so to speak, that he refers to as *noia*. Even in its ordinary usage this word is somewhat more diffuse than the English "boredom;" it includes as well an active state of irritation with something, as in the English cognate "annoy." For Dino it is "a malady of objects,"[83] a failure of the phenomena of the physical world to assume any meaningful or cognitive reality. The concrete world is undoubtedly there, since others seem to relate to it and deal with it effectively, but he himself is cut off or alienated from it in ways that are beyond his control. Since people too are conrrete bodies, this alienation extends to other human beings; the failure of cognition is also a failure of communication. Dino is unable to comprehend what goes on in the minds of others and unable to believe in the stereotyped and conventional phrases of their speech. Ceasing to believe in external objects, he turns to nonrepresentational painting: the blobs and cubes of modern experimentalism. But even this kind of painting is a simulacrum in some way of physical experience and as such *noioso* to a consciousness unable to believe in the physical world. On the first page of the novel Dino destroys the painting he has been working on with knife slashes, replacing it with an empty canvas which remains on the easel for the rest of the novel. At one point he quotes Kandinsky: "The empty canvas. In appearance: really empty, silent, indifferent. As though bewildered. In reality: full of tensions, with a thousand submissive voices, heavy with expectation . . . Marvelous is the empty canvas, more beautiful than many paintings . . ."[84] But tensions and expectations are the diametric opposite of achievements. The effect of art, like the effect of the sexual act, is to resolve tensions. This is Dino's problem, one that manifests itself in every aspect of his life.

Insofar as it deals with the theory of art *La noia* brings to a climax Moravia's growing dislike of modern experimentalism, a suspicion that modern painting in particular is deeply corrupted by the confusion of bourgeois society. In a 1959 newspaper article he described an insane asylum near Verona where the inmates were encouraged to paint for therapeutic purposes. These uneducated peasants and artisans began, sometimes, as representational painters, but they inevitably gravitated toward distortion and abstraction. The results, crude and untalented as they were, resembled Pollock, Klee, Max Ernst, Utrillo, and Grosz.

> Observing these paintings, one cannot help asking several rather disturbing questions. For example: in the time of Raphael, if the mentally ill had been allowed to paint, would they have painted in the manner of the Verona inmates or the manner of Raphael? I can't be too sure, naturally, but I suspect their painting would be abstract, that is more or less similar to what is done today. For madness is outside of history and for this reason always immobile and equal to itself. But it does not follow from this that abstract art too is outside of history; on the contrary. It corresponds to a historical moment in which there takes place a collapse of culture, a rejection of the processes of the past, the rupture of traditional relations with reality.[85]

It is significant that Dino in *La noia* is a nonrepresentational painter, at least up to the point where he turns into no painter at all. The antithesis to Dino in this respect and several others is the painter Balestrieri in the next studio. He paints nothing but portraits, on a huge scale, and invariably female nudes. When Dino first examines these paintings he finds them distorted and out of proportion, but later, when he has the opportunity to observe one of the models nude, he sees that the apparent distortions were merely a matter of Balestrieri's taste in the female form. He has a predilection for women with slender, almost adolescent forms onto which are grafted exaggeratedly mature breasts and flanks: a type of female body recurring throughout Moravia's work. Even though Balestrieri's painting is anatomically and aesthetically imperfect it has what might be called a biological logic to it; it is dominated by an aesthetic of reproduction. In this it resembles the fetish art of primitive peoples: art that is intended to effect magic rather than impress us by its beauty. Modern painters—Picasso and his contemporaries—briefly experimented with this style at one point, but abandoned it in favor of cubism and nonrepresentation. Balestrieri is not Picasso; but even art as fetish—Moravia implies—is better than art as chaos.

The figure of Balestrieri leads to the sexual theme of the novel, or rather to the sexual aspect of its single dominant theme. Initially, Dino is not very interested in women, in spite of his mother's effort to retain her hold over him by getting him involved with the servant Rita. Balestrieri, on the other hand, is a typical Moravian prepotent. Although he is small he has huge shoulders and a protruding nose; at one point he is compared to a Pompeiian satyr. His real interest in life is not painting but women. Painting, at first a ruse for attracting models to his studio, eventually becomes a means of glorifying the female form and a stimulus to his sexual activity. He is already an old man when Dino encounters him, and this behavior is not good for his health, but he himself knows this perfectly well. In fact there is a suggestion that sex for him is a sort of suicide. He tells Cecilia, the last of his mistresses, that his relations with her will very likely be the end of him, and yet when she tries to leave him he weeps and even tries to kill himself with sleeping pills. After Balestrieri dies of his sexual excesses Dino comments, "As I thought about that first suicide, the one caused by Cecilia's decision to leave him, I began to understand that the old painter, carrying his relationship with Cecilia to the logical end, had quite logically committed another and more successful suicide. Thus, in a way, he had attempted the first suicide because it seemed to him at a certain point that Cecilia, by leaving him, was preventing him from committing the second."[86] Sex, evidently, leads to death. But Balestrieri was an old man, and besides death is better than *noia*. Dino, in taking over Cecilia after Balestrieri's death, is half-consciously attempting to emulate not only Balestrieri's virility but the manner of his dying.

For this to happen, however, it would be necessary for him to love in the genuine and even obsessive way that Balestrieri has loved, and it is as impossible for him to do this as it is for him to become an artist. In spite of his efforts to "know" Cecilia, at first through the sexual act and then through inflicting his will on her in other ways, she remains as unreal for him as the glass on the table and the other objects around him. Cecilia herself is sensual, mindless, and enigmatic, one of the typical sibylline sex objects in Moravia's fiction. Dino's hope of using her as a link to the real world is futile. To be Cecilia's lover, he discovers, is not necessarily to be Balestrieri any more than to possess brushes and canvas is to be an artist. Thus the prepotence of Balestrieri is transferred, in Dino's mind, not to himself but to Cecilia. His relations with her become empty, a Proustian groping for phantoms.

To add a further complexity, the whole problem of *noia* or alienation in this novel is connected at the bottom to money. Cecilia is not basically mercenary. When Dino gives her money she takes it, but she shows no disappointment when he fails to offer it, as he does now and then as an experiment. On one occasion he offers to maintain her with a permanent allowance, but she says there is no need for this, since what he gives her has so far been enough for her needs. She lives entirely for the moment, and the center of her life is not money but sex. When she makes an important decision, as when she chooses between Dino and Luciani at the end of the novel, she does so entirely on sexual grounds, even when this results in a material loss. The diametric opposite of Cecilia in this respect is Dino's mother. Money plays for her the precise function that sex does for Cecilia; not only is it the center of her life and the means by which she exerts her influence over others, but it defines her identity in the absolute sense for herself and others. It is characteristic of her that she makes no objection to Dino's amusing himself with the servant Rita, even tacitly encouraging him in this, but refuses to talk about financial matters when Rita is in the room. Money is her prudery, not sex. In fact she keeps her household cash in the bathroom, in a safe hidden in the tiled wall—an irony that recalls the safe hidden behind the holy picture in the earlier tale "La disubbidienza." In *La noia* it is necessary for Dino and his mother to go into the bathroom together to conduct their financial affairs, as though they were discussing some delicate physiological matter. "My mother had taught me the combination of the safe, and I had learned it almost in spite of myself, perhaps simply because I have a good memory, but I disliked using it, especially when she was watching: it was unpleasant in the same way as taking part in a religious ceremony in which you don't believe."[87] Later, at a reception in his mother's villa, Dino contemplates the guests and reflects that money has molded these people into what they are, from their voices and gestures to the very lines of their faces. And he too, whether he wills it or not, is a part of the society that has made these people: " . . . it was precisely money, which I had renounced without succeeding in ridding myself of it, that had provoked the crisis of my art and in general of my whole life."[88]

Why is money at the root of alienation? The chief function of wealth, in the bourgeois leisure class that dominates capitalistic society, is to isolate the individual from physical experience. The material tasks that make his comfort possible, from building his house to cooking his food and fixing the plumbing, are taken care of by others. He is protected from heat and cold by insulated walls, and he travels hermetically sealed inside automobiles and trains. He has no need to deal with even the simplest physical problems, and thus the activities of his life are very largely abstract: financial transactions, social relationships, conversation, thought. Throughout Moravia's fiction the middle-class characters are outwardly patronizing toward workmen, artisans, servants, and others who do things with their hands, but inwardly and even pruriently curious about how these things are done. Physical love too is made with the body, and here too the bourgeois, especially the intellectual, is conscious of his ineptitude. His breeding has led him to believe that the body and its needs are something taken care of by other classes. In this way, through the habit of contempt for physical necessities, the bourgeois has systematically isolated himself from the concrete world to the point where this world is no longer meaningful for him and ceases to exist. Thus the "malady of objects" defined by Dino as the root of alienation.

In his encounter with Cecilia, Dino instinctively falls back on these defenses of his class, in spite of the irony and even contempt he feels for them. At one point he considers destroying Cecilia's power by marrying her and converting her into a *signora* like the others, preoccupied with social affairs and class distinctions. At other times he puts banknotes into her hand during the act of love, in order to give his amorous gestures a significance they would not otherwise have. The climactic encounter between Cecilia's sexuality and Dino's money occurs in a scene late in the novel when she announces her intention of going off to Ponza with her lover Luciani. This scene takes place in the mother's villa, a setting permeated by the power of money. Cecilia automatically disrobes and lies down on the bed, as casually as though offering a farewell handshake. But Dino proposes instead to cover her with money from his mother's safe if she will agree not to go away with Luciani. If there is not enough money in the safe, he tells himself, he can cover her up with industrial shares, which are as good as money, as his mother has often pointed out. But there is enough money, and Cecilia is soon covered with bank-notes from head to foot. This would be a rather clumsy symbol if it were not for Gino's, and Moravia's, irony toward the symbolism itself. The scene is sardonically compared to the myth of Danae, and Dino is conscious not only of the grotesqueness but of the futility of what he is doing. Cecilia giggles, contemplates the money, and tells him rather reluctantly that she cannot accept it. After a moment she adds, "Now let's make love." Her indefatigable monomania is a physical reality that cannot be obliterated by piling money on it. Money by its nature is abstract; the power that Cecilia represents is inexorable, wordless, and concrete. For this very reason it escapes the grasp of Dino. After Cecilia abandons him he can no longer believe even in his own existence and ends by driving his car into a tree. He survives, but tells himself, " . . . at least I had demonstrated to myself that rather than live as I had lived up to that time, I preferred death and preferred it in earnest."[89]

This is a considerable improvement over the ending of *Il conformista*, which it resembles somewhat in superficial incident, and the ideological statement of *La noia* is more complex and more carefully reasoned than anything in Moravia's earlier work. To the factual and psychological levels of the earlier work a plane of thought has been added which can justifiably be called philosophical, and this part of the novel is by no means naive or trivial. With *La noia* Moravia established himself as a leading exponent of the existentialist novel, a development which should have surprised nobody who had followed his earlier work with care. This ideological success, however, tends to obscure the serious technical difficulties of the novel as novel. *La noia* belongs to a genre of fiction that is sometimes called the *romanzo-saggio* or essay-novel: a narrative in which the action serves as a vehicle for the opinions of the author, opinions presented not only through dialogue but in long passages of more or less formal argument. Dostoevski is usually cited as the classic example. There is no fundamental reason why a work of fiction should be less powerful, or less effective, because it contains an ideological statement. But the *romanzo-saggio* is inevitably a mixed form; it lacks the room to explore ideas as thoroughly as the pure essay, and its effectiveness as a novel is impaired by the necessity of stopping every so often to lecture the reader on philosophical matters. The true novel operates on the reader in other ways: through powerful and vivid characterization, through incident, through the establishment of a concrete reality in which he believes as strongly as he believes in his everyday experience. Is it possible to do this and still use the novel as a vehicle for ideological opinion? Dostoevski succeeds in doing both, but can Moravia? This is the problem that lies at the heart of any discussion of *La noia* as novel rather than as ideological statement.

Regarded in this way, as pure novel, *La noia* is by no means a total failure. There is no doubt that, even beyond the essay sections of the novel, there is too much talk; Dino gives the impression of interviewing Cecilia about her previous relations with Balestrieri, sometimes for pages on end. Except for this talk nothing much seems to happen in the novel; the vivid incident of *La ciociara* or even of *Il conformista* is lacking. But Moravia has dealt with the problem of point of view at least as successfully as he did in *La ciociara;* the action is narrated by Dino in a language totally appropriate to the character and consistent with the mood of the novel. There are vivid characters; Balestrieri is the most obvious one, but some of the secondary figures are minor masterpieces. Cecilia's father, a shopkeeper dying of cancer of the throat, is a mute, desperate, and frightened figure who serves as a pendant to Cecilia's own vitality. As Cecilia's personality is focused in her sex, his is concentrated in his eyes, organs which unlike the mouth are totally passive in their function. "These eyes seemed to say things the mouth would not have expressed even if it had not been mute; more than the dumbness produced by disease they gave the impression of a subjugated impotence, of a person bound and gagged and left there, alone and helpless, in the face of a mortal danger."[90] Cecilia's mother, the servant Rita, and Balestrieri's widow are similarly characterized with a few bold and powerful strokes. Dino's own mother is one of the few effective and convincing women in Moravia's fiction, comparable to the Cesira of *La ciociara* even though she is seen only at second hand. Essentially she is a development of the mother figure found throughout Moravia's work, from *Gli indifferenti* through the later tales "Agostino" and "La disubbidienza." The difference is that the mother in *La noia* is unified as a personality through a single controlling trait: her avarice. Thus, instead of being presented as a finished character with certain qualities, she is seen as a person who became what she is through a visible process: the working of bourgeois economics on a normal and instinctive maternal temperament. The traces of her genuineness are still apparent; at one point Dino, remembering how she consoled him when he cried as a child, feels an unexpected vestige of affection for her. But a human personality is a sum of actions, and her warmness as a mother has been submerged in a lifetime of greed. Moravia seldom depicts women who are so clearly in this way resultants of complex forces.

In spite of the animal-like simplicity she presents on the surface, Cecilia is also a character of a certain complexity. At times she seems mercenary, at times pathologically oversexed, at times simply stupid; but she is none of these. She is fecund woman as seen by impotent or inconfident male, and thus there is inevitably a certain mystery to her in Dino's eyes. But even though he understands her less clearly than he does his mother, she affects him strongly and vividly, and she makes an equally strong impression on the reader. She is not intended as a complete figure in the sense that the mother is; her function is to serve as an embodiment of sensuality for contrast with Dino's alienation. Her mindlessness is therefore a sign of specialization rather than a deficiency; it is a strength and not a weakness. This characteristic Moravian view of female psychology is developed a step farther in *L'attenzione*.

The Novel of Authenticity

In many respects *L'attenzione** in 1965 resembles *La noia:* the heroes of both novels are artists *manqués,* in both cases this creative failure is intimately involved with a sexual crisis, and in both novels the special problem of the artist is associated with the general theme of alienation. The two novels even open with parallel incidents: in *La noia* Dino slashes the painting he has been working on, and the protagonist of *L'attenzione* tears up the manuscript of his novel in progress and throws the pages out the window. But *L'attenzione* is a more intricate novel thematically than *La noia,* and the thematic materials, instead of being merely talked about, are more fully converted to incident. The difference in novelistic apparatus—the means by which the story is presented—is even more striking. *L'attenzione* is Moravia's most sophisticated novel technically; in fact it is the only one of his novels in which the apparatus of presentation plays a major part in the finished product in the way it does, for example, in the work of Proust or Gide. Francesco Merighi is a journalist with ambitions to become a novelist. He abandons his first attempt to write a novel because the result seems to him purely literary, or as he expresses it, "inauthentic." Instead he begins keeping a diary in which he plans to record the most banal events of his daily life in order to use this material for a novel which will be genuinely "authentic." When he does this, however, he begins observing himself

* Literally "attention"; translated as *The Lie* (Farrar, Straus, 1966).

and those around him a little more carefully and makes a number of remarkable discoveries. The two most important of these are that his wife Cora is conducting a clandestine career as a procuress, and that he himself is in love with his step-daughter Gabriella or Baba. In short his life is full of the kind of artificially sensational or "literary" material from which bad novels are made. This development throws him into a profound crisis. He goes on keeping the diary, but he no longer has faith in its veracity; now that he recognizes it as more "literary" than a novel, he begins more or less consciously novelizing it as he writes. The novel in the hands of the reader therefore consists of Francesco's efforts to write a novel, or more precisely his effort not to write it by writing a diary instead.

All this resembles Gide's *Les faux-monnayeurs* and a number of other novels about writing a novel. The difference is that for Francesco not only his success or failure as an artist but his very existence as a human being depends on his solving this essentially aesthetic problem. For Francesco, as for Moravia himself, art is a means of comprehending existence, and behind this lies the implication that an uncomprehended or meaningless existence is no existence at all. In actual fact Francesco never succeeds in writing a novel, unless we are supposed to take the novel we are reading as the novel he is unable to write. But he nevertheless affirms, "Gradually, with the years, the novel became for me much more than a literary genre, it became in fact a way of understanding life."[91] A good deal of his diary consists of analysis of this particular point. Not only literature, he discovers, but a large part of life itself is "inauthentic." The typical novel portrays characters conforming to more or less conventional patterns of behavior; the characters enact the roles of lover, husband, or criminal instead of behaving like real human beings. But real human beings too enact roles: the mother portrays the mother, the lover plays the lover, the journalist pretends to be a journalist. Each acts not as his instinct or natural impulse would lead him to act but according to the accepted conventions of his role. The ordinary person's daily activities are performed in a state something like somnambulism: the words are spoken, the gestures repeated, according to a quite automatic pattern of conventional behavior. Francesco remarks of another character in the novel, "Consolo was not the editor-in-chief of my paper, instead he pretended to be, he played a part. But then who was he? A glance at Consolo's fixed and glassy eye suggested an idea that was bizarre but perhaps sound: Consolo was nothing but this pretence, this illusion of an editor-in-chief; beyond that pretence Consolo simply wasn't, he didn't exist."[92] In the same way Gide in his *Journal des faux-monnayeurs* speaks of people "completely permeated by their façades." Another example in Moravia's novel is the relation between Francesco and Baba. Francesco has had nothing to do with his family for ten years, most of which he has spent traveling. In any case Baba is only his stepdaughter, and the main emotion he feels toward her is that he desires her sexually. But early in the novel she asks him to behave "like a father" to her, and this implies that he must also behave like a husband to Cora. Attempting to comply, he dutifully asks Baba about her studies at the university, takes mother and daughter on an outing to the beach, and so on. But the whole attempt is "inauthentic" because Francesco's true impulses are inconsistent with this pattern. Cora's personality is equally sham; she pretends to be a housewife, a mother, a dressmaker, and she is none of these. A mother is someone who behaves like a mother, and in reality she attempted to prostitute her daughter at the age of fourteen. As for her business as a dressmaker, this is only an elaborate front for her real trade as a procuress.

As the novel advances it becomes clear that each of these people, if left to follow his impulses, would express a quite valid and consistent identity, although not perhaps one that society would approve of. By temperament Francesco is a genuine artist; it is his role as a journalist that has corrupted him and made it impossible for him to write honestly. When the conventions are stripped away Cora is interested in nothing but sex. She is perfectly consistent and self-contained, a vigorous animal dominated by a single impulse, corrupted only by a society that demands that she be something other than what she is. The natural inclination of Francesco and Baba is to become lovers. They have similar interests and are genuinely attracted to each other, and are not biologically kin. Only convention opposes this union, a concept of incest that varies from culture to culture and is nonexistent in some societies. Yet Francesco begins to wonder whether this very taboo is not perhaps at the bottom of his desire for Baba. Like Consolo, he is a prisoner of inauthenticity to the point where his false role becomes his whole identity.

This condition leads to a state of "inattention," another key term that Moravia defines in a rather special way for the purposes of this novel. For all practical purposes it is identical with the "malady of objects" of *La noia*. The inauthentic life consists of automatic words and gestures, that is, behavior that has no connection with reality. This being so, reality—concrete reality—ceases to have any meaning, and the individual fails to grasp the significance of the most ordinary objects around him. A stonemason, as long as he is a good stonemason, is thoroughly aware of what a stone is: he feels it with his hands, knows its hardness and texture, and hews and polishes it

every day. Similarly a person leading a normal sensual life, following his impulses and behaving in a biologically natural way, remains
aware of the complicated shape and texture of the world around
him. The sensory world is the datum from which his behavior takes
its beginning, and thus he always remains intimately in contact with
it. But once his behavior becomes conventional or "inauthentic" it
no longer has this basis in sensory impulse. Instead of being moti-
vated by the hardness or sweetness or warmness of things, the whole
sensory complex that leads us to seek pleasure and avoid pain, he
falls into a pattern of puppet-like gestures determined solely by convention. Consequently the world of objects soon ceases to have any
meaning for him, in fact atrophies until he can no longer grasp its
meaning or believe in its existence. This is serious enough for the
ordinary person; for the lover, or for the artist, it is fatal. Not to
believe in the bodies of others is to be unable to love; the result is
the empty and mechanical groping that passes for love in the world
of inauthenticity. To fail to grasp the significance of the external
world is to be unable to write meaningfully about it; the result is the
kind of formula journalism turned out by Francesco, to be con-
sumed by imbeciles with the minimum of effort. He is unable to
write for the same reason that the Dino of *La noia* is unable to paint.

Francesco's struggle to emerge from this crisis is unsuccessful,
but paradoxically it results in something like a work of art: the diary.
The fact that the diary is a diary and not a novel is a measure of his
failure, but at the same time the matter is not that simple. As he
records the events of his daily life in the diary he finds he is inevitably "novelizing" the material: sharpening a scene here, de-
leting the unessential, rearranging the elements. Soon, in a mood of
experiment, he is inventing whole scenes: a "pornographic" chapter
in which he makes love to Baba, and several passages in which the
author conducts Gidean dialogues with his character. Already the
line between diary and novel is blurred. At first this fictionalizing is
ironic and quite conscious, then Francesco himself seems to come to
the point where he can no longer distinguish between fiction and
truth. The truth of an incident becomes for him what he has written
about it, that is the entry in the diary. Moreover, another and even
more curious phenomenon begins to operate: the keeping of the
diary influences his behavior. Whenever he does anything he imagines his action as an entry in the diary, and soon he finds he is acting
out chapters instead of behaving naturally and normally. Seeking to
escape from the inauthenticity of social convention, he falls un-
wittingly into another kind of spuriousness: the inauthenticity of
literature. It is impossible to write a "true" diary, one that simply

and honestly records the events of daily existence; it is impossible for anyone, and it is even more impossible for a novelist. Although Francesco does not follow out the logic to its final step, behind this lies the implication that the very act of verbalization itself is formal, that it rearranges experience into the pattern of conventional syntax. And if, as some modern linguists believe, thought itself is largely verbal, then simply to think is to novelize.

Luckily, Francesco is a better novelist than he thinks. Or rather the method of this novel (Moravia's novel) rests on a subterfuge: the events seem to be observed through the passive and somewhat jaundiced eye of Francesco, whereas actually they are recounted with all the skill and inventiveness of Moravia himself. Some of the minor characters, those sketched only in a chapter or two, are particularly successful; in these vignettes Moravia's long experience as a short-story writer shows itself. About midway through the novel Francesco and Baba go to visit Cora's parents, former country folk who now live in a certain affluence with the help of their daughter. The degeneration of these simple but dignified peasants into parodies of the lower middle class is depicted in a masterful scene. Francesco remembers them from earlier days as figures from a Roman sarcophagus: plain, severe, the epitome of the antique Latin character. Now they live in a tasteless modern apartment and have grown into overfed caricatures of their former selves; the grandmother watches television and the grandfather spends his day drinking in the local tavern. Their transformation is the visible effect of Cora's money, which comes from a corrupt source and can only have a corrupting effect on those it touches. But the matter of inauthenticity or role-playing is also involved. The former peasants are ugly because they are trying to fit into roles which for them are inauthentic; they can only ape the gestures of the leisure class without comprehending or assimilating them. For the grandmother Cora is a good daughter for a single and simple reason: she gives them money. They know the source of this money but pretend not to know it, or manage with peasant shrewdness to forget it. "She's a good daughter, really a good daughter," the grandmother repeats in a curious singsong, as though she hopes to play a trick on someone. But the trick is on her; the secret she hopes to conceal is apparent in every detail of the inauthentic life she is living.

It is the grandfather who, assisted by wine, eventually expresses this truth. Just as Francesco and Baba are leaving he appears, like a drunken god in an old comedy, in the opening elevator door. He fails to recognize his son-in-law, or refuses to admit that he recognizes him. "But who knows him?" he shouts—*"chi lo conosce?"*—a vernac-

ular injury roughly equivalent to "Who does he think he is?" "And
yet," his wife prompts him in her crafty singsong, "you have a
daughter named Cora, a wife named Agnese, a granddaughter named
Gabriella, a son-in-law named Francesco, and your name is Antonio."
But the old man rejects this whole list of identities, including his
own. When he drinks he knows he is not the vulgar bourgeois who
goes by his name, and neither do the others have a right to the
spurious identities they claim. "I am what I am," he shouts at them,
and then he lurches into the elevator again. The last they see of him
is his legs, then his torso, then his face, and finally his hat disappear-
ing in the descending elevator "like a mummy in a sarcophagus."[93]
It later transpires that this scene is one of those invented by Francesco out of whole cloth and that the actual visit to the grandparents
was totally different. But Francesco, Moravia, and the reader share
the knowledge that this scene is more real than what "actually"
happened.

Several other minor figures are equally vivid, most of them
caricatural in the same sense. The editor-in-chief Consolo is sketched
with a few sarcastic strokes: energetic, puppet-like, insincere, his
character reflected in his fixed and glassy eyes. He describes his life
as "perfectly in order," but his wife makes violent overtures to Francesco in an automobile, explaining that she behaves this way whenever she has a chance. Francesco's brother Massimiliano is the subject of another chapter. His connection with the main line of the plot
is rather tenuous; he is a stockbroker and ostensibly Francesco goes
to see him about some investments Cora is interested in making.
They never get around to discussing the investments, and the real
purpose of the scene is to compare and contrast the four persons
involved: Francesco, Massimiliano, Baba, and Massimiliano's mistress Popi. Massimiliano is a vulgar sensualist, with apelike features
and a typical nouveau-riche brashness. After many years of marriage
he has separated from his wife and begun a flashy new life with
Popi, a former model. He is interested only in women, Popi's cooking, and his ostentatious apartment; he tells Francesco, "Women
should be changed every two or three years like automobiles. As soon
as they stop running well you should replace them with a later
model."[94] Popi is not running well already; she shows signs of
neurosis and is obviously on her way to the scrap-heap. Naturally
Massimiliano attempts to make love to Baba; she rejects him, but
later she tells Francesco she likes Massimiliano because "he is what
he is," all of one piece, consistent in himself and free of inauthenticity. This scene, like the encounter with the grandparents, is one of
those "invented" by Francesco or at least altered in many of its

essential details. But Massimiliano's character, and Baba's comment on it, are authentic parts of the novel as they are authentic in real life.

Baba's behavior in this scene is typical of her accuracy in judgments of others. She herself appears at first to be a spoiled and somewhat sulky young woman. But, in contrast to practically all of the other characters, she holds herself quite under control at all times and has no illusions about herself or the others around her. In Moravia's gallery of feminine psychologies she represents the Rosetta of *La ciociara* in a later stage of development. Both have been traumatized in childhood: Rosetta by the violence of the Moroccans, Baba through being corrupted by her mother at the age of fourteen. Rosetta's reaction is already evident at the end of *La ciociara* in the form of a willful and precocious maturity. Baba is seen a number of years later, when the childhood experience has been assimilated and become the center of a balanced and self-sufficient personality, although a deeply cynical one. Paradoxically she is protected by a kind of innocence or ironic simulacrum of innocence; nothing can touch her because everything vulnerable in her has been destroyed before she became an adult. On the surface she is as "inauthentic" as the others, pretending to be a good student, a daughter to Francesco, a fiancée to her friend Santoro. But her behavior makes it clear that she sees through this web of pretence and, in her private mind, accepts things as they genuinely are: Francesco as a man who desires her, the university studies as an empty ritual demanded of her by society, Santoro as a nonentity she plans to marry in order to have a place in life. Her characterization is a considerable literary achievement; these intricacies in her character are conveyed even though she herself is laconic to the point of crypticism, and even though she is seen only obliquely by Francesco who does not understand her very well.

The scene in which Baba is prostituted by her mother at the age of fourteen is one of the thematic pivots of the novel. It takes place a number of years before the main line of the action and is therefore told in flashback, or rather in a number of more or less fragmentary flashbacks that give the scene dimension by recounting it in different ways. Naturally all these versions come from Baba, and she herself has recovered from the experience only by convincing herself that it happened to another person, "the Baba of those days." Her behavior at the assignations arranged by her mother is a good example of her fundamental "authenticity." She refuses to behave like a prostitute or anything other than what she actually is: a schoolgirl with ink on her fingers. She simply lies like an inert object while the customers strive to elicit some reaction from her. "The men tried to make her feel something or do something, turning her this way and that way as they might have done with a doll to find the lever that made her talk and move. And finally they got fed up."[95] A similar scene serves as the key incident in Pirandello's *Sei personaggi in cerca d'autore,* where it is the father himself who inadvertently takes part in an assignation with his stepdaughter. In fact there are curious parallels between the two works: both deal with secrets in the background of an unhappy family, and in both cases the secrets are revealed through conversations which lead to flashbacks. This is also the theme, and the method, of *Oedipus the King,* and the parallel even occurs to Francesco at one point. But the difference between the classic tragedy and the two modern works is an important one: at the end of Sophocles' play Oedipus knows the whole truth in all its details, whereas for the modern writer there is no single truth and the events of the past are an elusive and fragmentary enigma. Is Baba telling the truth about her childhood experience? Francesco will never know, and perhaps the event itself exists only subjectively in the minds of Baba, Francesco, and the others.

The document that Francesco begins as a "true" diary therefore ends in a complicated plexus of fact and fiction, conjecture and analysis, invention and wishful thinking. As for what "really" happened, this does not exist, because the Moravia of 1965 no longer believes in the kind of omniscient novel where the novelist is permitted to know more than his characters know. This is not really Pirandellism because Moravia is not interested in this kind of philosophical sleight-of-hand; it is simply novelistic purity. Essentially it is a matter of the narrative problem that hangs over Moravia's work from the time of his earliest fiction: that of point of view, or more precisely the exact location and scope of the vantage point from which the reader views the action. In *Gli indifferenti* he switched rapidly from one consciousness to another so that the reader had a certain difficulty in empathizing with any one character, and this fragmentation was carried even farther in *Le ambizioni sbagliate* and *La mascherata.* In *La romana* he experimented with first-person narrative, with considerable success, and the technique was refined in *La ciociara.* But in *La ciociara* he still permits his narrator something of the omniscience of the author; at the end of the novel Cesira is fairly certain of what happened and fairly sure of the judgment to be made on the events. In *La noia* and especially in *L'attenzione* the exact nature of consciousness is portrayed with greater precision; in real life it is impossible for any one mind to encompass the objective past in the manner of the traditional novel. Francesco concludes that the true function of the novel is to record the state of its creator's consciousness. Thus all novels are realistic, even the most fantastic ones. "In other words," he writes on the last page of the diary, "if it was true as I was convinced it was true, that a novel cannot be anything else but realistic, my diary demonstrated that there were no limits to realism, that nothing could be excluded from reality, neither dreams, nor lies, nor that lie of life [*illusione vitale*] which in its time had made me ashamed of having lived."[96] In this way the novel-within-the-novel fights its way out of its fundamental dilemma, defending itself against the accusation that it is "about nothing" and "merely a novel about writing a novel." In its complexity *L'attenzione* is a greater novelistic achievement than *La ciociara*, although perhaps not as great an artistic success. If the two novels are compared it can be seen that in writing *La ciociara* Moravia had the advantage of a vivid personal experience, one that lent a power of incident and emotion found nowhere else in his work. In *L'attenzione* his experience—at least his concrete experience— was not involved in quite the same way. But if he was not assisted by personal experience neither was he limited by it. His imagination was therefore free to construct his most complex and technically sophisticated novel. Furthermore there is an ethical implication in *L'attenzione* that is even more central to Moravia's identity than the social-political ethic of *La ciociara*. In this study of inauthenticity he defined the authentic—that is, in the final analysis, the moral—in his own scale of values: the work of art in equilibrium with itself. In the sense, at least, that he believes such art to be possible Moravia can be considered an optimist.

The main impression that strikes the reader who works his way from *Gli indifferenti* and the early stories to *L'attenzione* is that of the consistency of Moravia's themes; or, to put it another way, the essential logic of his development from one interlocking idea to another. If he is an admirer of Moravia he tends to regard this as a kind of integrity; if he is not, the pattern may seem to him monotonous, the mechanical repetitiousness of a writer who has succeeded in popularizing certain psychological and philosophical ideas latent in the atmosphere of his time. It would be hard to argue that Moravia is an important primary thinker or that his fiction has significantly altered the course of modern thought; as, for example, the fiction of Camus may very well have done. It is also evident that he is not a highly original or revolutionary innovator in modern fiction technique. If there is anything "revolutionary" in his technical position, in fact, it is precisely the fact that he challenges the temper of his time by opposing the whole tendency of modern art to complicate technique at the expense of clarity and universality. Even his purity in the matter of point of view, the one area in which he coincides with the vanguard in modern fiction technique, is a position he arrives at through a desire for clarity and plausibility rather than any wish to be "modern." In short, he is a counterrevolutionary in artistic questions, as genuine as his radicalism may be in political and social matters. He is saved from being a "popular" novelist in the pejorative sense only by his fundamental integrity—an integrity which, apart from any biographical information we may have about his relation to his work, is evident in the aggressive consistency of his development. One of the chief marks he bears of an important artist is that his creation patently comes from inside himself, rather than from something outside in what he imagines the public or the *Zeitgeist* may demand. Even in the matter of technique it might be argued that his novels are commonplace only in the context of Proust, Joyce, and Virginia Woolf. If *L'attenzione* had been written in the eighteenth century it would be a remarkable achievement, comparable in its way to *Les liaisons dangereuses* or *Le neveu de Rameau;* yet it is something more than an eighteenth-century novel because it transcends Choderlos de Laclos and Diderot in the modern complexity and intensity of its statement. All the threads of the Moravian fabric are here: the association of sex with the will and with the fundamental problem of identity, the interweaving of this problem with that of the artist *manqué*, the concept of the novel as a way of coming to grips with a life that is in practically every other way unsatisfactory. Furthermore, these diverse elements are gathered together and expressed by a narrator who himself seems scarcely to understand them—who seems to be bewildered by the problems he somehow manages to communicate to the reader with clarity and even with a kind of eloquence. This is the essence of the Moravian method: that a rather complex thematic fugue is concealed for the reader through a highly developed technical competence, leaving a novel distinguished, at least on its surface, by an impression of simplicity or even banality. The real question in the evaluation of Moravia—a question that often seems to waver in the balance—is whether this portrait of banality, *noia*, "inattention" is in itself banal and "annoying," or whether it succeeds as a genuine and convincing literary construction. Looking backward from the perspective of *L'attenzione*, in fact, it can be seen that Moravia's whole work is an effort to portray human limitations and weakness in an art that does not in itself seem limited or weak.

Cesare Pavese

Cesare Pavese was born in 1908 in the town of Santo Stefano Belbo in the Langhe district of the Italian Piedmont. After a degree in letters at the University of Turin with a thesis on Whitman (1930), he went on to a versatile career as a poet, novelist, critic, and translator of American literature. His translation of *Moby-Dick* in 1932 was probably more influential in stimulating interest in American literature under fascism than any other single book. During the Thirties he served briefly as a part-time instructor at the Liceo Massimo d'Azeglio in Turin, and taught also in an evening school for adults. In 1935 he was arrested for clandestine political activity and exiled under police supervision to the small Calabrian town of Brancaleone, where he remained until the summer of 1936. After his return to Turin he was active in the newly formed publishing house of Giulio Einaudi Editore and served the firm in various capacities until the end of his life. His novels include *Il carcere* (1938-39), *Paesi tuoi* (1939), *La bella estate* (1940), *La spiaggia* (1940-41), *Il compagno* (1946), *La casa in collina* (1947-48), *Il diavolo sulle colline* (1948), *Tra donne sole* (1949), and *La luna e i falò* (1949-50). His short fiction is collected as *Racconti* (1960). His other works include the poetry collection *Lavorare stanca* (1936), the Platonic-symbolic *Dialoghi con Leucò,* a collection of criticism published as *La letteratura americana e altri saggi* (1941), and a remarkable diary, *Il mestiere di vivere* (1952). Along with Elio Vittorini he is considered primarily responsible for breaking the academic tradition that dominated Italian literature to 1930 and for introducing a vernacular and "American" element into it. His influence on the literary generation that followed him was considerable. Tormented by personal, political, and artistic problems, he died by suicide in Turin in 1950.

Toward a Poetic Novel

For whatever reasons, Pavese as a novelist lacks the broad popular appeal of Moravia. A considerable cult has been built up around his name by a limited group of initiates, but fundamentally these followers are more interested in the drama of his life, including his suicide, than in his fiction or poetry. There is no doubt that his reputation in the English-speaking world has been handicapped by the difficulty of translation. The apparent simplicity of his style is deceptive. His fiction attempts something much more difficult than it seems on the surface: the creation of a style utilizing the techniques and effects of poetry while at the same time remaining genuine narrative. It also attempts to combine vernacular and traditional literary Italian in a manner something like that of *La ciociara*, although Pavese carries the technique a little farther than Moravia: even though the vernacular is not dominant on the surface it becomes a kind of substratum, an underlying and informing structure, for the literary language. In most of the English translations of Pavese's novels (the exceptions are the versions made in 1967 and after by R. W. Flint) very little of this comes through. In fact, judged by certain widely read translations such as the 1953 version of *La luna e i falò*, Pavese gives the impression of a rather pedestrian regionalist who was influenced by American literature and succeeded in writing some pastiches of Anderson and Steinbeck. It has been left, therefore, to those who read him in the original to recognize him as probably the finest Italian prose stylist of his generation as well as a highly original contributor to the technique of the modern novel.

Pavese's work consists of nine short novels, a number of tales and stories, and a good-sized volume of poetry, plus miscellaneous material like the *Dialoghi con Leucò* and the diaries and criticism. This work is extremely diverse in style and genre, but certain consistent themes are evident in it from the beginning. The first of these is the contrast between the natural and the civilized, the rejection of *città* and the search for *paese*. In his own mind this took the form of a recovery of something lost, a search for his own origins comparable to Proust's search for lost time. Yet his birth in Santo Stefano Belbo was a kind of an accident. His mother came from a well-to-do provincial family and his father, originally from Santo Stefano Belbo, was a minor official in the Turin law courts; it was only because the family spent their summer vacations in the country that Pavese happened to be born there. Outwardly at least he was a typical Italian intellectual with a typical intellectual's background: the sheltered upbringing, the classical *liceo,* the university degree in letters. In person he was bespectacled, asthmatic, bookish, conscious of his own physical inadequacy and regarding sensory experience with the tentative and yet fascinated curiosity of the outsider. Certain of his early stories, particularly "Primo amore," very well illustrate this diffidence in the face of the physical, particularly in its cruder country forms. His attempt to "recover" Santo Stefano Belbo, therefore, was a kind of recognition of something atavistic in himself, or something he regarded as such, rather than a return to any setting or experience he had ever really known. But at a certain point in his career—and it was quite early—he did attempt to divest himself of his intellectual impediments and return to the simplicity, the primitiveness, and the naturalness of Santo Stefano Belbo, and he continued this effort for the rest of his life. His term for what he was seeking was *paese*—not so much village or country as some concept like "native ground"—a place to be rooted.

America and American literature were mixed up with this idea of *paese* in a complicated way. On the one hand America was an extension of *città:* the road from Santo Stefano to the "world outside" led through the slightly larger town of Canelli, then to Genoa, then across the sea to the skyscrapers of Manhattan. But in Faulkner, in Edgar Lee Masters, especially in Melville and Anderson, he discovered another America, "pensive and barbaric, blissful yet quarrelsome, dissolute, fecund; burdened with all the past of the world, yet youthful, innocent,"[1] an America that was *paese* not only for those who sprang from its soil but for all those who participated in the common experience of its literature. The American influence on Pavese's style, while important, has been overemphasized. But it is impossible to overemphasize the part this myth of America as primitive and elemental played in his inward development, his personal formation as an author.

Pavese all of his life suffered from a bad conscience. It is a little hard to get at what lay at the bottom of this, and even he himself was baffled by the mystery. Various ingenious theories of this guilt can be extracted from his personal life; it is surprising, for instance, that psychoanalytic criticism has not made more of the early death of his father, his failure to marry, his intricate friendships with other males like Augusto Monti, and the other classic Oedipal elements in his history. But this kind of conjecture, while fascinating in itself, leads to assertions that can be neither proved nor disproved and do not really throw very much light on the technical aspects of his work. For the purposes of literary criticism it is perhaps more valuable to approach the problem in another way: in what form, in what precise guises, does the theme of bad conscience appear in his work? Pavese's characters frequently—it can almost be said invariably— begin by evading a responsibility or running away from something, and then, after a certain period of exile, seeking a reconciliation which is sometimes successful and sometimes not. In the "Secretum Professionale" which opens his diary, written in exile in Calabria in 1935, he notes, "If there is a pattern in my poetry, it is the pattern of the runaway boy who returns with joy to his village . . ."[2] He is speaking here of the early poems of *Lavorare stanca*, but the comment applies as well to his entire work. Throughout his life he thought of himself more or less consciously as a "boy run away from home," and behaved like one: defiant independence mingled with nostalgia for the abandoned hearth. The boy runs away from the power and violence of sex, the man runs away from engagement or commitment, whether to marriage, to a political party, or to life itself. In his fiction and poetry the concept of escape is expressed in a number of recurring images. To the boy born in Santo Stefano Belbo the first escape is to the city, to Turin or Genoa. The sea too is escape; as elements of geographical symbolism the river and the Piedmontese hills are native, the sea foreign. The urban diversions— alcohol, easy sex, music, fashionable chatter, fast automobiles—are always connected in his fiction with evading genuine responsibilities. Work, including writing, is a form of commitment, but reading in the sense of "losing one's self in books" may be an escape, especially in wartime or in other times of crisis. The final evasion is suicide, the "absurd vice" that was Pavese's lifelong temptation and makes its way as a kind of subterranean motif through his work. Very few people die naturally in Pavese's fiction. For his characters death is less a result of disease or common human mortality than a conscious renegation, a failure to belong to life or find a place in it.

In spite of this constant search for the elemental and instinctive Pavese is a highly intellectual writer. Or, more precisely, he is that kind of a writer—like Lawrence and Rilke—who seeks out the elemental and primitive precisely because he is conscious of an over-intellectual tendency in his own personality. The main influences—at least the overt ones—in his early life were literary. In his schoolboy years he spent long hours with his friend Sturani at the Civic Library of Turin, and according to his biographer Lajolo he even taught himself Greek when the subject was not offered at the Ginnasio Moderno where he was a pupil. Later, at the Liceo Massimo d'Azeglio, he came under the influence of Augusto Monti, a remarkable teacher and a remarkable personality. Although Monti's Italian literature course dealt in large part with the accepted classics—Dante, Boccaccio, Machiavelli, Ariosto, Manzoni—he consistently attacked the tradition of the *letterato* in Italian culture, the writer whose experience was largely intellectual and literary, who wrote about books and things read rather than immediate sensory experience. This failure of commitment to life in any genuine sense resulted in empty metrics, Carduccian sentimentalism, the inflated *prosa d'arte* of the academic tradition. Monti's own critical position was antimetrical, antisentimental, and opposed to verbosity and pretentiousness in style. It was in this *liceo* period that Pavese encountered the poetry of Guido Gozzano (1883–1916), who is remarkable chiefly for having broken out of the traditional Italian metrics into a free vernacular line something like that of Whitman and Masters, and for mingling dialect with literary Italian. Gozzano's concept of verse, in fact, was essentially narrative rather than lyric, and it was around this concept that Pavese's own view of himself as a poet began to form. What he found later in Whitman, in Masters, in Melville was merely a reconfirmation of this original discovery in Gozzano.[3]

Pavese's effort to define himself as a writer can be expressed in a simple formula: from narrative poetry to poetic narrative. The early part of his career—roughly that to 1935—was devoted to the development of a poetry free from conventional metrics and expressed in a vernacular rhythm and diction: the poems of *Lavorare stanca*. During the Thirties he read the Elizabethans and especially Shakespeare, trying to get at the method of this combination of poetry and narrative, particularly the relation of plot to aesthetic whole. Shakespeare narrates and sings in such a way that neither can be separated from the other: what is the secret of this art? It was about this same time that he began reading and translating the Americans: his *Moby-Dick* appeared in 1932, the translation of Anderson's *Dark Laughter* the same year, and his first essay on Dos Passos in 1933. He read Robinson Jeffers as early as 1930 and expressed his enthusiasm in a letter to his American friend Antonio Chiuminatto. A great deal of discussion has been devoted to the question of how, in what way, and to what extent Pavese was influenced by American literature. He himself is not very helpful in this matter, and in fact confuses the question by commenting, "It is too simple to believe that translation has the effect of training your hand to the style you translate from. Translation—and I speak from experience—teaches us how we ought *not* to write; it makes us aware at every step of the way a different sensibility and culture express themselves in a given style, and the effort of rendering this style cures us of any temptation we might have to experiment with it ourselves."[4] When he wrote this in 1950 he was in a violent and somewhat irrational anti-American mood. It is also well-known that writers of any originality typically repudiate the notion that they have been influenced by anything at all outside themselves. The fact remains that Pavese—who thought of himself primarily as a poet and novelist rather than a critic—did devote long years of his life to reading, studying, translating, and writing about American literature. It is easy to explain that he did this for money, but he nevertheless gravitated toward American literature and not, for example, to German or Italian as certain of his university companions did. What interested him in part was the theme, or the whole mystique, of *paese* that he thought he had found in the Americans and especially in Anderson. But, even more important, American literature revealed to him the possibility of a poetic novel —the possibility that writing could remain primarily and genuinely fiction and at the same time make use of certain of the techniques of poetry, particularly the refinement of image and the rhythm and flow of language. After 1932 it was clear to him that his own bent lay in the direction of Melville rather than that of Shakespeare, Whitman, and Gozzano. After the writing of his first novel in 1938-39 he returned to verse only sporadically, and always on occasion of involvements with women; Italo Calvino has pointed out that all the poems after the first volume in 1936 are *to* women.[5] In Pavese's fiction, on the other hand, women are customarily regarded by the protagonist as enemies. In the diary entries from 1940 on, love is viewed increasingly as a vice that distracts from work, and poetry is no more than a kind of emotional by-product of this distraction. For the later Pavese poetry, in short, is another escape, an evasion. Just as the novels correspond to genuine life, to commitment, to work, the poems correspond to withdrawal into the private self-indulgence of eroticism. Pavese finished his last novel on November 17, 1949. In the ten months remaining in his life he devoted himself mainly to the poems of *Verrà la morte e avrà i tuoi occhi;** he made no more

* "Death Will Come and It Will Have Your Eyes."

effort to write fiction and seems to have had no plans for further novels. These final poems, written for the American actress Constance Dowling, are conventional in form and unashamedly sentimental; they are merely the momentary lyrical coagulations of violent emotion. Their logical conclusion, their confirmation, was the final gesture of August 27, 1950. After he finished *La luna e i falò* he wrote to his friend Aldo Camerino, "For a while—perhaps forever—I won't do anything else."[6] Poetry, evidently, did not count.

The early poems, on the other hand, relate in an important way to his fiction and are in fact the predecessors of the novels. Of these the most typical and probably the finest is the narrative poem "I mari del Sud"* which opens *Lavorare stanca.* All of Pavese is contained here in miniature: the theme is that of *paese* and wider world, the style anticipates the novels, the poem is dedicated to Augusto Monti. The assimilated influences of Gozzano, *Spoon River Anthology*, and Melville are evident. (Pavese's first article on *Spoon River* dates from 1931, but he refers to Masters with evident familiarity in a letter to Antonio Chiuminatto in early 1930, about nine months before he wrote the poem.) The central figure is the narrator's cousin who returns to the Piedmontese village after twenty years of wandering the world as a sailor.

> We walk one evening on the flank of a hill
> in silence. In the late twilight shadow
> my cousin is a giant clad in white,
> who moves calmly, his face bronzed,
> taciturn. Taciturnity is our virtue.
> Some ancestor of ours must have been very alone—
> a great man among idiots or some kind of madman—
> to teach us so much silence.[7]

The reference to taciturnity is among other things a piece of literary criticism, a comment on the verbose Carduccian rhetoric of the fin de siècle. But as a description of the Piedmontese character it reflects Pavese's view of his own personality, or more precisely the poetics he was in the process of constructing out of his personality: a precise and economic terseness with something of the quality of the native vernacular. This effort to combine vernacular and *lingua pura* continues throughout Pavese's work. It is achieved about as successfully in this poem as it is in any of the novels up to *La luna e i falò*. The essence of it is the effort to incorporate, not only the pattern and flow of common speech, but the mentality of the rural vernacular speaker—an intimacy with the earth, a sensitivity devoid of self-pity,

* "The South Seas." *Lavorare stanca* is literally "Work Is Tiring."

a strain of sarcasm—into the framework of conventional Italian. There are further complexities: another fragment of the poem suggests the way Pavese has made use of Melville in a manner that is simultaneously mythical and realistic, as well as the vein of irony that extends through the poem—not only an irony toward the ingenuousness of the youthful narrator but a self-irony as well, since Pavese associates himself with the boy.

> Just one dream
> has remained in his blood: he shipped out once
> as fireman on a Dutch whaler, the *Cetacean*,
> he had seen the great fins soaring in the sun,
> had seen the whales fleeing in a foam of blood
> seen the chase, the flukes rising, the battle with the lance.
> He talks about it sometimes.
> But when I tell him
> that he is among the fortunate who have seen the dawn
> over the fairest islands of the earth,
> he smiles, remembering, and replies that when the sun
> came up the day was already old for them.[8]

When Pavese first read this poem to his university friends it seemed "Homeric" to Massimo Mila, and Pavese himself consciously associated the cousin with Odysseus.[9] But there is more to the comparison than the figure of the "giant clad in white." Entirely apart from the relative importance of the two poets, the technique of Pavese's poem is closely parallel to that of the *Odyssey* as Auerbach describes it on the first page of *Mimesis:* "Clearly outlined, brightly and uniformly illuminated, men and things stand out in a realm where everything is visible; and not less clear—wholly expressed, orderly even in their ardor—are the feelings and thoughts of the persons involved."[10] Very basic to this effect is the kind of tension that comes from the simultaneous presence of intensity and simplicity. The high emotion of the whale-hunt ("the great fins soaring in the sun . . . the whales fleeing in a foam of blood") is balanced and thrown into relief by the cousin's laconic comment ("when the sun / came up the day was already old for them"). It is important to note that the emotion is not achieved through the effect of what is told—the spectacle or event in itself—but through a gathering and arrangement of imagery that is essentially poetic. The thing that occurs is the death of an animal amid blood and violence, but there is no appeal to sensationalism. What is achieved is a lift and not a shock. And any appeal to sentiment that might linger in the brief passage is deflated by the cousin's comment. The scene takes place in

Auerbach's "realm where everything is visible" and clearly illuminated: the name of the ship, the exact job that the cousin performed
on it, the designation of a weapon. The effect is natural to Homer
because he writes in a period of literary history before the separation
of styles that banned realistic detail from high poetry. For Pavese it
involved a deliberate attempt to reconstruct a poetics based on this
tension between the detail and the total effect. When he turned later
to the novel the task, as long and hedged about with difficulties as it
proved to be, was simply that of transferring this technique from the
form of verse narrative to that of fiction.

Pavese was intensely serious about this craft of fiction-writing,
more serious than he was about the outward circumstances of his
life, or even about life itself. It is curious that there is virtually no
humor in his fiction or in anything he wrote about fiction, from his
criticism to the copious self-analysis of his writing problems in the
diaries. And this is in spite of the fact that he possessed a genuine
sense of humor and could express it in writing when he chose. Some
of the letters from the Calabrian exile, one of the most unhappy
periods of his life, are full of an elaborate and whimsical kind of
self-mockery. In the letters he could even joke about sex. But he
never joked about his craft as a writer, and it was to this craft that
he directed the total and serious efforts of his intelligence throughout a career beset with technical difficulties. Pavese has at least one
mark of an important writer, or at least a writer of unmistakable
integrity, and this is a characteristic shared also by Moravia and
Vittorini. From beginning to end his work is self-consistent and
seems to be groping its way, book by book, toward the expression of
a single rather complex statement. It is what used to be called an
oeuvre, a career that in itself can be regarded as a single literary
work visible through a long course of development. There are mistakes and wrong turnings in this development, but no actual dead
ends like, for example, Steinbeck's *The Moon Is Down* in which the
author abandons his natural material and turns to propaganda.
Pavese's mistakes are in the main stream of his work, and they are
never total mistakes; he always manages to salvage something and
convert it to at least a partial success in a later novel. He did this
with the somewhat contrived use of country mythology in *Paesi
tuoi* and the treatment of rural aristocrats in stories like "Primo
amore," for example; both were rewritten and improved later in
La luna e i falò. There is only one narrator in the main body of
Pavese's fiction, and he is essentially an autobiographical narrator.
More precisely, since not all of Pavese's fiction is in the first person,
this "narrator" is simply a consistent and identifiable consciousness

through which the action of all of his fiction is seen. He appears in all the various epochs and stages of Pavese's own development, with a single exception: he is never the established novelist, the mature man haunted by the problems of approaching middle age, and on the brink of suicide. Sometimes he is thinly disguised as a law student, an engineer, a mechanic. In two curious cases (*La bella estate* and *Tra donne sole*) the autobiographical identity is switched in sex and becomes that of a woman. But it is still a consciousness that, transcending social class and even sex, remains fundamentally that of Pavese himself. It is a consciousness, for example, preoccupied with certain chronic problems: isolation vs commitment, work and the temptations that distract from work, the problem of transcending crude sex to arrive at some kind of genuine union of the spirit. It is even possible to trace a consistent imagery through Pavese's work: hills, crickets, sea, nudity, sun, moon, America, harvest, earth, perform the same symbolic or imagistic functions from his earliest published poems to his last novel. And yet in another sense he never repeated himself; each time he began a new work he struggled for a new framework, a new expression for his basic statement. In a 1949 article he explained how writers become self-imitators: by "surrendering to the perfectly legitimate temptation of exploiting an already known and conquered territory."[11] Sometimes he did take up an old story and rewrite it; *Il carcere* and *Il compagno* are expanded versions of earlier stories. But these are really revisions rather than new treatments of the old material. Furthermore they are not his best work and Pavese himself was aware of this; the material that was unsatisfactory in story form is only partly successful as a novel. His best work he wrote spontaneously, almost in a rush; *Paesi tuoi* was written in six weeks, *La luna e i falò* in slightly over seven. The search for spontaneity, in fact, was a large part of his personal technical problem. The difficulty with his earlier fiction, particularly *Il carcere* and certain stories, is that on the one hand it follows the autobiographical experience too closely and on the other hand its thematics and symbolism are too contrived, too overtly literary. The difficult task of surmounting this synthetic method, of forgetting at least on the surface the sophistication he had gained as a university student of letters, he accomplished fairly successfully before the end of his career. In a radio interview in the last month of his life he explained that when he began a piece of fiction he never had in mind a given setting, character, thesis, or social milieu. Instead he began from "an indistinct rhythm, a play of events that, more than anything else, are sensations and feelings."[12] The usual path of education, or *Bildung,* is from spontaneity to consciousness.

For Pavese, as for a number of other modern writers from Rilke to Lawrence, it is the other way.

To put the matter somewhat more precisely, Pavese is typical of a certain kind of modern writer whose problem is simultaneously technical and personal. It is relatively possible to separate the personal biography of, let us say, E. M. Forster from his technical career, but this is not possible in the case of Rilke or Pavese. Around 1940, the period of *La bella estate*, Pavese's diary is preoccupied with the concept of "style as a way of thinking," a style in which the ambience, the action, the secondary characters, are seen always through a mentality that influences the language and even the cadence in which the story is told. It is not primarily a question of whether the story is told grammatically in the first person or the third person; there is always an implied consciousness through which the narrative is processed on its way to the reader. It took Pavese some time to grasp that this fictional consciousness was his own, or a projection of his own transformed in a highly complicated way into an ideal or abstract alter ego. He finally seems to have realized that to create such a consciousness was to create something inside himself: a knowledge or mastery that is always latent in the act of artistic creation. By 1949 he could write that "the final—and primary—reason for making a story is the impulse to bring into focus the irrational and indistinct that lurks at the bottom of our experience."[13] The discovery of this Sleeping God was the real triumph of Pavese's life and the underlying matrix of his work. The recurring themes like the search for the primitive or the mysterious violence of sex are only aspects, subdivisions, of this primary matrix. And the technical problems he grappled with—point of view, the combination of dialect and literary language, the creation of a poetic fiction—were only tools that, like the Golden Branch of Aeneas, would enable him to enter this underworld. It is perhaps for this reason that Pavese's work, unlike Moravia's, appeals to a relatively limited circle of readers; its psychology and scheme of experience are highly special. But it is precisely for this reason too that, for these few, it has an effect of such extraordinary immediacy, the shock of recognition. In this sense Pavese belongs with Stendhal and Rimbaud, all those who write for a "happy few"; or an unhappy few as the case may be.

Breaking Out of Jail

"I mari del Sud," the first poem that Pavese considered worth publishing, dates from the fall of 1930. From this time until 1935 his creative effort was devoted chiefly to poetry. Meanwhile he supported himself by the usual expedients of the struggling young writer: articles for literary quarterlies, reviewing, part-time teaching, tutoring the *enfant terrible* of a family of country aristocrats, translating American novels. This poetic activity came to a climax in 1934 and 1935; in slightly more than two years he produced forty poems, most of them occupying a page or more in the volume of his collected verse. At this point there intervened a personal accident curiously parallel to the one that happened to Dostoevski at the beginning of his career: he was arrested for clandestine political activity, imprisoned, and then exiled to a remote part of his country. Pavese was not really very interested in politics, at least not as much as some of his friends like Massimo Mila and Leone Ginzburg. He had even joined the Fascist Party in 1932, probably because it was necessary for his planned career as a teacher. But he attracted the attention of the fascists precisely because of these friendships and because of his connection with the "subversive" review *La Cultura*. On May 15, 1935, about two hundred persons were arrested by the police in Turin, among them most of the intellectuals belonging to the movement "Giustizia e Libertà" and the entire staff of *La Cultura*. Pavese spent ten weeks in the Carceri Nuove in Turin and in Regina Coeli prison in Rome, and then was sent to exile under police supervision (*"mandato al confino"*) in the remote Calabrian town of Brancaleone. His original sentence of *confino* was for three years; of this he actually spent a little over seven months in Brancaleone. It was as a result of this same mass arrest that Carlo Levi was exiled to another southern Italian town, the experience he later described in *Cristo si è fermato a Eboli*.

No one mistreated Pavese in his two prisons or in the period of his exile, and compared to some others involved in this incident he escaped fairly lightly. But the experience was a crucial one for him personally as it was for his technical formation as a writer. Like Moravia's illness, it was an intrusion that broke into the normal routine of his life, disturbing the forming pattern of his identity, and then gave him long months to think while the pieces were rearranging themselves. After these months he knew a good deal more about isolation—not only the exile itself but the spiritual isolation he had felt from the time of his childhood—than he had before. His career as a writer takes a sharp bend at this point and never returns to its original direction. He wrote a number of poems during the Calabrian exile, including some of his best ones. But the poems taper off after 1935 and finally, around 1940, come to a stop entirely except for occasional spasms of love lyrics. His first fiction (unpublished until after his death) was written in July 1936; it is a story about the Calabrian exile. The novel *Il carcere,* written in 1938-39, is simply an expansion and rewriting of this story. From this point on the notion of *carcere,* of confinement, of feeling one's self enclosed actually or symbolically within some kind of walls, is a recurring theme in his work. A number of characters in his fiction are convicts or have been in jail, and several stories are actually set in prison. But the real importance of the Calabrian experience extends beyond the matter of thematics. In Brancaleone Pavese thought out his personal problem as a writer and saw more clearly the direction his literary influences and his own nature were leading him, and the interlude of the exile enabled him to make a clean break with what he had done before. His first volume of verse, *Lavorare stanca,* appeared while he was in Calabria, but this event really marked the down-turning of his career as a poet rather than the beginning as it might have seemed. He still wrote poems, at a slowing rate, for several more years. But it was precisely at this point, in the winter of 1935-36, that he turned seriously for the first time in his life to the writing of fiction.

*Il carcere** is a novel with many technical faults or unresolved difficulties. The first of these is insufficient conversion of the autobiographical experience. In this connection it is interesting to compare Pavese's first attempt to produce a work of fiction out of this experience (the story "Terra d'esilio"†) with the later novel as it was finally published in 1949. The story, actually written in Brancaleone shortly before Pavese left to go back to Turin in the summer of 1936, is narrated in the first person by an engineer who is in Calabria solely for reasons of work; he is supervising the paving of the provincial highway. He is therefore only an observer of the central action of the story, which turns around a semiliterate Turin worker who has been sent to Calabria as a *confinato.* The worker, Otino, is jealous of his common-law wife in Turin. When she is killed by another lover he is tormented by a confusion of emotions: grief for the woman he loved, satisfaction that her faithlessness has finally been punished, impotent rage that the revenge has been carried out by somebody else. This story is tentative and sketchy in style, lacking in the hard concrete details that characterize Pavese's later fiction, but it is successful in at least one crucial respect: the relation of narrator to protagonist. The engineer is a spectator and yet he is not

* Literally "Jail." Translated as *The Political Prisoner* (London: Owen, 1955).
    † "Land of Exile."

only a spectator; when Otino asks him if he is a *confinato* too he says, "We all are, more or less, here."[14] The two men are totally different in background, culture, and temperament, and yet they are linked by a powerful bond of common condition. Between them they share, not only the personality, but the empathy and emotional commitment of the author; just as Marcel and Charlus are two sides of the author in Proust's novel, the engineer and Otino are two sides of Pavese in this story. Probably this technical device was the result of the accident that Pavese, hoping to publish the story, was writing to avoid censorship. Thus the narrator is made not a political exile but a perfectly law-abiding engineer, and even Otino is not a political *confinato* but was exiled for striking a militiaman who flirted with his girl. And yet Otino is fundamentally a persona of the author, the murder of Otino's girl a projection of Pavese's own jealousy of the woman he had left behind in Turin. Meanwhile the engineer represents the more rational and intellectual objectivity with which Pavese, in another part of his mind, viewed his own predicament. In this way the effort to conceal the autobiographical basis of the story resulted in a complexity of relation between narrator and protagonist that is the story's chief merit.

When he rewrote this material in 1938-39 in novel form Pavese was evidently not quite so anxious for immediate publication, or perhaps he now foresaw a period in which fascist censorship would no longer be a problem. The result was that he wrote closer to the real events, even though this would seem to be a reversal of the normal process by which a writer fictionalizes an experience. The point-of-view character is now a political *confinato* and a kind of intellectual, even though he is an electrical engineer by profession. Otino is still present, converted to a *confinato* anarchist who lives in another village on top of the mountain and no longer performs any central function in the mechanics of the novel, although there is an attempt to make him serve as a personification of the engineer's bad political conscience. A good many of Otino's characteristics, for example, his complicated sexual problem and his obsession with mail from Turin, are now attributed to Stefano, the engineer. But the author backs away from his character now in another sense: the action is related in the third person instead of the first. This is the main tactical mistake in the writing of *Il carcere;* not that the first person is always and inherently better, but that in this case the basic psychology of the novel, the involvement of the writer in his material which in turn becomes the involvement of the reader, demands the intimacy and immediacy of first-person narration. The recurring technical problem of Pavese's whole career, in fact, was that of combining a genuine personal commitment to his material with the objectivity of a finished work of art, and he was never successful at this except when he used one specific point of view: the first-person narrator who is basically a spectator but in another sense involved in or committed to the action. This is the method of *Paesi tuoi* and *La luna e i falò*, his two most successful novels, as well as some interesting half-successes like *Il compagno*. His attempts to experiment with other techniques always resulted in at least a partial failure of empathy. In *Il carcere* it is all "he" and "him" and it seems to be happening to somebody else, somebody neither the author nor the reader knows very well.

There are other difficulties: there are too many characters (again probably because Pavese was following his autobiographical experiences too closely) and they are not well enough defined, the necessary details of Stefano's previous life in Turin are lacking, the plot seems to be moving toward some resolution or statement and never gets there. In the earlier story version there is the climactic murder, even though it takes place in Turin instead of at the scene of action. In *Il carcere* we continually expect some such event which will tie together the diverse threads of the narrative, but it never happens. When his period of exile is commuted Stefano simply gets on a train and goes away. As, of course, Pavese did himself.

In a number of other technical matters *Il carcere* is an improvement on "Terra d'esilio," so much in fact that it is possible to say that the main function of the novel was to serve as a school of narrative technique for the author himself. Naturally there is the greater richness inherent in the form; *Il carcere* is a short novel but structurally a true one rather than an extended tale or novella. But a more important difference is that in *Il carcere* Pavese begins to sketch out the major themes of his later fiction. In the story there is a girl named Concetta who is brought to town for a few days and kept in the butcher shop, "nourished on meat and olives" and available to the members of a cooperative who have contributed to her expenses. But the engineer himself becomes only slightly involved, and very little is made of the matter. In the novel Concetta is divided into two: the cooperative harlot is still there but there is a new character called Concia, a gypsy-like local servant girl who evokes complicated meridional desires in the northern engineer. Barefooted, goatlike, arrogant and yet elusively tempting, she represents one side of Stefano's somewhat confused sexual needs. The other half is represented by a new character: Elena, the "no longer young" daughter of his landlady, who not only cleans his room but shares his bed and brings him pathetic bunches of flowers to win his affection. Her tremulous maternalism (she even calls herself his "mammina") and her mute air of sacrifice are necessary to Stefano and at the same time annoy him. She represents home, family, woman as mother, and in the dynamic pattern of the novel this is associated with confining walls and the deprivation of independence. At the other pole stands Concia, the animalesque and uncomplicated peasant. But is she really as uncomplicated as she seems? "It occurred to him that, instead of Elena, he might have Concia in his room. But his numbed blood felt no excitement. 'It would be the same, even she isn't a savage, she would want me to love her.' "[15] Here the novel begins attacking its theme in a major way. Stefano longs for domesticity and yet is stifled by it, hungers for pagan sensuality but knows in a part of his mind that pure sensualism is impossible for an intellectual like himself, or for any human being ("even she . . . would want me to love her"). Entangled with this is the matter of isolation vs commitment. In a letter to his sister in March 1936 Pavese wrote, "I find it completely stupid to have believed in the past that individual isolation, even for an instant, could be happiness."[16] But in the tavern of the Calabrian town Stefano feels awkward and alienated among the gregarious southerners. The price of union with other men—or with women—is to give up a piece of one's integrity, one's wholeness. Is he to be alone and independent or in some way involved with others, thus necessarily surrendering a part of his independence? This problem, in its sexual aspect as well as a number of others, is a crucial one of the novel.

It is here that the word *carcere,* the key image of the novel, becomes involved. Stefano's rented room is a jail and Elena is his jailer. So is every mother and wife, in the sense that family limits independence. But in the tavern of the Calabrian town, amid the chattering and joking southerners he now calls his friends, Stefano feels "a vacuum, a futile pain," and reflects, "the cell was made of this: the silence of the world."[16] The real reason the family is a jail is that one is limited by it, is left unfulfilled and lonely in the midst of domesticity. Thus the family is only a microcosm of the world, and the world itself becomes a prison. This is the *carcere* of the title: not the cell of Regina Coeli, not the rented room by the railroad tracks, but the very immensity of a world in which the individual feels himself in some elusive and intangible way an exile, longing to establish contact with other men yet cut off from them by mysterious and invisible walls. And paradoxically it is this very sense of being cut off from others that leads Stefano to a realization of the kinship of all men, a kinship that subsists precisely in their common isolation. If everybody is in jail then at least everybody is in jail together. This does not mean that they are innocent or that they do not deserve to be in jail, in fact precisely the opposite. Like Kafka, Pavese concludes that the fact that all men are punished demonstrates that they are in some way guilty. Toward the end of the novel Stefano "imagined the whole world as a jail in which people were shut up for various reasons but all correct ones, and in this he found comfort."[17]

Is it possible, then, to break out of jail? Pascal remarked that all the unhappiness of men arises from the fact that they cannot stay quietly in their own room. The very fact of being in jail, even justly, even accepting one's isolation, leads to the instinct of wanting to break out. At least for ordinary men; those who feel no impulse to break out are monks, hermits, and saints. "Our convent is the prison,"[18] his friend Giannino remarks to Stefano, and in a number of other places in the novel isolation is associated with the religious life. (We learn from the letters to his sister that Pavese at one time even half-seriously considered the idea of becoming a priest.) But not very many men are saints. In his rented room Stefano lives out of his suitcase; to unpack it would be to accept, not the justice, but the *fact* of incarceration. When Elena unpacks the suitcase he packs it again. Yet in some mysterious way he is not free to go, while the others are free to come and intrude on him. Stefano comes back to the room once and finds the door open. Was it Elena again? "This too reminded him of the cell: whoever came to the door could enter and talk to him. Elena, the goatherd, the water-boy, even Giannino, could come in like so many turnkeys . . . Stefano was astounded by so much uniformity in so strange an existence. The immobile summer had gone by in slow silence, like a single dreamy afternoon. Of all the faces, the thoughts, all the anxiety and the peace, there remained only vague ripples, like the reflection of a pail of water on the ceiling."[19] The door is open, but if he leaves through it with his packed suitcase where would he go? In a poem he wrote in Brancaleone Pavese remembered autumn in the Piedmond, the hares fleeing over the frozen ground, the pleasure of warm rooms, wine, and good food.

> You think that afterward life will start over
> that you'll breathe easy again, winter will come back
> with the smell of wine in warm taverns,
> a good fire, the stable, the food. You think,
> as long as you're locked up you think. They let you
> out one night,

and the hares have been taken and eaten in
warm rooms
by the others, the happy ones. Look at them through
the windows.[20]

And yet possibly there is a way to break out. Not in any real
world; but for the artist at least there exists a possibility of operating
in a realm other than the real world. Or rather, even though the
artist must reflect this real world with its limitations and insoluble
dilemmas in the artificial world he creates, he stands in a special
relation to this artificial world precisely because he is its creator and
thus outside the structure of its limitations. God is not bound by his
own laws, and the poet is not confined within his poem; he stands
above it. Pavese's personal achievement in *Il carcere* was therefore
not any resolution of the problems it expressed, or even any particular understanding of these problems that he had not had when he
began to write, but simply the first step toward a technical competence that was to be his self-fulfillment. He had invented a metaphor
for his predicament. Thereafter whenever he wrote well he was free;
when he wrote badly, or was distracted from writing, he was in
prison. The theme of *carcere* recurs chronically in his writing to the
end, under a variety of different names.

Oxen and Women

*Paesi tuoi,** dating from the summer of 1939, is different from
anything in Pavese's earlier fiction. It is narrated in the first person,
and yet the narrator is neither a directly autobiographical character
nor a central figure in the events he relates. Instead he is that semi-
involved spectator that Pavese had been working toward for some
time, a spectator who is a projection of the author's consciousness
and yet is a character apart from him. The empathy of the reader is
broken into two parts. In one part of his mind he associates himself
with the narrator, as the author does himself. But this narrator is
empathetically involved with the central character whose story he
is telling, sharing to a certain degree the emotions and inward reactions of this character. Thus that part of the reader's empathy not
fixed on the narrator passes on to the central character, even though
he is seen only at second hand through the consciousness of the
narrator. The part played by this narrator is essentially the function
performed by Marlow in *Heart of Darkness* and *Lord Jim,* although

* Roughly "Native Soil." Translated as *The Harvesters* (London:
Owen, 1961).

Pavese seems not to have noticed this in Conrad and instead laboriously worked out the technique for himself. (His single article on
Conrad, dating from 1946, is devoted almost entirely to the subject
of exotic setting and makes no mention of narrative technique.) He
experiments with it in a few stories before his first major application
of it in *Paesi tuoi*.

But there is something in *Paesi tuoi* that is not found even in
the stories before 1939. Berto, the narrator, is an unemployed Turin
mechanic with a limited verbal sophistication and no literary background at all, and his way of telling a story is solidly based in
vernacular. The words he uses are those found in an Italian dictionary, but the rhythm of his telling, his inflexions, the flavor of his
mentality, are Piedmontese. The result is a style simultaneously
ironic and ingenuous, a style that permits itself all the possibilities of
psychological insight while at the same time retaining a fundamental
innocence and freshness toward the events it relates. Sentence by
sentence the novel resembles not so much Lord Jim as one of
Anderson's first-person stories like "I Want to Know Why." And this
stylistic quality, in Anderson as well as Pavese, is closely connected
to theme. "For Anderson the whole modern world is a contrast
between nature and little men,"[21] Pavese wrote in 1931. Although
his view of city and country was not quite so simple in 1939 as it had
been in 1931, this is essentially the thematic framework of *Paesi tuoi*.
Berto, released from jail after a short sentence, is uncertain what to
do with himself and besides has reasons for getting out of Turin.
Impulsively he decides to accompany Talino, a young peasant who
has shared his cell, back to his farm in the hills. Insofar as it involves
Berto, then, the action of the novel is the discovery of *paese*, of the
primitivism of the countryside. For Talino, of course, the journey to
the farm is a return. Pavese himself stood in exactly this double
relation to the primitive: on the one hand he had been born in
Santo Stefano Belbo and it was a kind of native ground to him in at
least an atavistic sense, on the other hand he had spent his formative
years in Turin and the country was something he was obliged to
rediscover through a conscious act of will. In this sense—relation to
the setting—Pavese equals Berto plus Talino. But there is an important distinction to be made. Unlike the protagonist of *Il carcere*,
Berto is not an intellectual; he is a mechanic. This gives him the
freedom to view things unlimited by any literary preconceptions,
but it also results in a technical problem. Pavese is willing to confine
himself to Berto's frame of rhetoric, but not to his intellect or his
aesthetics. It is here that he creates for himself a difficulty that
Conrad was not confronted with, since Marlow is by no means an

average or normal seaman any more than Conrad was himself. The limitations of his narrator involve Pavese in a kind of stylistic subterfuge. The language of the novel is that of Berto himself, but the underlying mentality, the aesthetic viewpoint, is that of a much more complicated consciousness—one capable, for instance, of perceiving the mythological implications of the action and of attributing symbolic significance to various details of the setting. This aesthetic consciousness permeating the narrative, this substructure of myth and symbol, Pavese refers to in his diaries somewhat confusingly as "style." "The style of Berto is not attributed to Berto, but assimilated to a third person. Instead of naturalistic it should become a revelatory *way of thinking*. It is this that cannot be done in poetry, and ought to be possible in prose."[22] Thus it is necessary to speak of style in *Paesi tuoi* on two levels: style as vernacular or regional rhythm (the element of Berto), style as "way of thinking" (the element of Pavese himself). The first is proletarian, the second is "poetic" in the general sense, i.e., highly metaphorical and associative in its use of language. The first is naturalism; the second is the mythic suggestiveness that Pavese in his best work shares with Melville, Conrad, and Anderson.

Pavese's diary in this period is full of comments on narrative technique, especially on the relation between "style" and theme, or central statement, of the novel. At one point he decides, "The style should not influence the formation of the story: preceding style there exists a nucleus of realities and persons that *have happened . . .* 'Literature' is when the style precedes the imaginative nucleus.' "[23] But only a few days later this conclusion is reexamined and rejected: "Now I see that the very act of telling about an incident or character is idle fantasy-making, because this *telling* itself is what the traditional concept of poetry is reduced to. In order to write with *any other* end in mind, it is necessary to work through style, in other words seeking to create a way of understanding *life* that will be a new kind of knowledge."[24] This opposition of life and literature is only one of the many dichotomies implied in the novel. Can a work of literature, words on a printed page, represent life in some kind of sense that is opposed to literature? This paradoxical task is one of the aims of *Paesi tuoi*.

The "way of understanding life" in the novel is involved with "style" in a number of intricate ways. First there is the mixture of vernacular language and mythic imagery in which Berto tells his story. This technique corresponds to a quite personal aim of Pavese himself: the rejection of the "literary" along with the recovery of some kind of archetypal or mythic contact with nature. Then there is the even more directly autobiographical question: to what extent is Pavese's own personal problem, or his own personal experience, expressed in the novel? The important event of this epoch of his life was the rediscovery of Santo Stefano, yet this rediscovery he made not through any physical return to the place of his birth (he had returned there frequently throughout his childhood and youth) but precisely through the writing of the novel. The title of the novel is drawn from an Italian proverb: *Donne e buoi dei paesi tuoi,* [Look for] women and oxen in your own village. But what was Pavese's own village? In this novel he is both Berto and Talino. Or, more precisely, he divides himself into three: Berto, Talino, and the unifying consciousness that hovers over the action. Talino goes home to his *paese* and is involved there in a dark and violent family drama, a drama that began long before the action of the novel opens. He himself is hardly aware of his motives, and these motives are not very clear to Berto or to the reader either. There is a side to *paese* whose power can only be measured viscerally, and it is not attractive side. Since Talino personifies this power, he is not really in a position to understand it. But Berto does understand it, at least partially, before the end of the novel. When he decides to accompany Talino home to the farm he anticipates it as a refuge where he will be able to restore himself with plain food and healthy outdoor work. The farm is presided over by the old Vinverra, a tyrant who is half Silenus and half rustic brute. His dominant element is wine, as his name suggests. Except for Talino the others of the family are all female: an old grandmother and three younger women, including Adele, who has children of her own, and Gisella, the youngest and most attractive. At first Berto finds something fundamental and satisfying in this family in spite of its crudeness. The whole setting of the farm and countryside, in fact, impresses itself on him in sexual terms. The images that dominate the early part of the novel are moon, stubble, heat, the odor of hay, apples, crickets, cold water. Two of these, stubble and crickets, occur all the way through Pavese's work as suggestions of harvest and rustic abundance, of fertility. The farm and the countryside around it are dominated by a conical hill whose associations are obvious even before we have been told that it looks like a breast. In a diary entry shortly after the writing of the novel Pavese refers to the hill as a kind of Homeric epithet that "expresses the sexual reality of the countryside."[25] The difficulty with this symbol, in fact, is that it is too consciously contrived, too "literary" in Pavese's own pejorative sense. Much better is the image of Gisella "made of fruit"—she has a clean astringent odor, her flesh is whiter than the others, and Berto associates his own physical relations with her with the sensation of biting into the tart firm apples he finds in the storeroom. When he inquires why these are called Gisella's apples he is told they come from her tree; when a child is born the peasants plant a tree so the two will "grow up together"—through sympathetic power the tree will share its vitality and other qualities with the child. ("Who knows what they planted when Talino was born," Berto thinks. "Either firewood or a pumpkin."[26]) Not only do the apples suggest Gisella's physical qualities—whiteness, firmness, tartness—but through their association with harvest and abundance, perhaps even with Original Sin, they provide a pivotal image around which the action of the novel turns. In this way, unobtrusively and naturally, a piece of folklore is converted to symbol.

In the early part of the novel Gisella, and the whole farm, seem to represent for Berto that return to the natural he has instinctively hungered for, although he does not put it in exactly these terms. He begins more or less contentedly repairing Vinverra's farm machinery and courting Gisella in his spare time. The significance of the fact that he is a mechanic becomes apparent. Assuming that Gisella represents some kind of natural element, the primary fecundity of the farm, the question is: who is going to control or possess her? Can the machine come in from outside, from the city, and effortlessly dominate the scene? At first it seems that it can. There is something strange about Gisella and this is connected to her family and especially to Talino, but Berto does not worry about this very much. Instead he continues to regard the situation as a rustic idyll, and behaves accordingly. "The old woman sent Gisella to draw water from the well—a hole with a wall around it, the only spot where it was cool—and I tried to help her by turning the windlass but she didn't want me to and seized the handles and drew up the bucket that sang like a woman, while she stretched over and showed her legs. Then when the bucket arrived we took it and I was close against her; and, watching each other's reflections, we drank a water sweeter than cherries."[27] Shortly after this he arranges a tryst with her by the well after dark; in fact it is she who suggests it. He waits for her behind the wall and in the darkness hears a voice "like an old woman" laughing at him, but it turns out to be a she-goat that blunders off into the canes.

> I was tranquil then, as though I had been bled. But Gisella didn't come, and I lit up and smoked and the stubble was a little white and a little black, as the moon came and went, and the wind rose and the crickets screeched in the canes, and all

the dogs were asleep. I began to get sleepy too. Then the clouds went away and everything was like a sea on the moon, so that behind the farm you could see the dark teat of Monticello. When I laughed now it was from rage, and I decided I had known from the beginning that Gisella too was kidding me. "This is Talino's *paese*, Berto. Maybe she's even fixed up with Talino, and you stand here while they laugh at you." I threw away the butt and started walking.[28]

This passage is a model in miniature of the whole technique of *Paesi tuoi:* the mixture of vernacular and symbolism, the repetition of the key images of moon, stubble, and crickets, the appearance of the goat to lend a somewhat ironic Dionysian note, the flowing style made up of long phrases linked by commas.

Berto is finally on the right track when it occurs to him that Gisella is "fixed up" with Talino. Another way in which this passage is a key one is that the progress of the novel involves a shift of interest from Berto's own story to that of Gisella and Talino, and it is in this passage that he begins to realize that in the end he is only a spectator—that he is not destined to play any important role in the drama going on around him. From this point Talino emerges as the central character of the novel. At first Berto has regarded him as a kind of village fool, associated with firewood or pumpkins; now he begins to take shape as a primitive demon whose leitmotif is fire. Pavese was to make more of this image of fire in *La luna e i falò;* here, in a less complicated way, fire simply stands for a dangerous and crazy kind of passion. It was for setting fire to a farm building belonging to the neighboring Del Prato family that Talino was sent to jail in the city, although this fact takes a while to emerge. It is also in this crucial portion of the novel that Talino and the image of crickets are brought together for the first time, in a casual way that is more important than it seems. In Pavese's private imagery crickets signify summer, harvest, abundance. But in popular Italian idiom "to have eaten crickets" or "to have crickets in the head" means to be a little pixilated, "to have notions." Talino shaved in the city, in prison, but now his beard has been growing longer. When Berto finds him behaving rather lunatic one morning he asks him. "You beast—have you eaten crickets?" But Talino only answers clownishly, "Come on, let's fight," and assumes a wrestling position—like Proteus? These possibilities remain unfocussed suggestions, but it is clear that by this time Berto is beginning to recognize Talino as an antagonist rather than a companion. It is clear also that the association of Talino with crickets not only sharpens the characterization of Talino himself but prepares the way for the whole statement the novel makes on the subject of *paese* and country life: that under the fecundity of the earth (crickets as abundance) there is something primitive and "demented" (crickets in the head). There is no real danger of overinterpretation here, since Pavese's diaries are full of sketches and notes for these complexities.

As for the burning of the farm building, an incident that for a long time remains rather mysterious, Berto eventually learns that it was Gisella who informed on her brother and caused him to be sent to prison. Is this, then, the origin of the enmity between the two? Evidently not, since this theory still fails to explain why Gisella should betray her brother to the police, a reprehensible act by country ethics. The enmity, then, precedes the barn-burning. It is shortly after he fits together the facts about the fire that Berto succeeds in enticing Gisella out into the fields, on a single occasion, to make love. Here he learns about her scar, which is in such a place on her body that only one who was intimate with her could know about it. She attributes it to an accident of falling on a rake, but it is obvious instead that Talino had something to do with the wound, that it dates from far earlier than the fire; Gisella tells Berto, perhaps truthfully, that it happened when she was fourteen years old. Much earlier, in the second chapter, Talino has told Berto that he likes white-skinned women. As for the motive of the barn-burning, Berto learns that in the summer of the incident Gisella had been "going with" (*parlava con*) Ernesto del Prato, the son of the family that owned the barn. Thus the theme of a fated and long-lasting incest dawns gradually on the reader as it does on Berto.

The dénouement is rather skillfully foreshadowed. There is Gisella's scar, the predecessor of the second and mortal wound she is to receive; there is the warning Berto gives Gisella without realizing fully what it means ("But you, Gisella, be careful. If you keep scratching him he's going to hurt you. You know he's a brute"[29]); and there are the two carabinieri that Berto and Talino meet on the eve of the climax, symbols of justice who seem to detect some unspoken guilt on the part of Talino. All the instruments of injury involved are agricultural tools: the rake that Gisella says she fell on (a false lead), Talino's *roncola* or brush-cutting scythe which is probably the real cause of her earlier injury, and the pitchfork (in Italian *tridente* like of a pagan god) with which he finally kills her. When violence comes it is unexpected and yet inevitable, exactly as a dénouement should be. While men and women are working together on the threshing floor—a setting rich in mythological implication—Talino appears with the pitchfork in hand and straw in his hair. When Gisella offers him to drink from a bucket (Berto has already drunk, and it seems to him she offers the water "as though she wanted to be kissed") Talino thrusts his whole face in the bucket, and Gisella cries, "No, that way you're dirtying the water." Talino, with "eyes like an animal," gives a leap backward and thrusts the pitchfork (here again the Italian is richer in implications: "plants the trident") in her neck.[30] All this is related absolutely without comment and almost without emotion; the reading of the passage moves as swiftly as the incident itself. It is only after Gisella cries "Madonna" and falls that Berto feels the sweat turned cold on his body. This is one of the most skillful passages in Pavese's fiction; only in *La luna e i falò* was he to come up to this level of economy and power.

Thus the pastoral idyll ends in violence and death. For Berto the point of the country interlude is that the *paese* is too primitive and too elemental for his temperament. It is not that the violence of the country is unnatural; in fact it is precisely because violence is "natural" in the country that he is unable to accept it. Earlier, before he has witnessed Talino's violence, Berto reflects that losing blood in the country is less shocking than in Turin. "Once I saw some on the wheel of a tram after an accident, and it was frightening; but here it seemed to me that someone bent over in the stubble, losing blood would be more natural, like a slaughterhouse."[31] This is precisely what chills him when Gisella is killed: after the first cries and the perfunctory efforts to pursue Talino, the peasants carry her to bed and let her bleed to death as though what is happening is perfectly natural. As soon as she is dead they stoically return to their work on the threshing floor. "And the anger mounted in me, because they all seemed to be agreed to let her die as though she were something that belonged to them"[32] Yet it is their right to deal with their own drama and their own tragedy on their own terms. What, then, was Gisella for him? He concludes that his place is in Turin.

But here the three-level point of view of the novel becomes important again. Over Berto hangs the hovering consciousness of the storyteller; just as Berto knows more than Talino, this conscious-ness knows more than Berto. It knows, for example, that the country is only an analogue or metaphor of existence itself, that the dark and violent side of life is present in the city as well as the country. The difference, perhaps, is simply one of manners—the superficial ap-paratus of civilization that Pavese had sought to strip off in his search for *paese*. To return to myth is to return to the savage, to the animal. This was the discovery that Melville had made in *Typee,* which Pavese had read as early as 1930. Yet in order for this knowledge to be a part of him it was necessary for him to rediscover it himself, through the writing of *Paesi tuoi*. Not long after finishing the novel, on December 10, 1939, he compares himself in his diary, quite humbly, to Dante. The poet puts himself in his poem, and this self at first seems a mere spectator, sometimes compassionate, sometimes indifferent or even contemptuous. But the story of the poem is not really the story of the sinners; it is the story of the traveler-spectator who is a mask of the poet, and who becomes, if the poem is skillfully done, another self of the reader. The writing of the poem serves, then, not to elucidate sin, but to clarify the poet's own condition to himself. In 1940 Pavese was not yet out of the darkling wood, but he was able to identify at least some of the beasts that were menacing him.

The Other Point of View

At this point is useful to depart from strict chronology and consider two novels together: *La bella estate,** dating from 1940, and *Tra donne sole,†* written almost at the end of Pavese's career in 1949. In some respects these two novels are markedly different in style, but they share a number of technical characteristics. The settings in both cases are urban; *La bella estate* is the first of Pavese's novels to be set in Turin. The themes are similar, involving in some way the problems of self in relation to others, work vs love, producing and consuming. And, most important, both stories are told from the viewpoint of a female character. There are a number of examples in the history of fiction in which a male author succeeds in telling a story through a female narrator. Some that immediately come to mind are *Moll Flanders,* which Pavese had translated in 1938, Moravia's *La romana* and *La ciociara,* and Giraudoux's *Suzanne et le Pacifique.* In addition there are novels, of the type of *Madame Bovary* or Crane's *Maggie, a Girl of the Streets,* in which the story is told grammatically in the third person but psychologically seen, in large part, through the consciousness of the heroine. Since a novel centering in a single consciousness can succeed only if the author identifies to a certain extent with his character, there is a certain inherent handicap in switching sexes in this way, and the novelist can hope to succeed only if there is a certain element of ambivalence in his attitude toward the two sexes. Flaubert was able to say, "La Bovary, c'est moi." James might have said the same of Isabel Archer.

* *The Beautiful Summer.* Included in *The Political Prisoner* (London: Owen, 1944).

† *Among Women Only* (Farrar, Straus, 1959).

But a writer like Hemingway or Malraux, one whose narrative psychology is strongly masculine, is unable to say this, and the heroines in such authors tend to be projections of male desire or imagination rather than fully rounded human beings. It is clear that Pavese is this second kind of writer. Women always remain objects rather than subjects for him; he never succeeds in transcending his own sexuality to the point of understanding and regarding them as they understand and regard themselves.

Considering this, it is curious that he should have attempted these two novels related from the feminine viewpoint and concerned very largely with erotic relations. A clue is perhaps to be found in a diary entry of 1939, shortly before he began *La bella estate*. "Every artist tries to take apart the mechanism of his technique to see how it is constructed and to make use of it, if he can, coldly. Yet a work of art succeeds only when there is something mysterious in it for the artist himself. This is natural: the story of an artist is the successive replacement of the technique used in a preceding work by a creation presupposing a more complex aesthetic law. The artist who does not analyse and continually destroy his technique is worthless."[33] This was one of Pavese's peculiar kinds of puritanism: the technical apparatus devised for any one work could never be repeated in a succeeding work. Each time it was necessary to reinvent the novel as though a novel had never been written. The diary entries around 1940 suggest that in this period he conceived of his art as developing constantly from the personal, the subjective, the autobiographical, toward the objective and detached. *Il carcere* was practically pure autobiography, *Paesi tuoi* less so. In *La bella estate* he evidently felt the necessity of converting and concealing the autobiographical element to an even greater degree; the technical apparatus of the novel is an elaborate mask. This tendency is continued in *La spiaggia*, which followed in 1940-41, even though it is related by a male narrator. It was only the war and the traumatic effect it had on Pavese's view of himself that made him realize his identity as an artist was inextricably involved with the complex and anguishing problems of his personal life—that all of his writing, whether he willed it or not, was about himself. It is for this reason that the point of view of *La bella estate* is somewhat unsatisfactory, and the novel along with it. It was not published during Pavese's lifetime and appeared only posthumously in 1952. Why he returned to this technique in 1949 with *Tra donne sole* is another and somewhat more complex problem.

The central character of *La Bella estate* is the sixteen-year-old Ginia, who works as a seamstress for a Turin modiste. (After literature and agriculture, *haute couture* was the trade that interested Pavese the most, and in some way he acquired a considerable body of information about it.) She is a healthy and cheerful girl of working-class stock, and the early chapters are full of the kaleidoscopic excitement of adolescence in the city.

> In those times it was always a holiday. Just leaving the house and crossing the street was enough to make you go crazy, and everything was so beautiful, especially at night, that even coming home dead tired they hoped that something would happen, a fire would break out, a baby would be born in the house, or even that day would break suddenly and everybody would come out in the street and you could go on walking and walking all the way out into the fields and into the hills.[34]

This is the "wonderful summer" of the title. But living in this way like happy savages is only permitted to children—or to the idle rich, as Pavese was to portray them in his later novels—and Ginia, a little precociously, is on the brink of adulthood. One of the merits of the novel is that Pavese makes no attempt to show her as "typical"; she is no ordinary child. She lives in an apartment with her brother Severino and keeps house for him, and in this way she has, as she herself reflects, all the work and responsibilities of being married without any of the advantages. In the course of the novel she attempts to break out of this domestic situation, out of her immaturity, out of the petty-bourgeois environment that surrounds her, into some kind of self-fulfillment. The steps in this process are first her female friends Rosa and Amelia and afterward the men she meets in the Turin world of artists and would-be artists. Her curiosity about art is mingled with her fascination with the world of sexual maturity; at first the two attractions seem parallel, then it becomes clear that they are conflicting elements in her life. Her girl friends are older or at least more experienced, and her attitude toward their experience is highly ambivalent. When Rosa confesses that she is afraid she is pregnant, Ginia's reaction is not sympathy, not disapproval, but a vague feeling of having been left out of something.

> Ginia told her she was a stupid thing and they quarreled on the street-corner. Then it blew over, because Rosa acted that way only because she was scared, but meanwhile Ginia was more worked-up than she was, because it seemed to her that she had been tricked and left to play the child while the others were enjoying themselves, and this from Rosa who didn't even have

any ambition. "I'm worth more than her," Ginia said, "at six-teen it's too early. All right for her if she wants to throw herself away." She talked this way but she couldn't think about it without feeling humiliated, because the idea that those others without saying anything about it had all gone off in the bushes, while for her, who lived alone, a man's hand made her heart pound, this idea took away her breath.[35]

This passage gives a good idea of the style of the novel: the flowing phrases linked by commas, the language superficially in the third person but centering in a single consciousness, the condensation of the thought that slips from one idea to another without apparent logical connection. (What was Rosa's "not having any ambition" to do with her sexual experience? But in Ginia's mind it has a great deal to do.) This kind of interior monologue or *erlebte Rede* is different from the technique of *Paesi tuoi* in which the first-person narrator seems to be telling his story in retrospect to an audience or listener. Ginia seems to be talking, or thinking, to herself. She would, in fact, be incapable of telling her story in any systematic form. This is why the third person is necessary for Pavese's purposes—in order to allow entry into a mind which is not aware it is being watched— and this also lies at the bottom of a good many of the difficulties of the novel.

Rosa is a factory worker, and Ginia is just snobbish enough to feel superior to her for this. But her second friend Amelia is an artist's model, and through her Ginia is introduced to a world that seems to her far more fascinating than Rosa's factory or her own *atelier*. At first she is surprised—not so much shocked as incredulous —that Amelia poses in the nude. Then Amelia takes her to an appointment with an artist, a fat and somewhat cross old man with a gray beard who is called only Barbetta. He sketches Ginia too, commenting with interest on the strength of her face, "since every-one says virgin's profiles are formless."[36] He seems to take no interest in either girl as a sexual object, and this baffles Ginia. Amelia play-fully accuses him of "betraying" her with other models, and he shouts back at her, "With the whole world I betray you . . . Do you think you're worth more than a plant or a horse? I work whenever I take a walk, what do you think?"[37] This is Ginia's first real encounter with professionalism—with a serious and total devotion to one's own craft. No one in her own world behaves this way; Rosa would un-hesitatingly abandon her factory, or Severino his job as an electri-cian, the instant some personal gratification like a sexual experience offered itself. Yet she has enough intelligence to see that Barbetta's way is a superior one, and the conflict is left in her mind: art or love? personal self-indulgence, or the creation of something outside one's self? The crucial middle part of the novel is devoted to her search for selflessness in the world of art.

Through Amelia again she meets a pair of younger artists or self-styled artists, Guido and Rodrigues. For a while she imagines that through her friendship with these people, even through becoming sexually involved with them, she can fulfill herself in some way and find out what life is all about. But she gives herself, she comes to know Guido and Rodrigues and Amelia intimately, and nothing is changed. Guido is not a very good painter and only half serious about it, and Rodrigues is not a painter at all; he is one of the poseurs who hang around the world of art and build a reputation by sitting in cafés and talking. Both of them are ready to drop the whole thing as soon as there is a chance to go to bed with a girl. As for Amelia, she is a lesbian, and finally she confesses that she has syphilis. Ginia is not sure what all this means, but at least she understands that the people she is condemned to live with are fakes; her vague longing for a world where work is done and beautiful things are made has led her instead into a circle of weak and self-indulgent failures. Her encounter with them is in part a victory, and she has enough intelligence to know what her victory consists of: her basic good sense that the others lack in spite of their sophistication, and her knowledge that there is something more in life than self-indulgence. Yet she lacks a guide to lead her into some other world where people act out of higher motives than egotism, and she is too immature and uncertain to find her way there alone. At the end of the novel the bored Amelia reports that there is nothing worth seeing at the movies that evening, and Ginia tells her, "Let's go wherever you want. You lead me."[38]

The root of the trouble with *La bella estate* is not Ginia's weakness of character, although this is a factor. The real difficulty is that Ginia's weakness of character, her deficient culture, her sex, and a number of other qualities make her so different from the author that the result is a failure of commitment, of empathy between author and character, and the characterization is only partly convincing. To a degree the point of view is a technical tour de force, but the difficulty is that it remains only that. In the end the main value of the novel is that it was a lesson for Pavese himself, if only a negative one, in narrative technique. In many ways it is smoother in its storytelling than either *Il carcere* or *Paese tuoi,* but never again was Pavese to confine himself to a narrative consciousness so limited and so different from his own.

Tra donne sole is narrated in the first person by a character with a good deal more sophistication and maturity, in short with a culture approaching Pavese's own. Yet the world of Turin *haute couture* is the same, a little more elegant and genuine perhaps, and seen a little more from the inside, and the Clelia of the 1949 novel is really only Ginia in a later stage of development. The basic conflict is still that of producing vs consuming, or useful work opposed to self-indulgence. Clelia, a mature businesswoman, returns from Rome to her native Turin to set up a fashionable boutique for her firm. But this project comes into conflict with her personal erotic needs, which exist even though she is hesitant to admit them to herself. Under other conditions she might have resolved this purely personal problem on her own terms. But the nature of her job leads her into contact with a certain class of women, for the most part narcissistic women with more money than they know how to spend, and soon she is involved with the whole world of Turin salons: lesbians and demilesbians, bored nobility, artists *manqués*, and spoiled children. In the face of these influences, these temptations, she is unable to maintain her hard professionalism; like the Ginia of *La bella estate* she is simply too weak.

At this point it is useful to return to the hypothesis that good novels, Pavese's novels specifically, are always autobiographical in some sense. Leaving aside the superficial matters of setting and milieu, what is the parallel element in the situation of this novel and Pavese's own experience? Both Pavese and Clelia have a job to do; Clelia's pseudo-creative and "artistic" trade is a kind of caricature of the métier of the artist. In a letter to Rino del Sasso, a reviewer of the novel, Pavese calls her "a restless and irritable bourgeoise who believes in only one value, work."[39] After a number of failures and setbacks she carries out the task her employers expect of her, but in her own mind the episode has not been a success. In her private thoughts she knows, or believes, that her commitment to "art" in its purity has been insufficient. As a result she has been diverted from her task, at least in part, by two distractions: her own sexual needs, and the opulent and fake-artistic salon life of the Turin rich. In this sense her life is at least partially a betrayal, and betrayal is a latent theme in Pavese's work from 1940 to the end. More than once he had sacrificed his work to erotic experiences that came to nothing and left him exhausted and despondent, experiences he believed to be essential to his function as an artist but were in fact distractions. In each case, after the initial fever was over he had excellent insight into the nature of the mistake he was making, although he was probably wrong in believing that he differed in this respect from the average artist. The point is that, rightly or wrongly, he believed this tendency in himself to be a weakness. Five months before his death he wrote in his diary, "You don't kill yourself for love of *a* woman. You kill yourself because a love, any love at all, reveals you in your nakedness, poverty, isolation, nothingness."[40] If he was not an artist he was nothing. But how could he be an artist when he was so easily distracted by a pretty face, the curve of a breast, a weekend on the Riviera? In his own intensely puritanical system of values the very successes of the end of his life, the Premio Strega and the acceptance of the fashionable literary world, seemed to him in at least a part of his mind capitulations. It is not hard to read a self-portrait into the "restless and irritable bourgeois who believes only in work."

Pavese's inner struggle, as he himself viewed it, was therefore that of a weakness with a strength—rather than a strength with a strength as Mann, for instance, views the conflict between love and duty in the mind of Hans Castorp. And it is tempting to conclude that it is because he thinks of this susceptibility as a weakness that he attributes it, in *Tra donne sole*, to a female character, a woman who tells her own story in the first person. It makes very little difference whether Pavese himself was aware of the parallel—and the letter to Del Sasso suggests that he was not—or whether it took place in a subliminal part of his mind. From a technical standpoint the device has certain advantages. Both men and women have weaknesses, and struggle in complicated ways with these weaknesses in their private thoughts. But for a male writer to discuss these weaknesses publicly, in his own voice, creates an effect that is not quite what is intended. Flaubert, for instance, had a weakness for sentimentalism, and in order to avoid seeming unmanly or affected he attributed this quality, in his chief treatment of it, to a woman. This is the real meaning of his confession that Emma Bovary was himself. The alternative is to describe the "feminine" complexity of one's own thought in a frankly autobiographical way, as Proust did, with the result of creating a hero who seems somewhat less than virile. (Proust, of course, committed another kind of mendacity in converting his homosexual lover to a woman.) Thus Pavese's Clelia: an alter ego who is permitted the doubts, the vagaries, the sentimental and petty regrets the author will not permit himself.

Considering the handicaps involved, this characterization is carried off with a certain degree of success. Clelia is of working-class origin, and throughout the novel there is a kind of Marxist orientation in which the proletarian is regarded in a favorable light and bourgeois values unfavorably. As a concrete sign of this polarity

Clelia has two coats: a practical cloth coat which is "for work," and a fur which she wears in the fashionable salon world, and for love. Chapters set in the salon world alternate with chapters in which Clelia, in her cloth coat, struggles with the technical problems of remodeling and furnishing the shop. Yet one of her two problems, the personal sexual one, really lies outside of this whole polarity of working vs wasting. Clelia wants not only satisfaction of her feminine needs but also companionship and hopes to find this in the world of work. For a time she seems to be making friends with the young *geometra* or artisan-architect Febo, who is supervising the remodeling of the shop. They drink grappa together in lower-class taverns, and they share sarcasms about the bourgeoisie. But when he finally makes love to her, in a vicious little scene involving three in a bed, "he didn't trouble himself much and it was soon over."[41] Instead of the union of mutual understanding she longs for there is only a brief and cynical physical contact. This is love among the "workers." What else, then, is there?

Clelia's penetration into fashionable Turin society is never more than partial, if only because, as a worker and not a waster, she is only partially accepted there. She thus remains more or less on the periphery of that part of the action that takes place in this society. Her special status in this respect has a double function: it influences Clelia herself, and Pavese utilizes it as a technical point-of-view device. Once again, as in *Paesi tuoi*, the crucial action is seen from the viewpoint of a partially committed spectator. In fact, given the completely different settings of the two novels, the structure is almost the same. There is a spectator-narrator (Berto, Clelia) who moves up to the edges of a milieu more or less new to him, and cannot decide whether he wants to enter and become a part of it or not. For a while the narrator imagines that the story that is taking place is his story. But he eventually recognizes that far more intense dramas are taking place in the milieu he is trying to enter, and he slips back into the role of a passive spectator. In both novels the climactic event is a death: the murder of Gisella in *Paesi tuoi*, a suicide in *Tra donne sole*. And in both cases this event is prefigured or rehearsed before it is finally carried out: Talino has attacked Gisella before, and the death of Rosetta at the end of *Tra donne sole* is anticipated by her attempted suicide in the first chapter.

But the fashionable society plot of *Tra donne sole* (it might be called the inner plot, as opposed to the outer plot of Clelia's own personal problems) is much more complicated than the Talino-Gisella plot in *Paesi tuoi*, and probably this is a natural result of the difference in complexity of the two settings. Pavese portrays the aimless and decadent brilliance of the salon world with a certain skill, even though the reader is left with the feeling that it is not quite his material. The technique is kaleidoscopic: the action shifts from character to character, place to place, with a kind of jerky impulsiveness. On Clelia's first night in Turin she happens to open the door of her hotel room and sees Rosetta, an unsuccessful suicide, being carried out of her room on a stretcher. Later she learns a good deal more about this unhappy girl who is the finest and most sensitive character in the novel. In fact Rosetta becomes a kind of alter ego for her, what she herself might have been if she had been born into the salon milieu. There are other such characters; the complexity of the novel is built on the multiplicity of women who serve in this way as projections of different parts of Clelia's identity. There is Momina, a bored society woman who experiments with lesbianism more out of restlessness than out of viciousness. For Rosetta she is a "mirror," what she herself will become if she continues on the path she is following. For Clelia herself Momina is a friend, a possibility of love, and at the same time a warning, a demonstration that it is not enough to have money to be happy. All these people are wasters; they have nothing in particular to do in life but spend their money and pursue an illusory happiness. On the other hand there is Nene, an artist, ingenuous, impulsive, not very attractive, with "big lips and bangs, and an impudent way of laughing like a child."[42] Clelia is a little contemptuous of her because she is poor—Nene's position on the fringes of the salon world is even more precarious than her own —and at the same time she senses that Nene is doing something that is important to her and gives her personal satisfaction, and in this way fulfilling herself in a sense that nobody else in the novel is. She also has a man—another artist named Loris—with whom she gets along in some way although she isn't married to him, and this too intrigues Clelia. At the age of thirty Nene still has enough innocence to be confused when Loris is mentioned. Reflecting on her eccentricities, her queer manners, her odd appearance, Clelia concludes, "Probably she really had something, and this was the way an artist had to be."[43] Above all Clelia is impressed by Nene's purity in the middle of a corrupt society. It is significant that whenever the action gets particularly squalid, for example in the *amour à trois* scene mentioned earlier, Nene disappears.

These four—Clelia, Momina, Rosetta, and Nene—and a number of others who play less important roles are linked together in an intricate way: their sex unites them while practically all their other qualities divide them and set them apart. They are the women of the title who are "among themselves"—not independent of men, but preoccupied with a quite special struggle that is among women only. It is Rosetta who finally emerges as the key character in this circle.

She is pulled in various directions by conflicting impulses: to be a painter, to get married, to become a nun. If the others, especially Clelia, are able to save her, then by implication there will be some hope for themselves. But in the end she finds life "a dirty business." The pace of the novel accelerates toward the end; the final chapter is only about three pages, and the climax is related briefly, almost sarcastically. "One day I said to myself— 'I wonder about Rosetta,' and I telephoned Momina. 'I'll come to your place,' she told me—'I don't know what to think. The stupid thing has killed herself again.' "[43] There are various deft touches at the end: instead of a hotel room Rosetta this time rents an artist's studio, she shuts herself up with a cat that "betrays her" the next day by whining and scratching at the door. The whole story of Rosetta, in fact, is well done. What happens to her, why it happens, the details of its happening— these are well conceived and convincing. The difficulties of *Tra donne sole* are the complexity of the plot, which seems cluttered in so short a novel, and the characterization of Clelia. The device of the semi-involved spectator, relatively successful in *Paesi tuoi,* is somewhat less successful here. The difficulty is that the reader senses that Clelia's voice is actually Pavese's, that her personality is really only a kind of synthetic platform from which the author himself views his story. Her manner of reacting in the play of egos among persons is basically masculine. She gropes instinctively for the initiative and seizes it whenever she can; and when this initiative is denied her— for example in an erotic relationship—she is hostile and resentful. Even if we concede that such personalities might have existed in the Turin salon world of 1949, or in other milieux where women are required to play a semimasculine role, the characterization stops short of verisimilitude; we cannot believe in, or at least cannot understand, the mental processes of such a person in such a time and place. She is really only the author clumsily disguised, and this leads to a kind of sex-switched *roman à clef* in which the protagonist is neither Pavese nor a real woman. The experiment was a particularly unfelicitous one for an author whose understanding of women was so subjective and so emotional. In his last novel Pavese did not repeat this mistake; the women in *La luna e i falò* are seen only through the clouding filter of male consciousness.

Among the Lotus Eaters

La spiaggia* is a novel that in its setting, its characters, its superficial incident, might have been written by Moravia. Pavese

* *The Beach* (London: Peter Owen, 1963).

himself was not very well satisfied with it. In 1946—in the period when he regarded his work and everything else from a Marxist viewpoint—he called it "a distraction, even though a human one," and "the little novel neither brutal nor proletarian nor American."[44] It was written in 1940-41, but it appeared in his lifetime only in installment form in *Lettere D'Oggi* and in a limited edition published by this same review. Yet taken simply as an exercise in construction and technique it represents a considerable step beyond the three novels that preceded it. It is the first treatment of the theme of producing vs consuming that dominates *Tra donne sole*, and it forms an obvious bridge between his early "naturalism" and his later symbolistic style. Pavese was right in considering it his least characteristic novel in its ambience or narrative texture. But this is not the real source of its difficulties. Instead these are chiefly structural, the result of embarking into a far greater technical complexity than Pavese had attempted before.

The setting, a villa on the Riviera, was one he never used either before or after for a novel. But its possibilities obviously attracted him, and he experimented with it earlier in the fragment published in the collected tales as "Casa al mare," dating probably from 1940. The basic dynamic of the characters in their relation to one another is sketched out in another story written two years earlier, "La casa in collina." Between them these two short narratives explore the technical alternatives that were later to be developed fully in *La spiaggia*. "Casa al mare," a fragment with a female protagonist, exists in two manuscript versions, one in the first person and the other in the third. "La casa in collina" is told by a male narrator who is partly involved in the plot and partly a detached spectator, the point of view that was later adopted for *La spiaggia*. This narrative framework, in fact, is used in all of Pavese's subsequent novels—although, as we have seen, it is not entirely successful in *Tra donne sole* where the narrator is a woman—and it reaches the end of its logical development in *La luna e i falò*. The problem of point of view, one that preoccupied Pavese throughout his career, was fundamental to the nature of his work and his own relation to it. How can the novel be a personal expression and yet objective—simultaneously intimate and detached? In his diary a few months before the writing of *La spiaggia* he notes, "The equilibrium of a story depends on the co-existence of two persons: one is the author, who knows how it will end, the other the characters, who don't know. If the author and protagonist are merged (*Je*) and know how it will end, it is necessary to increase the stature of other characters to restore the equilibrium. Yet the protagonist, *if he tells the story*, must remain essentially a spectator (Dostoevski: 'in our district.' *Moby Dick:* 'call me Ishmael').”[45] In the solution of this problem *La spiaggia* represents a kind of breakthrough to the technique later to be used in *La luna e i falò.* This is probably the chief importance of this somewhat unsatisfactory novel, at least for Pavese himself.

The basic situation of *La spiaggia* is a triangle, but a triangle of a special sort that recurs more than once in Pavese's work: two male friends with a woman who comes between them. Doro and Clelia are married before the action begins. Doro's friend, the anonymous narrator of the novel, is at first resentful of the marriage, then accepts it partially and comes to stay with the couple in their Riviera villa, although he feels a certain embarrassment at the idea of intruding into their intimacy. The situation is Jamesian and the style is to match: this is the most sinuous and verbally complicated of Pavese's novels. (Clelia's letters are full of "amiable items selected with intelligence from the mutable congeries of thought and deeds in another life and another world.”[46] After sketching out the characters and their relationship the novel turns to a kind of flashback: Doro and the narrator go off to the country, to Doro's ancestral hills, on an escapade that they both tacitly regard as an attempt to recapture their adolescence. The second chapter is devoted to a somewhat ironic account of this rustic orgy. Under the window of a pair of country girls the wine-filled Doro and his companions sing, howl, dodge a flowerpot, and are finally dispersed by a gunshot. At first glance this episode seems to have little to do with the rest of the novel. But the country scene is part of the rather complex mythology of city and country that underlies Pavese's whole work. The return to *paese* is the return to the primitive and a rejection of "culture," thus a return to youth and innocence. But adolescence is innocent only in its spontaneity, its unconsciousness. Adolescent sexuality in another sense is perverse because it is basically irresponsible; it denies the biological implications that lie at the bottom of the impulse. It is a curious paradox that, at least in the framework of this novel, *paese* does not represent fecundity, in fact it stands for the opposite of fecundity. In *Paesi tuoi* the uncontrolled sexual instinct ends in incest; in *La spiaggia* it ends, unconsummated, in the throwing of flowerpots.

After this interlude the novel returns to the Riviera setting and its major action. In these early chapters the setting seems to the narrator a kind of Land of the Lotus Eaters, a gilded and slightly perverse playground of the rich. Doro's name is literally "golden;" he smokes gold-tipped cigarettes. Clelia describes herself as "a spoiled child who doesn't know how to do anything.”[47] On the surface at least there does not seem to be any particular intimacy between Doro and Clelia, the only married pair in the novel. The narrator tells Clelia something—but not all—about the escapade in the country, and she only comments, "What egoists."[48] The major lines of the conflict are established. The narrator imagines that this conflict is between spontaneity and naturalness on one hand and the artificial and affected life of the Riviera on the other. In this he is rather profoundly mistaken. It is true that Doro and Clelia live a life that is superficially somewhat trivial. Doro has his little divagations like the escapade in the hills, and Clelia has the "rich and bovine" Guido, a conventional admirer she does little to discourage. Doro, who pretends to paint, is a bad artist, and Clelia is not exactly a model wife. On the surface, therefore, their relationship is almost totally corrupt. But under the surface is something the narrator has failed to notice, and the reason is that he does not understand marriage. The narrator (it is significant that we never learn his name) is a bachelor and a *liceo* professor; in this he resembles Pavese. He is a projection of the author as well in his suspicion of the entanglements of marriage and at the same time his loneliness and desire for companionship, his unfulfilled sexuality. He imagines that he and Doro ought to be friends as they were in adolescence, and that Clelia has come between them; in other words he imagines he is jealous of Clelia. But it is really Doro he is jealous of. What he really envies, and what he needs without knowing it, is the profound biological attachment that holds Doro and Clelia together in spite of their superficial differences, an attachment that is "natural" in a far more fundamental way than the Dionysian capers of the country episode. This is why Clelia merely smiles when she hears of the incident, even if her smile is a little surly. She is sound where the narrator is shakiest, at the roots of her life.

Soon after this basic situation is established, about a third of the way through the novel, another character is introduced: the student Berti, a former pupil of the narrator who happens to be spending his vacation near the villa. Gradually he intrudes his way into the plot. First he proposes to the narrator that they should read some books together—"not lessons, but reading as I had done sometimes at school, explaining and discussing, teaching him a lot of things he didn't know."[49] From this he advances to a rather prurient curiosity about Doro, Clelia, the whole circle and their private lives. It soon becomes clear that his interest in books is only a pretext—or is it? How can the narrator be sure of this when Berti is confused about it himself? He is aggressive and shy by turns, resentful, naive, eager, unconvincingly cynical. He is fascinated especially with the women

121

of the circle, with Clelia and the attractive young Ginetta, but blushes when they are referred to and talks about something else. In short he makes a fool of himself, but he is a fool who is presented in the context of the novel with a certain ironic sympathy. "He began explaining to me that every so often he had an urge to work, a compulsion, a craving to do something, not to study so much as to have some strenuous place of responsibility, so he could throw himself into it night and day and become a man like the rest of us, like me."[50] This naive remark is at the same time a *cri du coeur* that echoes through Pavese's whole work. Like many other writers Pavese here has split the autobiographical presence into more than one character; Berti resembles the Pavese of the student days, while the narrator resembles the Pavese who wrote the book. At the same time Berti is a kind of caricature of the narrator himself; Berti's attitude toward books, toward the villa circle, toward women, is a parody of his own behavior. The real function of Berti is that he serves for the narrator as a mirror of his own foolishness, his sterility.

The attitude of the narrator, or more precisely of the novel itself, toward the Riviera setting changes as the action progresses. In the early part of the novel the sea represents escape, irresponsibility. The narrator remarks several times that days at the beach "don't count," that the things people do naked in the sun commit them to nothing once they put on their clothes and go back to the city. This pagan freedom (as he imagines it) attracts him and at the same time produces a certain apprehension in him. It was undoubtedly this aspect of Riviera life that made it seem attractive to Pavese as a setting. Like country life, like the exoticism of books like *Typee*, the beach strips away the amenities of civilization and reduces experience to its elementals: sun, food, sex. The narrator is not quite ready to surrender himself to the life of these Lotus Eaters; he takes refuge in the "superiority" of his intellectualism. But even if he were ready to surrender to this life he would be unable to do so, because he is mistaken about its fundamental nature. At the end of the novel an unexpected incident dissolves away all the falseness, the triviality, the flashy smartness of the setting: Clelia announces that she is pregnant. This event seizes hold of the characters—not only Doro and Clelia but the narrator himself—and obliges them to acknowledge the fundamental forces at work under the superficiality of their lives. Doro abandons his artistic pretensions and makes plans to take Clelia to a Genoa specialist. Clelia, glancing resignedly at the narrator, comments, "You see, it's paternity beginning. Now he gives the orders."[51] The Lotus-Eating dream is over; the narrator goes back to the city and takes Berti with him.

Before he leaves he tells Clelia he is "happy to have spent with her the last summer of her girlhood."[52] Now even he seems to have grasped what the naive Berti already knew: that the elemental is not idleness in the sea and sun, instead it is working, having a "strenuous place of responsibility," making children.

The difficulty with the ending of the novel is perhaps that too little is made of this new view of elementalism, that the reader is not convinced by it. It seems to be presented suddenly, and yet the way has been prepared for it from the beginning of the novel. Whether or not it is successful, the *deus ex machina* of the ending is deliberate. If the reader is not "convinced" by this dénouement neither, in a certain sense, is the narrator. It stupifies him, it eludes his comprehension. But at least he understands that Doro and Clelia have something he has not, and that whatever this thing is they shared it even before Clelia's pregnancy. "I began to understand that no place is more uninhabitable than the place where you've been happy. I understand why Doro one fine day had taken the train to go back to the hills, and the next day came back to his destiny."[53] As for him, his destiny is to go back to Turin and be a professor.

Here it is necessary to depart once more from strict chronology in order to deal with a recurring pattern in Pavese's work. *Il diavolo sulle colline,** written in 1948 and published the following year in the volume *La bella estate,* is similar in tone to *La spiaggia* and shares some of the same qualities and difficulties. The parallel would be evident even if it were not for a diary entry (October 7, 1948) that clarifies the relation between the two novels. "October 4th finished *Il diavolo in colline* [*sic*]. It has the look of something big. It's new language. To dialect and cultured style is added 'student discussion.' For the first time you've really planted symbols. You've revived *La spiaggia* grafting onto it youthful discovery, the life of discussion, mythical reality."[54] Pavese at this point, only a few days after finishing the novel, lacked the perspective to see it in its proper proportions; in any case his most successful treatment of "mythical reality" in *La luna e i falò* had not yet been written. But his explanation of the way the component parts of the novel were fitted together throws a good deal of light, not only on the nature of *Il diavolo sulle colline,* but on some of its difficulties. Can symbols really be "planted?" Or can a more or less unsuccessful novel be revived by "grafting onto it" something new? One of Pavese's chronic problems in the later years was the search for spontaneity, or at least

* *The Devil in the Hills* (Farrar, Straus, 1959).

for a semblance of spontaneity even if this were achieved through contrivance. Even without the diary entry it is obvious that this spontaneity had not yet been achieved in 1948.

The setting of *Il diavolo sulle colline* is Turin and the country-side around it, especially the Piedmontese hills that recur constantly as a thematic element in Pavese's work. It is not quite so easy to establish the period of the action. There is no indication that the war has taken place or that the countryside or characters have suffered any damage from it, and on the other hand there is no mention of fascism or the prewar political scene. But the narrator and his two friends Oreste and Pieretto are university students, and certain other minor elements (rowing on the Po, white nights on the hill above the city) connect the story to Pavese's own student days. This failure of the novel to be meshed with any specific chronology is more serious than it may seem at first glance. Both the novels written in 1948, *La casa in collina* and *Il diavolo sulle colline*, are about responsibility and the evasion of responsibility. But where the first meets this problem squarely, with an almost painful candor, the second hints at it only obliquely. Thus it is possible to argue that the novel itself, coming as it did from the period of Pavese's own grave political and personal uncertainties, represents a kind of evasion; the prewar setting, the nostalgic memories of student life, reflect an unwillingness or inability to come to terms with the contemporary reality that oppressed him at the time. It is very likely that the writing of *La casa in collina* left him empty and spiritually exhausted, and in the summer of 1948 he slipped back to the materials he had dealt with earlier in *La spiaggia*.

Il diavolo sulle colline, insofar as it can be taken as veiled auto-biography or conversion of autobiographical experience, regresses even farther than *La spiaggia*: the narrator is not yet a *liceo* teacher but only a student. Where *La spiaggia* takes place in the mid-Thirties, then, this novel is set ca. 1927-28. It is probably because the story takes place before fascism became oppressive, before Pavese himself was arrested and exiled, that there is no mention of politics. Once the emergence of the theme of responsibility has been noted in Pavese's work, it becomes apparent that the chief quality of the characters in *Il diavolo sulle colline* is their irresponsibility. The narrator and his friends Oreste and Pieretto are ostensibly university students but do very little studying; they spend most of their time roaming the Turin streets and the hills around the city at night. On one of these nocturnal expeditions they meet Poli, a wealthy and somewhat spoiled young man a little older than they are. At first they are a little sarcastic about his "advantages"—an expensive automobile, mistresses, liquor, drugs. But after a while they realize he is behaving about as they would if they had his money—what else, they ask themselves with a kind of sophomoric profundity, is there? For a good part of the novel they serve as somewhat ironic disciples of Poli's epicureanism. There is a certain amount of philosophizing about life, love, freedom of choice, and the futility of human endeavor (the "student discussion" of Pavese's diary), a good deal of drinking, and expeditions in Poli's car to hilltops and country roadhouses. These diversions end when Poli's mistress Rosalba, who suspects she is about to be abandoned, shoots him and narrowly misses killing him. This is the first of two turning points in the novel and in the development of the characters, especially the narrator.

The following part of the novel, roughly the middle third, corresponds to the country bacchanal scene early in *La spiaggia*. The three friends go to stay with Oreste's family in the country, in a primitive Piedmontese village on a hilltop. There, among the vineyards in the sunshine, the narrator begins to recapture the contact with the earth he has lost in the city. The three friends swim and take nude sunbaths; the idea of being naked in the sun is an image, or perhaps merely a form of behavior, that Pavese returns to frequently. The white stripe left by a bathing suit is a mark of prudery, of sickly artificiality. In *Il diavolo sulle colline* the cult of nudism is taken half seriously even though the manner of telling about it is whimsical: "The aim was to roast the groin and buttocks too, cancel the infamy, blacken everything."[54] There are other elements of life in the village that fit into the same pattern of pagan elementism: the candid and mysterious chastity of the girls, the voice of the crickets, the mysterious presence of the moon, the odor of the vines, the naturalness of Oreste's rustic Mombello cousins. This is the "mythical reality" of the diary entry; the moon, the crickets, nudity, are the symbols of a pantheism that develops and becomes more complex in each succeeding novel of Pavese. In spite of the attraction of this frank paganism the narrator of *Il diavolo sulle colline*, like the Berto of *Paesi tuoi*, is a little ambivalent toward it. If he surrenders to it completely what happens to culture, progress, the fine ideas he has learned at the university? "This thrill of going consciously naked, of hiding ourselves from all glances, of bathing, blackening ourselves like tree trunks, had something sinister to it, more bestial than human."[55] The two poles of his life are the boredom of studying dry books and the bestiality of going naked in the sun. And so he comes to believe, at least for a time, that the way of Poli—a kind of overrefined epicureanism that it is perhaps fair to call perversity—is a third alternative.

As it happens—by a coincidence perhaps a little too neat—the country village of Poli's family is on a hill (the "Greppo") not far from Oreste's village. Inevitably the three friends go to see what he is up to there, and their visit marks the second major turning point of the novel. They find Poli living on top of the hill with Gabriella, a wife nobody knew he had. Gabriella is moody, flirtatious, changeable; Poli is detached and indifferent. There is some kind of tension between the two. Gradually the three friends are drawn into this intrigue, into the life of Poli, into his system of values. The center of this system is the idea of absolute liberty, freedom of choice. For Poli this means the freedom to follow his sensual whims, to drink too much and take drugs, to engage in profound discussions about the meaning of life and yet be basically indifferent to the fate of others. It transpires that his former mistress Rosanna has committed suicide, but Poli dismisses this with a shrug; she too is free to do as she pleases. He even explains to the narrator that being shot by Rosanna was an experience he found valuable, since it made him more keenly aware of the sensation of consciousness. This Italian Dorian Gray, as shallow and artificial as he is, is convincing precisely because his spuriousness is made real and believable; he is one of Pavese's more successful characters.

The three friends end by spending several weeks in this new Land of the Lotus Eaters on top of the hill. They play records, drink, go hunting for game birds, stay up all night discussing freedom with Poli and trading badinage with Gabriella. At this point the medical student Oreste emerges as a character distinct in certain ways from the others. Earlier, in the Turin scenes, he has already been established as more studious than the narrator and Pieretto. Halfway through the novel it comes to light that he has a fiancée, a country girl named Cintra he hopes to marry after he is established as a doctor. Yet it is Oreste now who, because of his very seriousness, takes Gabriella's flirtation seriously and becomes involved with her in a futile and dangerous love affair. The situation is obvious to everybody; Poli becomes even more indifferent and sarcastic.

In the working-out of this crisis there is an ingenuity which is one of the best touches in the novel. The reader constantly expects the action to resolve in an act of violence, something like "The Short Happy Life of Francis Macomber." In the hunting scene Gabriella even takes the gun in her hand at one point; this is her chance to be Margot Macomber if she wants to. But Pavese is, perhaps, more realistic, more faithful to the banality of life, than Hemingway. The hunt ends without incident and everybody goes back to the villa. The hunting scene, which seemed about to become a climax, is only a feint. The real climax of the novel is the following scene in which two automobile loads of Milanese friends arrive at the villa and turn the night into a farcical bacchanal. The game progresses from drinking and sex to blasphemy: Pieretto and one of the guests clown at falling down and worshipping a picture of Poli. But Pieretto objects that the true god bears a wound in his side. "Let the accused take off his clothes . . . Show us the wound."[56] The whole tone of the night is typified by its final and most vulgar incident, in which a guest named Cilli appears with a piece of woman's underwear asking everybody to smell it and guess whom it belongs to. This party in itself is enough to demonstrate, not only to the narrator but to Oreste, that the way of Poli and Gabriella leads into a descending spiral of corruption. But they have not yet seen how Poli's own hubris is to work itself out; they have not yet seen him naked and offering the wound in his side. The next morning the narrator comes unexpectedly into his room and finds him holding a handkerchief full of blood. He is already in the advanced stages of consumption, and comments only, "At least it'll soon be over."[57] This turn of events is unexpected and yet logical and convincing. Poli has already been shot at by one woman, and he might quite plausibly have ended like Francis Macomber. But the blood he shows to the narrator is not the result of external violence; it comes from inside him as a result of the life he is leading. This is the end of his freedom. The novel closes as his expensive car takes him back to the city to die; in the last glimpse the three friends have of him he "agitates his hand"[58] in farewell.

This ending is moving and succinct. The whole characterization of Poli—his sham philosophizing, his spasmodic generosity, his triste experiments in vice—is the best part of the novel. And yet the work in its totality is only partly successful, probably less successful than *La spiaggia* of which it was in a certain sense a rewriting. Part of the difficulty is that Pavese is not really comfortable in this milieu of the idle rich he attempted to deal with in both *La spiaggia* and *Il diavolo sulle colline*. It was not that he possessed no experience of this world; he had had a good deal of contact with it by 1948. But he never succeeded in assimilating it to the point where it became a part of his nature, something he could regard simply and intimately as he regarded, for example, the life of the Piedmontese countryside. In dealing with the "mythical reality" of country life the novel is somewhat more successful. But here it suffers from a somewhat synthetic quality, a too evident effort to make the moon, crickets, nudity, wine into meaningful symbols. It was only in the later *La luna e i falò* that he succeeded in forming this private mythology into a pattern that gave an impression of true spontaneity—vivid, mysterious, and yet simple and natural. And a final difficulty with *Il diavolo sulle colline*, the reason why it seems even more fragmented and diffuse than *La spiaggia*, is that Pavese here tries to deal with three basic elements of conflict rather than two: the artificiality of city life, the "bestiality" of nature, and the refined vice represented by Poli. This complexity of conflict leads to a profusion of scenes, half-developed characters, images and suggestions that at first seem important and are then abandoned. Pavese's love of rowing on the Po, for example, might have played an important part in the novel; it serves as the center for several stories. But in *Il diavolo sulle colline* it is taken up, dealt with tentatively for a chapter or two, and then dropped. Pavese is not the kind of a writer who can juggle a great many characters, scenes, ideas, and settings at the same time. His best novels follow a single and graceful line that conceals, under the simplicity of its curve, an inner complexity.

The Bad Conscience

After he finished *La spiaggia* early in 1941 Pavese abandoned the novel form for over five years, until he began *Il compagno* in the fall of 1946. During much of this time he worked on stories, many of them left unfinished. It was the least productive period of his career and a time of confusion and uncertainty in his personal life. A good deal of it was devoted to his involvement with Fernanda Pivano and to the painful political vacillations culminating with his espousal of the Communist Party in 1946. Part of the war period he spent in Rome, part in Turin, and part in the Piedmontese village of Serralunga where his sister Maria had taken refuge from the Allied bombings. His diary in this period, especially after 1943, is concerned chiefly with his reading: Shestov, Kierkegaard, Greek tragedies, Milton, the more obscure Elizabethans. His biographer Davide Lajolo, a Marxist and after the war a Communist deputy, regards this period in his life as a kind of betrayal. "At Serralunga he shut himself up in a trench made of books and when he raised his head from the printed page it was to contemplate nature, the hills, and to build symbols on this horizon of his childhood. It was a way, the usual way, of escaping the remorse that tormented him for his failure to come forth and risk himself with the others."[59] Many of Pavese's friends were in the Resistance; Lajolo himself was the commander of a partisan division. At least two of his friends, Giaime Pintor and Leone Ginzburg, lost their lives in the struggle against fascism. There is no doubt that Pavese felt restless, dissatisfied with himself, guilty, during these years and in fact for the rest of his life, and there is no doubt either that there was a political element in this sense of guilt. The one novel in which he dealt specifically with the Resistance, *La casa in collina,* was published after the war in a volume called *Prima che il gallo canti* (*Before the Cock Crows*). When Pavese handed the book to Lajolo he added the rest of the quotation: "Three times you will deny me."[60] Unfortunately Lajolo's biography brings a political orientation to bear on everything to the point where any interest of Pavese in purely literary problems is regarded as a kind of betrayal; an example of this is his annoyance in the quotation above with the word "symbol," almost as antipathetic to Lajolo as "fascism." But this is to oversimplify the situation to the point of falsity; in fact another remark quoted by Lajolo himself suggests that for Pavese political commitment was only a kind of metaphor for the more fundamental commitment or fulfillment he was seeking. Lajolo had written a kind of diary of his Resistance experience under the title *Classe 1912.* After Pavese read this he commented, "Your whole partisan book lives in the breath of your little girl. I have no children and it's for this too that I feel alone and suffer a sense of lacking."[60] If he had been forced to choose between the two, it is possible that Pavese would have found it more important to be a father than a division commander in the Resistance. In any case, in his private thoughts as in his fiction these two kinds of failure are mysteriously linked.

This kind of ambiguity in which the political (commitment vs isolation) and the sexual-creative (producing vs consuming) are mingled is especially evident in the two novels written immediately after the war: *Il compagno* and *La casa in collina.** In only one of these, *La casa in collina,* is the political element overt and obvious. In *Il compagno* the political implications might escape notice if it were not for the title; *compagno* is literally "companion" but also suggests the idea of "comrade" in the Communist sense—a hint that is followed in the title of the English translation. On the surface the novel deals with a purely personal conflict. The narrator Pablo is a youth who works in his family's tobacco shop in Turin. His companion Amelio is injured in a motorcycle accident and confined to bed, probably permanently, with a broken back. Through his visits to the sickroom Pablo meets Linda, Amelio's girl friend, who was also involved in the accident but not injured. Since Pablo is attracted to Linda, and Linda is a girl of somewhat flexible virtue, the inevitable

* The first is translated as *The Comrade* (London: Owen, 1959), the second as *The House on the Hill* (Walker, 1961).

happens: he finds himself vacillating between his sexual desire and his loyalty to his helpless friend. On the surface there is no overt reason for Pablo to feel guilty about anything. It is not even certain that Amelio would object to his relations with Linda. Pablo is not "responsible" for Amelio's suffering except in the existentialist sense that every human being is responsible for every other human being, but this is exactly the source of his guilt. The narrator of Camus' *La chute* tells the story of a man whose friend was in prison and who slept on the floor of his room in order not to enjoy a comfort of which his friend had been deprived. "Who will sleep on the floor for us?" asks Clamence. Pavese's novel, written ten years before, expands the implication of this ethical question into a major theme: Pablo, in the end, finds himself unable to offer a token and useless sacrifice as a sign of his common human involvement with Amelio.

The idea of *Il compagno* is sketched out in a 1938 story manuscript, unpublished until after Pavese's death, called "Fedeltà."* As is the case with several other stories of this kind that grew into novels, "Fedeltà" is told in the third person and the later *Il compagno* in the first. There are other important differences between the story and the novel. The story deals almost entirely with the conflict between desire for the girl and loyalty to the injured friend. In the novel Pablo's involvement with Linda leads him into a circle of dancers, nightclub habitues, and parasites centering around the theatrical impresario Lubrani, and in this way a second theme of the contrast between a working class and a wasting class is introduced. Except for the implications of the word *compagno,* this is about as political as the novel gets. The protagonist of the story manuscript, who is called Garolofo, is a tobacco clerk and nothing more; his personality is not sharply defined. In the novel Pablo is a talented amateur guitarist, and in this way the theme of the artist, or a kind of parody of this theme as it is treated in the usual *Künstlerroman,* is introduced: can the artist survive the temptations of a materialistic society, or will his standards be corrupted by these temptations and he himself destroyed? One of Pablo's problems is whether he is to become a good guitarist or a kind of parasite in Lubrani's entourage. A final intricacy of the novel is that Pablo little by little takes possession of the former life of Amelio—his girl, his friends, his habits—until he begins to feel like a kind of identity thief, a Doppelgänger. Because of this diversity of themes the novel has a tendency to fall apart structurally; the various elements have not really been molded into a homogeneous whole. In particular

* "Faithfulness" or "Loyalty."

the part of the novel dealing with Lubrani seems tacked on or in-completely assimilated. Lubrani is probably of interest chiefly as a prototype of the more fully developed Poli of *Il diavolo sulle colline,* written two years later.

The most striking innovation of *Il compagno* is a certain pecu-liarity of its style: its tendency to form into little self-enclosed cap-sules of narrative, sometimes only a paragraph or two long. The best of these passages resemble the "vignettes" of Hemingway's *In Our Time;* they might be taken out of the text and printed by themselves as complete, if somewhat cryptic, miniature narratives. The novel opens with one of these vignettes:

> They called me Pablo because I played the guitar. The night that Amelio broke his back on the Avigliana road, I had gone with three or four others for supper on the hill—not very far, you could see the bridge—and we drank and joked under the September moon, until it got too cold and we went inside to sing. Then the girls started dancing. I played—Pablo here, Pablo there—but I didn't enjoy myself, I always like to play for somebody who understands, but these people just wanted to see who could shout the loudest. I played the guitar a little more on the way home and somebody sang. My hands were wet with the fog. I was fed up with that life.[61]

Pavese might have stopped right there, and he would have had a piece of narrative more perfect in its way, if less complex, than the novel he published. The reader would never have learned what happened after Amelio broke his back, but he would have under-stood that there was some dark connection in Pablo's mind between his own guitar playing, Amelio's suffering, and the vulgarity of the people who "wanted to see who could shout the loudest." This skill in the miniaturization of narrative possibly came from the five years of writing stories, or trying to write stories, that preceded the novel.

The theme of responsibility, latent and "metaphysical" in *Il compagno,* becomes overtly political in *La casa in collina* (1947-48). Again there exists an earlier story as a prototype: a fragment written in the fall of 1944 and published in the posthumous collected tales as "Il fuggiasco."* This piece of narrative, along with another attempted revision dating from early 1947, is in a confused state and seems to have difficulty locating the thread of its story; Pavese evidently struggled with this material over a period of years. Lajolo calls the hero of the novel "the character into which Pavese poured

* "The Fugitive."

the most of himself."[62] In this he is referring chiefly to Pavese's political vacillations and particularly his sense of guilt over the Resistance. The political element in the novel is undoubtedly important, but Lajolo's interpretation is oversimplified. In the first place there is a strong personal element in practically every novel of Pavese, and especially in *Il carcere, La spiaggia,* and *La luna e i falò.* He probably "poured more of himself" into this last book than any other, although the autobiographical element is converted and concealed in various oblique ways. Furthermore *La casa in collina* is about a great many more things than politics; it is even possible to argue that politics in this novel is only a metaphor for the whole problem of human solidarity, as the device of the paralyzed friend was a metaphor of solidarity in *Il compagno.* The narrator himself, in fact, seems to go out of his way to make this point:

> I ought to say—beginning this story of a long illusion—that the blame of what happened can't be put on the war. In fact the war, I am certain, might even have saved me. When the war came I had been living for a while in the villa there where I rented some rooms, but if it hadn't been for the work that kept me in Turin I would already have gone back to the house of my folks, among those other hills. The war simply relieved me of my extreme scruples over being alone . . . With the war it became legitimate to isolate yourself, live by the day, not regret any more your lost opportunities. But you might say I had been waiting for the war a long time and counting on it, this war so strange and so vast that, with a little effort, you could just curl yourself up and let it rage, out of the sky onto the city, while you went home to the hills. Things happened then so that just living without complaining, almost without talking, seemed to me dignity enough. That kind of deaf rancor in which my youth had ended found in the war a place to hide, a horizon.[62]

This passage contains at least one direct autobiographical reference: by the time of the action of the novel Pavese himself had no work in Turin and had "gone back to the house of my folks, among those other hills" of Serralunga. The "lost opportunities," the "scruples," suggest the personal defeats in his own life for which the war became a kind of refuge: the disappointments in love, the uncertainty over his writing. But undoubtedly the question still haunted Pavese as it haunts the protagonist of the novel: what kind of a man is it who, brooding over his private sorrows, retreats to the hills with his books while others are suffering? In this way the political element, pushed out one end of the novel in the passage just quoted, comes back in the other end. It is not enough to sleep on the floor for our friend; if possible we must help him break out of jail.

Corrado, the first-person narrator of *La casa in collina,* is a teacher in a Turin *liceo.* Even before the bombings he has formed the habit of going on summer nights to sleep in a villa on the hilltop above Turin, a terrain he likes because it reminds him of the hills where he lived as a child. In the summer of the air raids, in spite of his urge to "curl himself up" in his private isolation, he finds himself involved with two women. The first of these is his landlady's daughter Elvira, a reincarnation of the Elena of *Il carcere:* an anxious middle-aged spinster who smothers him with unwanted attention, worries when he is below in the city, and is jealous if he pays the slightest attention to another woman. There are jokes about Corrado marrying her, but to Corrado it is no joke. Elvira combines the least attractive sides of both mother and wife; she represents exactly the kind of feminine influence Corrado detests and seeks to escape in remaining independent. He himself says, "I was happy not to have in my days any real affection or encumbrance, to be alone, not tied to anyone."[63] But the price of this freedom is a vague loneliness or sense of incompletion which he only gradually recognizes in himself. The second of the two women is Cate, a girl with whom Corrado has had a love affair some eight years before. Finding her now living in the nearby tavern of Le Fontane with a group of other refugees, he almost fails to recognize her. When he remembers there is a flashback chapter that economically sketches this earlier encounter. In those days he behaved like the immature youth that he was, refusing to admit any responsibility for the relationship and regarding it merely as a passing adventure with a working-class girl. "Once in a while I bought her a lipstick that filled her with joy, and then I began to see that you could maintain a woman, educate her, bring her to life, but if you know what her elegance is made out of, it loses its savor."[64] Because of this he abandons her, or the affair comes to an end of itself, and he thinks no more about it. But the Cate who appears unexpectedly in the darkness of that June night is another person. She is a mature woman with a son now, and her gaucheness has been replaced by a kind of good-natured and ironic cynicism. It is significant that the re-encounter with Cate, beginning with sexual memories, then reawakens in him his sense of political guilt. "You aren't a fascist by any chance?" she asks him half-seriously. He tells her: "We all are, dear Cate. If we weren't we would revolt, throw bombs, risk our skins. Whoever lets things go and is satisfied is already a fascist."[65] The lines of the conflict are laid down. How to be independent, retain one's personality and freedom of choice, and still come to terms with this nagging sense of responsibility that calls for some kind of commitment? The rest of the narrative consists of Corrado's efforts to work himself out of this dilemma.

The scene of the first encounter with Cate, like the rest of the novel, hovers in the vague region between the political and the sexual, if the sexual is understood to include the family-forming instinct as well. Cate's child Dino plays at the game of war; he knows more about the Resistance than Corrado does, and later in the novel he actually escapes to the hills to join the partisans. The thought occurs to Corrado that Dino may be his own son. If this is so then Dino is not only a figure of the youthful idealism of the Resistance but an echo of Corrado himself as a child. Dino is the child that Corrado would be again if he could retrace his steps and correct the wrong turning he made somewhere in the past—but where exactly was this? Corrado's search for a mature identity ironically leads him to a regression into nostalgia, into childhood. Meanwhile the events of the war accelerate; he becomes, rather than a participant, a passive victim of its vicissitudes. Cate, her family, and the refugees at Le Fontane are arrested; only the child Dino escapes. Corrado himself takes refuge in a seminary where he pretends to serve as a teacher; Dino is sent to the seminary too but soon runs away to become a partisan. Corrado understands clearly that in taking shelter among the priests he has committed an evasion, a betrayal. And yet this novel is the only one in Pavese's work in which the protagonist shows any genuine religious impulse. Corrado's predicament is similar to that of Jake in *The Sun Also Rises*, who tries to pray but finds himself thinking of money, friends, everything but God; he has gone too far along another road. He finds a kind of peace in the seminary, but he understands that his position there is that of an impostor. Later when (as he believes) the fascists come looking for him at the seminary, he sets out on foot to go back to "those other hills" where his family has taken shelter from the war. Here memories of Serralunga, where Pavese stayed with his sister during the war, and nostalgia for Santo Stefano Belbo, where he was born and spent his vacations as a child, are mixed. On the way he happens to witness a terrible event: the ambush of two truckloads of fascist soldiers by the partisans. The dead are described with particular precision: one fallen on his face with his feet still in the truck, another "kneeling stiffly against the barbed wire, as though alive, blood flowing from his mouth and eyes, a wax boy crowned with thorns."[66] That night, continuing his flight through the hills, he sleeps in a hut that in the morning he recognizes as a ruined and abandoned chapel. His choice of the hut was an accident; but not even if he went looking for it, he recognizes, would he be entitled to the grace the chapel represents. Nevertheless he "says in silence an old word" to himself as he leaves. The fundamental religious vein in this novel has been overlooked by most of Pavese's critics, Lajolo included.

The only grace Corrado can expect is that of being received, as a child, into his welcoming family. It is strange and unacceptable to him that war should have disturbed his past; in coming home he expects to find the objects and events of his childhood waiting there for him unchanged, "like a room kept shut." Outwardly at least he succeeds in shutting himself up in this room. The fascists occasionally search the hills but, warned by his mother and sister, he is always able to take shelter in some ditch until they are gone. Yet the "grace" he hopes for in this blind retreat into childhood never comes. In his secret thoughts he knows that it is not for him to act like a child while Dino, the child, is behaving like a man. Sometimes he wonders whether Cate, Dino and the others will come out of the war alive, but when he hopes to see them again this very hope makes him afraid. At the end of the novel these thoughts lead him to one of the most vivid and eloquent soliloquies in Pavese's fiction.

> I have seen the unknown dead, the fascist dead. It is they who have awakened me. If an unknown, an enemy, becomes this kind of a thing as he dies, if he stops us and makes us afraid to step over him, this must mean that even vanquished the enemy is somebody, that after having shed blood it is necessary to placate it, give a voice to that blood, justify those who have shed it. To look at certain dead is humbling. They are no longer somebody else's business, you don't feel that you have stumbled on them by accident. You feel that the same destiny that has made those bodies fall has fixed us here to look at them, to drink in the sight. It's not fear, not the usual cowardice. You feel humble because you understand—you see with your own eyes—that in place of the dead we might be there ourselves: it wouldn't be any different, and if we are alive we owe it to these smeared corpses. And so every war is a civil war: every fallen soldier resembles those who remain, and demands justification from them.[67]

And yet his reflexions take him even farther than this. In the end he understands that the war itself is not responsible for the vague incubus that troubles him; the war is only a catalytic factor, a pretext. Whatever this incubus is, it will not simply evaporate after the war is over. "War" in this book, like "jail" in Pavese's first novel, becomes a metaphor for deeper and more fundamental problems. "Now that I have seen what war is, what civil war is, I know that, if it ends one day, everybody will have to ask himself: 'And what do we do with the fallen? why are they dead?' I wouldn't know what to answer. Not now, at least. Maybe only the dead know, and only for them is the war really over.' "[68] This war for Pavese ended only with his suicide.

The Geography of the Moon

La luna e i falò* was written in fifty-three days of intense activity in late 1949, about nine months before Pavese's death. He had finally achieved the spontaneity he sought, or at least the semblance of it; this last book gives no impression of contrivance and yet is the most finished and structurally symmetrical of his novels. A number of technical problems that had plagued him throughout his career were finally resolved. The first of these was point of view, or more precisely the psychological and linguistic relation of the narrator to the story he is telling. Like the earlier *Paesi tuoi*, *La luna e i falò* is told in vernacular language by a narrator who—at least on the surface—is only semi-involved in the story he relates. Because both narrators are of uncultured origin they speak naturally and simply, without literary affection. Thus Pavese in these two novels was able to achieve the vernacular or pseudo-regional language he had always sought for from the time of his earliest poetry, a style impossible in novels like *Il diavolo sulle colline* where the narrator is a person roughly of the writer's own cultural background. But *La luna e i falò* has an advantage in this respect over *Paesi tuoi*. The Berto of the earlier novel begins and ends as a Turin mechanic; his culture is insufficient to provide the proper language for the events he is relating, especially in their mythic or symbolic aspects, and Pavese himself was conscious of this difficulty. The unnamed narrator of *La luna e i falò* has grown up in a primitive Piedmontese village; his initial culture is even less adequate than Berto's. But he spends the middle part of his life wandering over the world, to Genoa and then to America, talking to many different people and working at many different jobs. With this relative sophistication he then comes back to the village and views it, in a sense, as a stranger, an American. But the very return to the village provokes in him a nostalgia that reawakens the dialect, the

* *The Moon and the Bonfires* (Farrar, Straus & Young, 1953).

simple language rhythms, of his childhood. If he had never left the village he could not have told his story at all. He could not have told it as well if he had remained in America, cut off from the vernacular he had spoken naturally and unconsciously as a child. Returning to the village as a man of forty, he is able to speak in two voices at once, or even in three: the country boy, the objective traveler from America, and the returned emigrant who is a complicated mixture of the two.

This three-angled viewpoint is somewhat more complicated than that of *Paesi tuoi,* and the difference is reflected in the time scheme or chronological plan of the novel. The narrator begins quite simply telling the story of his return to the *paese:* "There's a reason why I came back to this place, here and not to Canelli, or Barbaresco, or Alba. I wasn't born here, that's almost certain; where I was born I don't know; there isn't any house or piece of earth around here, any bones that belong to me so I could say, 'Here is what I was before I was born.' "[69] Then, as he begins explaining in an apparently random way his reasons for coming back as he did, he falls into talking of the two other epochs of his life: his boyhood in the country and his lonely years of exile in America. For the rest of the novel these three time levels are then alternated, and at the end of the story a fourth is added: the period of the Resistance, when the narrator was to all intents an American and the events in the Piedmontese hills might have happened on another planet. And yet the complexity of this time scheme is concealed in the simplicity with which the narrator turns from one epoch to another, the transitions always effected by chance associations in his mind. The reader is not conscious of the chronological structure any more more than he is in the *Odyssey,* where the poet naturally and simply begins telling his story *in medias res.*

Pavese was not an orphan like the narrator; he did not grow up in the countryside, he never went to America, and he actually was in the Piedmontese hills during the period of the Resistance. And yet under the surface *La luna e i falò* is his most autobiographical novel. This is another of the technical problems that are resolved in this final work: the autobiographical elements are powerfully present under the surface but are assimilated to the point where they are hardly visible and become an organic part of the work of art. The narrator grows up in the countryside and yet as an orphan, an illegitimate waif; he has no true roots there. Pavese felt the same rootlessness for different reasons; his intellectual experience had cut him off from contact with the soil. When the narrator comes back to the Gaminella farm where he was raised by foster parents he finds it is now occupied by Valino, another tenant farmer, who has a crippled son named Cinto. The narrator seeks to become a kind of friend or elder brother to Cinto, and tells him stories of travel, America, the wider world. In these conversations Pavese is speaking to himself: just as the narrator with his knowledge of America, his sophistication, is a projection of the educated side of Pavese that traveled in the realm of books and read American literature, so Cinto personifies the naive and "primitive" side of his own nature that Pavese hoped to recapture. Or rather, since this element was already present in his own nature but inaccessible, he hoped to assimilate it into his conscious identity in some way, to "make friends with it." The difficulty of the relation between Cinto and the narrator, the relative schism that separates them, is a measure of the unresolved conflict in Pavese's own personality. Parallels of this kind could be pursued indefinitely. The most important of them is the relation between the narrator's exile in America and Pavese's own "emigration" into American literature, which he came in time to regard as a kind of betrayal or wrong turning in his effort to establish his identity. In one of the American scenes the narrator meets a fellow Piedmontese, a truck driver who gestures contemptuously toward the narrator's girl and says, "Do you like these women?" But the narrator tells him, "That's our fault. It's their home, in this country."[70] Pavese did not really belong in the realm of American literature and his love affair with it was "his own fault"; his home as an artist was the Italian language. Or so he came to believe at the end of his life when, for political reasons and others, he repudiated the American element in his own formation. *La luna e i falò* is full of such thinly veiled allusions to the conflicts in Pavese's own mind.

The most significant success of this novel, however, is the skill with which the symbolic or mythopoeic element is incorporated in an ostensibly realistic action. This was the most difficult of Pavese's problems, and the primary reason at least for the partial failure of both *Paesi tuoi* and *Il diavolo sulle colline*. And yet in its creation of a complex system of nature images *La luna e i falò* goes far beyond the earlier novels that had experimented tentatively with the technique. The images of crickets, moon, vines, bonfires, blood, hills, play a part in *Paesi tuoi* as they do in all of Pavese's fiction involving a country setting. The unlettered Berto of *Paesi tuoi* is aware of the power of these things, but the language he uses to express it is necessarily too subtle, too literary, to be wholly convincing. In certain other novels the problem is the opposite. The relatively sophisticated narrators of *La casa in collina, Il diavolo sulle colline,* and to a certain extent *La spiaggia* are capable of expressing the symbolism but not of believing in it in any mythic sense; the whole trend of their background and education inclines them to skepticism. In this regard the narrator of *La luna e i falò* is in a uniquely advantageous position. Within the framework of the novel it is necessary for both narrator and reader to accept certain premises: that the moon has an influence on crops, that bonfires "wake up the earth," that there is a mysterious connection between the body of woman and the body of the land. The narrator did believe in these things as a boy, as all Piedmontese peasants do. In the time of his "American" sophistication he becomes skeptical, and he remains skeptical even after his return to the village. But under the influence of his friend Nuto, and under the very influence of the land, the moon, and the crops themselves, he comes to believe, or more precisely to return to his childhood belief; and in this gradual acceptance of belief the reader accompanies him. In this process Nuto, in his arguments with the narrator, serves not only as a kind of shaman but as a spokesman of rural folklore.

> "The moon," said Nuto, "you have to believe in that. Try to cut a pine in the full moon, the worms will eat it. A wine-tub you should wash when the moon is young. Even the grafts won't take if you don't make them in the first days of the moon."
>
> Then I told him I had heard a lot of stories in the world, but the ones he told were the biggest. It was no use running down the government and the sermons of the priests if you went on believing in these superstitions and old wives' tales. And it was then that Nuto quite calmly told me that superstitions were only things that caused harm, and if anybody used the moon and the bonfires to rob the peasants and to keep them in the dark, then he would be the ignoramus and they ought to shoot him in the piazza. But before I talked about it I would have to become a country boy again.[71]

In the earlier novels, especially in *Paesi tuoi*, this whole structure of symbolism is simply imposed as a *fait accompli;* here Nuto as raisonneur introduces and justifies it step by step. The reader, if he accepts the apparatus of the novel at all, thus undergoes a process of conversion parallel to the conversion of the narrator, which in itself reflects Pavese's own effort to recapture the innocence and mystery of his childhood. It is obvious that this mechanism would be impossible without the complex point-of-view or psychological standpoint from which the narrator views the action.

Nuto, who plays no active part in the plot, is nevertheless a key figure of the novel in this and in another sense as well. In the earlier flashback scenes of the narrator's boyhood Nuto is only a little older than he is. But he has already come into a man's estate; not only is he a carpenter but he is an amateur clarinetist who plays at country fairs, "sought after and listened to, talking with the grownups, with us boys, winking at the women."[72] His real fame in the countryside is that of a musician, and this lends him a sort of Orphic function in the mythopoeic pattern. There is even a scene in which he leads a kind of Dionysian procession down the country roads, playing his instrument which resembles the Bacchic pipe, while peasant women lean out the windows to sing. Scenes like this would seem affected or contrived if it were not for the narrator's laconic and matter-of-fact way of telling, his undercurrent of irony. In its final effect the procession scene is half playful, half a kind of submerged symbolism that contributes to the general mood of the novel. On a more specific level Nuto's music identifies him as another of the artist types who recur in Pavese's fiction; his most obvious predecessor is the narrator of *Il compagno*, who is "called Pablo because he played the guitar." But Nuto is also a carpenter and a good one, where Pablo is only a grudging and indifferent tobacco clerk. In other words there is a tension in Nuto's identity, and in this he provides another analogue of Pavese's own inner conflicts. When the narrator comes back from America he finds that Nuto is married and settled down—*un uomo fatto*—and has hung up his clarinet on the wall. He has had to decide; it is impossible to be both carpenter and musician. "Of course I still like music . . . the trouble is it's a bad master. . . . It becomes a vice, you have to stop."[73] The place of clarinet playing in his life corresponds exactly to the place of poetry, or pure literature, in Pavese's. There is a charismatic power, something Orphic, about the artist, but at the center of his calling there is something dubious. It is significant that Nuto marries only after he has given up music. The artist is not a complete man, a *uomo fatto;* he is a half-man half-god whose human side is condemned to unhappiness, to sterility in his relations with others. Pavese's view of the artist approaches Thomas Mann's, especially in the Leverkühn of *Doktor Faustus*. The life that Nuto finally selects for himself is that of the artisan; that is, the half-artist who nevertheless makes something concrete and useful, and makes it for others rather than for himself. (There is no reason why art should not be made for others, but Pavese, at least, regarded pure poetry as a self-indulgence.) The mature Nuto is the type of the maker, a Daedalus, and this is more valuable for others and more fulfilling to himself than the Orphic role he has abandoned.

At the opposite pole from the makers, in Pavese's scale of values, are the wasters. It was his preoccupation with unproductive hedonism or "wasting" that led him to devote so much of his attention, in novels like *La spiaggia* and *Il diavolo sulle colline,* to the idle rich, a class with which he had little rapport and basically mistrusted. Another of the successes of *La luna e i falò* is that this theme is dealt with in a really satisfactory way for the first time. At thirteen, when he is old enough to leave his foster parents, the narrator goes to work as a servant on the prosperous farm of La Mora. The master here is Sor Matteo, a country landowner of old-fashioned cut, rather rustic in manners, competent and abstemious even though he has never had to work the land with his own hands. But his second wife is weak and flighty, and his two elder daughters by another marriage, Irene and Silvia, "have pretensions"; they demand flowers and piano lessons, flirt with provincial swains, and call the narrator Anguilla or Eel because he is so skinny. Here the sexual element in his attitude becomes apparent—"To let off steam I thought about the things we boys talked about when he went to hide in the canebrake."[74] To the boy this family, as provincial as it is, seems a fable of beauty and elegance; his sexual awakening is confused by reveries of Silvia in which she is simultaneously princess and enemy. It is unimportant whether they are truly aristocratic; they seem so to the boy, and they serve as emblems of aristocracy at least in the framework of the novel as it is structured in his mind. Pavese knew families like Sor Matteo's thoroughly from his own boyhood, and yet, Turin-raised as he was, he could view them with an objectivity or irony that was impossible for him with the truly rich. In the course of the novel this family falls apart like the family in *The Cherry Orchard,* and for the same reasons; it represents a social class in the state of disintegration. Even before he leaves La Mora the narrator begins to perceive that his masters are not really at the top of the social scale—that they are snubbed, for example, by their more genuinely aristocratic neighbor, the Nido countess, who plays the part of the Yaroslavl aunt in *The Cherry Orchard.* And an even more basic discovery is that he comes to comprehend their essential fleshliness, their mortality, equal to his own.

> The thing I couldn't get through my head in those days was that all women are made alike, they're all looking for a man. It must be that way, I used to think to myself; but the idea that all of them, even the most beautiful, even the ladies, liked that kind of thing was stupifying. But I was noticing more things now, I had heard a lot of things, and I knew, I saw how even Irene and Silvia ran after this man and that. Still it baffled me.

It was Nuto who told me: "What do you think? the moon is the same for everybody, just like rain, just like sickness. It doesn't matter whether you live in a hole or a palace, blood is red everywhere."[75]

The narrator's disenchantment with this race he imagined of a finer substance than his own is the first step in his own maturity; he sees now that his reverie of the rich has been a childish daydream, a fable.

This discovery is not the only part Sor Matteo's family plays in the development of the narrator. Irene and Silvia, and especially the younger Santina, are held in reserve under the surface of the novel until finally they emerge to play an important role in its climax. Meanwhile intervenes the narrator's long sojourn in America. This section of the novel involves one of the most curious and revealing pictures of America in modern Italian fiction, not only because Pavese had a complicated set of emotions on the subject but because, since he never visited America, he was free to construct a totally mythic setting out of emigrant lore, his reading of American literature, and the countless American movies he sat through in his student days and later. In 1947, about two years before the writing of *La luna e i falò*, he recalled this earlier enthusiasm for America in an article for the Communist daily *L'Unità*. "Towards 1930, when Fascism commenced to be 'the hope of the world,' a lot of young Italians looked in their books and discovered America: an America pensive and barbaric, blissful yet quarrelsome, dissolute, fecund; burdened with all the past of the world, yet youthful, innocent."[76] This was the America of Edgar Lee Masters, of Anderson's *Dark Laughter,* of *Moby-Dick.* But the war, the influence of his leftist friends, and especially his violent and hopeless love affair with the American actress Constance Dowling has replaced this image with another. The dedication of *La luna e i falò* is "For C," and the English epigraph that follows was a phrase Melville had underlined in his copy of *Lear:* "Ripeness is all." The America of the novel is a desert, a wasteland of inedible food and flashy automobiles, populated with the soulless and narcissistic women of the fashion magazines. The narrator goes to California and wanders from job to job, as rootless as the other Americans. In fact it is for their very rootlessness that he likes them at first, seeing in it a parallel to his own bastardy. "In Fresno where I lived, I went to bed with a lot of women, one of them I almost married, but I never found out where they had their mothers and their fathers and their land."[77] America is the opposite pole of *paese,* a place with no past, no myths, bloodless. As he tells the Piedmontese truck driver he meets in the café, "There's nothing. It's like the moon."[78] He meets a girl named Rosanne and she becomes his mistress for a time. She is casually, almost indifferently, promiscuous and yet totally passionless; when he asks her what he means to her she remarks that he is after all a man. Or, she adds in English, "Put it the other way round, you come with me because I'm a girl."[79] The narrator grasps finally that there is more than one way of being rootless, that the Americans are linked together in some strange and invisible way he will never understand because their rootlessness is not his own. Whatever his blood is, it is not the pale and chemical substance that flows in the veins of the Americans. Even more than the bitter *L'Unità* article, this novel is Pavese's farewell to the "pensive and barbaric" America of his youth.

There is no doubting that the moon, the lunar landscape of America, has its own kind of power. In the earlier part of the novel, before America is involved, the moon is associated with night, magic, the feminine mooncycle, the invisible influence that rots pine trees and sours wine if its laws are not observed. Gradually, as the novel progresses, the lunar element is associated with America. A paradox is involved: as synthetic and "unnatural" as the American landscape may seem, the moon is simply the mysterious and indifferent working of nature. "Mysterious" and "indifferent" are appropriate adjectives for Rosanne. The Piedmontese peasants fear and respect the moon because, like all peasants, they recognize nature as their enemy. And in 1949 America too, with its Marshall Plan and its Bomb, seemed to hold the power of life and death over Europe. Opposed to the moon in Pavese's symbology, and especially in this novel, is fire, the *falò* of the title. On St. John's Night the peasants light bonfires to "wake up the earth"; the power of fire is Promethean, man-contrived, opposed to the natural power of the moon. To shift the framework only slightly, the moon is associated with the feminine principle, with female sexuality, and fire with the masculine principle, with male sexuality. Men work the fields; women, attuned to the moon cycle in a mysterious way, produce children. The force of the bonfire that wakes up the earth is equivalent to the force of male passion for women. This rudimentary mythology is the basis for the whole imagistic pattern of the novel, especially the latter part of it.

Earlier in the novel, in the narrator's conversations with Nuto, fire is presented almost totally as a positive force, the tool of man's determination to wrest a living from the earth. But as the novel progresses this quasi-sexual force begins to assume other and less savory aspects. The boy Cinto, as we have seen, represents in a certain sense the naive or unformed innocence of the narrator's own boyhood. (His name is short for "hyacinth".) His father Valino is a stupid and rather surly peasant, an extrapolation of the peasant temperament to the point of sheer brutishness. Mute and passive for most of the novel, this brutishness finally expresses itself in a definitive act: Valino murders the two women of his household, burns the house, and hangs himself. The narrator and Nuto arrive to find Cinto speechless and trembling before the burning house that illuminates the hills like daylight; this is the first of the two climactic bonfires of the novel. The thread that runs from Pavese himself to the narrator, to Cinto, and finally to Valino is a tenuous but important one. As a projection of Pavese himself the narrator sets out to recover the primitive and "mythic" in his own boyhood. The quest for Santo Stefano Belbo leads to the peasant, not only the natural inhabitant of the *paese* but in a sense its psychological equivalent. Like Melville attracted to and then horrified by the Marquesan natives. Pavese draws back from the final consequences of his search. "The people who practiced the worst and most frequent sacrifices were the agriculturalists," he wrote in his diary in 1945. "Neither the shepherds, nor the hunters, not the artisans were ever as cruel as the peasants."[80]

This was written while the bloody events of the war in the Piedmontese hills were still fresh in his mind. Bloody and flaming, it should be added; the two best-known tactics of the occupying Germans were the massacre of hostages and the burning of villages. But this is not really, or primarily, what the ending of La luna e i falò is about. The point is really that the surrender to the primitive, the search for some kind of Rousseauistic innocence, unleashes in the human character forces that deny its very humanity. There is no turning back in the progress from savage to civilization, which is also the progress of boy to man. Valino is a brute, but for a civilized man, a reasoning being, to reject his social heritage in an attempt to resemble Valino is something more than brutishness; it approaches perversion. This breakdown of values is illustrated particularly in the decline of Sor Matteo's family. The three daughters of the family have none of their father's austerity and feel no particular inhibitions; they simply follow their impulses. Their father is a producer, they become consumers, wasters. It is this self-indulgence that leads them individually to disaster and eventually destroys the family. Silvia dies of an illegitimate pregnancy, and Irene, too spoiled and capricious to choose among her beaus, ends married to a mediocre husband who beats her. The end of their younger half-sister Santina is most striking. As her name suggests, she is typified in the early part of the novel mainly by her innocence; carefree and playful, with "flowerlike" eyes, she is pampered and indulged by the others. It is she who turns out the worst. During the war she takes up with the fascist militiamen, repents and goes into the hills to join the partisans, then betrays them and returns to the fascists. Her promiscuity is both sexual and political; she floats in a vacuum without values. When she falls into partisan hands again she is taken out and shot in her white dress. Over her body they cut dried vines, the final Dionysian ritual of the novel. "Then," explains Nuto, "we poured on gasoline and lighted it. By noon it was nothing but ashes. Last year you could still see the place, like the bed of a bonfire."[81]

All this is told by Nuto and happens while the narrator is away in America. Could he have prevented it if he had stayed in the land where he belonged? Could Pavese have prevented the agonies of 1943-45 if he had not retreated into the "trench made out of books" of which his biographer Lajolo complains? But the Pavesian protagonist—in all the novels as well as in *La luna e i falò*—feels responsible not for events as they take place but for his own attitude toward them. "Whoever does not know how to live in charity and embrace the suffering of others is punished in feeling his own suffering with an intolerable violence,"[82] the diary notes in 1945. This final bonfire of Santina, and its ashes, are things that take place inside the narrator himself. There is a mysterious connection, which the narrative suggests rather than refers to explicitly, between Nuto's clarinet, the lame and goatlike Cinto, the bonfires of the midsummer night, the violence of the Resistance, and the male sexual impulse. At the other extreme, for the narrator, is the lunar landscape of America; Rosanne and Santina are the two impulses of his own nature expressed in sexual terms. Between them lies the way of Nuto, who abandons his Dionysian instrument to form a family and devote himself to something humble and useful, the making of things for others. For the narrator this fulfillment is denied. He resembles Kafka's Hunger Artist, who fasts not because he has chosen the way of fasting but because food is forbidden to him by some mysterious law within himself. The story of Valino and Cinto, of the war in the hills, of Santina's bonfire, is really his story; he is that peripheral and yet involved narrator that Pavese worked toward in all his fiction. He makes no comment when Nuto tells him of Santina's death. The novel ends on this note of unresolved longing, with the word "bonfire."

This final scene—an incident which is not witnessed by the narrator and is related only at second hand by Nuto—has an extraordinary intensity, comparable to that of Jim's leap from the *Patna* in *Lord Jim,* which in a similar way has not been seen by Marlow and is told only in a fragmentary and halting fashion by Jim. The scenes resemble each other also in that they are simultaneously realistic accounts of events plausible in themselves and fables rich in the mythic or symbolic. Jim leaps into an archetypal darkness out of which he struggles toward rebirth, the bonfire of *La luna e i falò* and the ashes it leaves behind are the narrator's final and annihilating image of himself. Pavese's achievement here is enhanced by his decision to use a narrator with obvious linguistic and conceptual limitations, although the novel is shrewd enough in its technique to turn this handicap, at least partially, into an asset. If Pavese had produced only this one novel he would be a writer of undeniable importance. Through *La luna e i falò,* and by implication through the rest of Pavese's work that prepared the way for it, the development of Italian fiction has advanced a significant step: a kind of Melvillization has taken place to enhance and enrich a neorealistic movement that was in danger, by 1950, of degenerating into mechanical imitation of American naturalism. There is rather general agreement among Pavese's critics that he did leave such a mark on the generation of writers that followed him. But to speak of influences in this way is to regard Pavese only as a kind of cog in a process of literary history. Such assertions of influence are hard to prove in a concrete or documentary way, and in any case they miss the real point: that a work of art, if it has any intrinsic value, is important of and by itself. In his last novel Pavese finally achieved the simple and powerful narrative, the narrative unaffected and even naive in style and yet rich in unspoken implications, that he had worked toward for a lifetime. The final proof of this must, in the end, be a subjective one. The proof is that, as the reader loses himself in *La luna e i falò,* the sensations and reactions of this narrator who has no name and only a rudimentary education become his own sensations and reactions; that the reader, in short, forgets he is reading a novel and directly shares the emotions of the storytelling voice.

Elio Vittorini

Elio Vittorini was born on July 23, 1908, the son of a minor railway official, in the Sicilian city of Siracusa. Most of his childhood was spent in remote towns in various parts of Sicily, and his formal education was slight. At thirteen he began roaming Italy on the free train pass he was entitled to as a member of a railway family, and at seventeen he left Sicily for good. After working for a time on a construction gang in northern Italy he became a proofreader for the Florentine daily *La Nazione*. It was in this period that he began acquring his impressive literary background and his knowledge of English, which he taught himself by translating novels with a dictionary. He began writing fiction as early as 1927; soon he was a contributor to the small but important Florentine review *Solaria*. In 1931 he published *Piccola borghesia*, a collection of stories; his first novel *Il garofano rosso* was written in 1932-33. Meanwhile he had begun a parallel career as a translator and critic of American literature. During the Thirties he translated *Light in August, Tortilla Flat, God's Little Acre*, and several nineteenth-century American writers including Poe. His best-known and most important novel, *Conversazione in Sicilia*, was first published in volume form in 1940-42. His fiction also includes *Uomini e no* (1945), *Il Sempione strizza l'occhio al Fréjus* (1947), *Le donne di Messina* (1949, revised 1964), and *Erica e i suoi fratelli*, written in the Thirties but published along with *La Garibaldina* in 1956. A semifiction-alized travel book, *Viaggio in Sardegna*, appeared in 1936, and a collection of American literature under the title *Americana* was published after mutilation by the censors in 1940. A collection of excerpts from Vittorini's criticism and literary journalism appeared in 1957 as *Diario in pubblico*. During the Forties Vittorini served as editor of the independent leftist review *Il Politecnico*. He died in Milan in 1966.

Collectivizing the Furies

The fiction of Vittorini is intensely personal, but he never reveals himself in it in even the disguised and oblique way that Moravia and Pavese appear in their own novels. In his best and most characteristic work the narrative is seen through a single personality that is always the same, always the author, and yet this personality is reticent about its innermost emotions and impulses; the persona of the author lacks candor. The dominant storytelling consciousness becomes a receptor, a photographic apparatus. This apparatus is capable of perceiving and communicating the most subtle and intricate impressions from the external world, but its relation to the world of impressions is essentially a passive one. At the bottom Vittorini's deepest loyalty, the loyalty of his reflexes, so to speak, is to the task of finding a poetic language for these impressions. But this aesthetic tendency is in profound conflict with his politics—his external view of himself as a leftist and revolutionary—and the tension that results is a recurring problem throughout his career.

Vittorini's education was rudimentary even for the construction worker he became at one time, let alone for a writer. His literary culture was very largely self-acquired. The first fiction that made an impression on him was a child's adaptation of *Robinson Crusoe,* a book that is an important key to his whole personality and his outlook as an artist. Much later, in 1930, he taught himself English by laboriously translating this novel with the aid of a dictionary. In the meantime there intervened his *Wanderjahre,* another important influence in his literary development. At thirteen, with his railway pass in his pocket, he set out to see the world. This was the first of three such flights in four years. In the daytime he visited the cities of Italy; at night, because he had no money for hotels, he slept in trains. The fourth time, when he was seventeen, he did not come back.

In the northernmost corner of Italy he repudiated his petit-bourgeois origins and became a proletarian, a member of a construction gang building a bridge near Udine. "Building a bridge is not the same as building a table or building a house. Once you begin you cannot stop the work until it is done, at least as far as the piers are concerned. There are cement caissons that have to be driven into the riverbed little by little, excavating beneath them and pumping the water out from inside. If it starts raining you have to work faster than the rain, whether digging or pumping. And then you work night and day without relief, no longer aware that you are working to earn your bread, thinking of nothing but winning, breaking through. This was a milestone in my life."[1]

There were two lessons here for Vittorini, and two clues for his serious reader. The first is that there are some tasks that have to be done at a single leap without stopping halfway; building a bridge, or writing a novel. The second is that there is a joy in the surrender of self involved in collective action. The two extremes of his personality are defined: the first lesson is technical or aesthetic, the second political. It was out of a combination of these two impulses that he began contributing to Alberto Carocci's *Solaria* and became an active member of the group that gathered around it: antitraditionalist, humanist, European, and thus by implication antifascist. It was in this period, while he was still a proofreader for a Florentine newspaper, that he began translating *Robinson Crusoe*. The fascination that this book exerted on him is a rather complex matter but a crucial one in his development as a writer. Most of his fiction is about wandering or exploration in one form or another. Two of his best books, *Viaggio in Sardegna* and *Conversazione in Sicilia,* are about journeys to islands, in fact psychologically and metaphorically about "discoveries" of islands. Another, *Le donne di Messina,* is about an effort to carve a little Eden out of an unpopulated wilderness left by the war. At the period a little later in his life when he "discovered" America in books he regarded it more or less in Robinsonian terms, as a virgin world where man could redefine himself in individual confrontation with nature. The element of solitude is important in this myth of the primitive. Robinson Crusoe is alone on his island and, rather improbably, provided with all the basic necessities. He is thus left free to analyse his sensations: sun, rain, food, sleep, the cryptic twittering of the jungle. Later he meets his savage, but Friday is really only an alter ego, a primitive side of himself that he is half fearful and half curious to discover. The main feature of Crusoe's life is that he is alone, and (in spite of his protestations) not really displeased with his savage independence. There is religion in the book but no politics, since religion can be engaged in by a castaway but politics demands a society. *Robinson Crusoe* is not really an allegory of human ingenuity but a defense of solipsism and the rejection of civilization. Or, at least, so Vittorini read it in the important formative period when the themes of his fiction were working their way to the surface of his consciousness.

Even more important than this thematic element is the matter of stylistics in Vittorini's work. The turning point in his artistic development is *Conversazione in Sicilia*. It is accompanied by his only major work of autocriticism—the preface to *Il garofano rosso* written only slightly later, in 1948, in which he discussed the differences between the two novels—and it is the only one of his novels to be completely successful as a unified and self-sufficient work of art. The books that followed it were plagued with problems that are simultaneously artistic and personal, involved with politics and the conflict of individualism and social responsibility. But they are all essentially in the same style: a flowing, imagistically subtle, evocative, highly personal idiom that in many ways resembles lyric poetry more than it does conventional prose. It is hard to find precedents for this style either in previous Italian literature or in the American fiction he translated during the Thirties. It is easy to point out certain superficial resemblances to Verga or to Faulkner, but essentially this style (Vittorini preferred the term *linguaggio*) was a thing he worked out deliberately and painstakingly for himself. It is simultaneously a personal expression of emotion and a quite contrived and conscious literary technique. At least in *Conversazione in Sicilia* he succeeded in the task he had set for himself: that of bypassing the whole apparatus of bourgeois "culture" and arriving at a poetry that would be a totally personal expression of his identity, his emotions, and his world outlook. The fact that his fiction output is relatively small in bulk and of uneven quality is undoubtedly connected to this highly personal nature of his aesthetic. His talent is more special than that of either Moravia or Pavese. He does not possess a wide range as a writer, and when he attempts to break out of the narrow range where he excels these experiments are usually disappointing. In spite of his quite conscious effort after *Conversazione in Sicilia* to diversify, to grow and acquire complexity as an artist, he is primarily the author of one novel. But he is that kind of a one-book author, like Rabelais and Cervantes, who adds a new artistic dimension to the history of literature.

The novelistic language of *Conversazione in Sicilia,* a language reflected as well in the novels that follow, is not essentially a realistic one. In a 1933 article he distinguishes between two kinds of writers: those who make you think, "Yes, that's the way it is," and those who make you think, "I had never supposed it could be like that," and in this way suggest a new mode of experience, a new "how" to existence.[2] The experience communicated in a work of fiction is of course specific, fixed to a single place on the map and a single point in time; in this at least Vittorini is a realist. But the effect on the reader (and Vittorini is as much interested in the psychology of the reader as he is in the creative process) must not be bound to or limited by this specific. "Poetry is poetry for this reason: because it does not remain tied to the things from which it originated and can be related, if it is born out of pain, to any pain."[3] This approaches the aesthetics of Mallarmé and the Symbolists; poetry is concerned not with things but with the general emotions generated by things. For the Symbolists, in fact, the poem itself is the thing, more comprehensible and more aesthetically satisfying than the imperfect world of objects. But Vittorini does not go this far. His fiction remains tied to a world of sunshine, melons, wine, rain, human voices. But one of the points of his method is to demonstrate that melons and sunshine are the same for all men, to affirm the universality of sensory experience. Underlying this is a notion of solidarity, of the resemblance that links all men together in the human condition. Men feel heat and cold in much the same way, and this is a reminder that all men hunger and suffer in their lives, know love and hate, and finally die. This concept of the community of experience is the connecting link, a tenuous and not very satisfactory one, between Vittorini's aesthetics and his politics. The sensations of the novelistic hero, which are also those of the author, are projected as possibilities for the reader and for all men. (It is important to note that they are "possibilities"; Vittorini's fiction does not so much evoke the reader's own experience as suggest new things that might happen to him.) The solidarity of feeling thus becomes the solidarity of politics; or at least Vittorini attempts to bring the two together. The difficulty is that, while all men feel heat and cold in the same way, they may not necessarily feel the same about such political questions as freedom and the artist's relation to the state. The relative failure of Vittorini's later books turns around this difficulty.

Vittorini's political beliefs are complex and often somewhat unfocused, but if it were necessary to find a single word for his position throughout his lifetime it would be "revolutionary." This is a term that, roughly, will apply equally well to his embryonic notions as an Udine bridge-worker and to the complex ideology he worked out many years later as the editor of *Politecnico*. Something is wrong with the world and whatever it is that is wrong is basic. No amount of tinkering, of bourgeois liberalism, is going to get at the root of the difficulty. Something fundamental must change—but where? inside men, or outside, in the economic and political arrangement of society? This is merely another disguise of the problem of the solidarity of feeling and the solidarity of politics. Vittorini concludes that the change must take place inside, and even that this internal change must precede any external change in the organization of society. Here—although it took him quite some time to realize it—he parts company with the Party Communists and even with the Marxists. His ideology or intellectual identity consists of a set of concentric rings. On the outside, at the most superficial level, he is a revolutionist and therefore a Marxist. At the next level down he is an artist interested in the commonality, the universality, of sensory experience. At a still deeper level is the most fundamental of his identities: the warmness and empathy that gropes for warmness and empathy in others, the quality that led the Udine bridge-worker to feel a sense of fulfillment in sharing a task with other men. This is the true sense in which Vittorini is a "collectivist," although—again—it took him some time to recognize this complexity in himself. The sense of losing self in another, of communion, that Moravia finds in sexual relations Vittorini attributes to any common human effort. This is best expressed in two novels that artistically are below the level of *Conversazione in Sicilia*: the Resistance novel *Uomini e no* and *Le donne di Messina*, a novel about a "collective" effort to build a community out of the ruins of the war. The question that is raised without really being solved in these two quasi-political novels is a basic one: how does the individual fit into this collective urge, what happens to the ego, to identity, in the surrender of personality to a common effort? The problem has an artistic side: novels are about characters, about human beings whose feelings the reader comprehends and shares. Is it possible to empathize with a community? The relative failure of *Uomini e no* and *Le donne di Messina* demonstrates that, if not impossible, it is at least difficult. Even in *Conversazione in Sicilia* this tendency toward the shadowy hero, toward abstraction of character, is apparent. The protagonist attempts in a certain sense to be everybody: the author, the reader, all humanity. In fact a curious feature of *Conversazione in Sicilia* is that the hero or narrator is the least clearly defined character in the novel. This might be acceptable in a narrative technique like Pavese's, where the narrator is only a semi-involved spectator of the events he relates. But Vittorini's narrator is in the forefront; the things that happen in the novel happen to him and not to others. The technique is an attempt at pure subjectivism, an effort to show the "how" of experience by putting the reader inside the quite spontaneous consciousness of the protagonist. In this Vittorini resembles Joyce or Virginia Woolf more than he does the orthodox Marxist novelist.

Conversazione in Sicilia opens with the well-known reference to furies: "That winter I was prey to abstract furies. I won't say which, that's not what I want to tell about. But I have to say they were abstract, not heroic, not alive; some sort of furies connected with the doomed human race."[4] The furies are both inside the narrator and out. They have something to do with the newspaper placards (the Spanish war, the chest-pounding of fascism) and yet the narrator implies that he is quite privately responsible for them. Instead of an impulse to counterattack he feels a kind of passive anesthesia. "That was the terrible part: the quietude of hopelessness. Believing the human race to be doomed and yet feeling no fever to do anything about it, an impulse, for example, to share the doom myself."[5] Did all men feel this? How to convince all men that they ought to feel this, or might feel it? "Putting the reader inside" implies at least some degree of universality, if not in the experience itself then at least in the work of art that reflects it. This is the basic task of his writing in the middle period of his career: to objectify the subjective. *Conversazione in Sicilia* is not a travelogue of Sicily, and it is not really a portrait of regional manners in the style of Verga, even though there are certain resemblances. For Verga the important events of the narrative happen to the fisherfolk who are the real characters of *I Malavoglia;* for Vittorini the events happen to the protagonist, a visitor who sees the train travelers and Sicilian villagers from the outside, much as he may empathize with them. These secondary characters are important, in fact, only insofar as they provoke impressions, emotions, and inward processes in the narrator. Vittorini's mature style, the style of *Conversazione in Sicilia,* is an effort to find the verbal equivalent of certain emotions. The narrator's disclaimer that the furies are "not what he wants to tell about" we may take as an artistic feint, a tactic to direct the reader's attention to the surface of the narrative before it is led to what is underneath. This is the real meaning of Vittorini's statement that poetry "does not remain tied to the things from which it originated" and "can be related, if it is born out of pain, to any pain."

Yet the view that Vittorini is a regionalist is not entirely unsound. Sicily is used as a major setting in only two of his novels,

Conversazione in Sicilia and *La Garibaldina*. But underlying his whole work there is a matrix of personal experience: the abandonment of primitive Sicily for an urban north, and a later attempt to recover this innocence and primitivism of his youth. The finest tale of the early collection *Piccola borghesia* is about a Sicilian boy who, in the middle of the war in Gorizia, plays with his northern cousins at games of the Wild West and Mato Grosso. *Viaggio in Sardegna* five years later is a slightly ironic search for the primitive, the poetic, in another island resembling Sicily; in fact when he reissued the book in 1952 he retitled it *Sardegna come un'infanzia*. This search is simply objectified, fictionalized, in *Conversazione in Sicilia*. In Vittorini's work there is always the implication of a kind of geographical polarity: on the one hand the north, cities, civilization, white collars, books, intellectualism; on the other hand the south, the land, wine, sunshine, the basic and primitive elements of existence. Fascism he associates with the north, even though fascist policemen and bureaucrats (Baffi and Senza Baffi in *Conversazione in Sicilia*) are often southerners. The "screaming newspaper placards" are of the city; fascism in made out of paper, it takes over the apparatus of the city and civilization and uses it as a weapon against the country. Vittorini's origins were small town and petty bourgeois, and in spite of his bridge-building experience he never quite made the transition to the proletariat. The workers are ostensibly the heroes of his Resistance novel *Uomini e no* and of the "Autobiografia in tempo di guerra," but his deepest emotions are always tied to childhood, to Sicily, to the sea and sun. This is precisely the difficulty with his leftist or "collectivist" fiction: the tension between the outward political apparatus and his innermost emotions is unresolved. In *Viaggio in Sardegna*, an extremely revealing book, he begins what is ostensibly a travelogue by confessing, "I know the joy of spending a summer afternoon reading a book of adventure half-naked in a chaise-longue, by a house on a hillside overlooking the sea. And many other joys as well: of being hidden in a garden and listening to the wind barely moving the leaves (the highest ones) of a tree; or of hearing in the sand infinite sand-existences crumble and fall; or of getting up before dawn in a world of chickens, and swimming, alone in all the water in the world, by a pink beach."[6] These are not precisely the joys of a dedicated revolutionist. Vittorini's retreat into primitivism is analogous to Pavese's; and like Pavese's, it is a retreat that the political part of him regarded as a kind of betrayal. The tension is apparent in his whole work and especially in the badly unresolved conflicting themes of *Le donne di Messina*.

In short, Vittorini's career as a writer is in some respects an unfortunate case of mistaken identity. At a certain point in his life, regarding himself as a poet in the most technical sense of the term and addressing himself to purely poetic problems, he produced a single novel that transformed the Italian literary scene to a greater degree, probably, than any other book of his generation. But he was able to maintain this purity only during a brief period of his life, the ten years or so that came to a climax in 1942. The years before 1932 are apprentice years, devoted to learning his craft against the tremendous handicaps of his lack of education. And with *Uomini e no* in 1945, and perhaps even earlier, with the "autobiographical" fragments written during the war, he turned from this poetic vocation to the problem of *littérature engagée,* to the attempt to make a "collective novel" that would reconcile the individual and political elements in his own nature. By 1946 he had practically abandoned fiction to devote himself to political questions as editor of *Politecnico.* But the true artist is "engaged" only with the problems generated by his own nature as an artist. If these are political, as in Malraux, or metaphysical, as in Kafka, then pursuing such problems is a necessary condition of his own fulfillment. If the artist's innermost nature is not political then it is impractical to impose a political framework on his talent; abstract furies are difficult to collectivise. Basically Vittorini turned from individualism to the political novel, and to the political activism of the *Politecnico* period, not out of inward impulse but out of conscience, which is not precisely the same thing. It can be argued that there are cases in which the voice of one's own nature, the voice of his identity, should take precedence even over conscience. But this is primarily a moral question rather than one lying within the realm of literary criticism. Insofar as Vittorini is to be criticized and judged as a novelist, the matter to be considered is the way this decision affected the technical quality of his fiction.

The Apprenticeship

Vittorini's knowledge of literature before 1927 came solely from private reading, and it was a kind of reading that was wide-ranging and highly selective. Precisely because he was not obliged to read everything, as a student or professional critic might, he read only what appealed to his special curiosity. One of his early personal discoveries was Svevo. Probably he had read all three of Svevo's novels before he began writing fiction himself; by 1930, the era of the first stories, he had contributed an article on Svevo's *Una vita* to *Solaria*. In 1931 his *Solaria* stories, along with some previously unpublished pieces, were collected in the volume *Piccola borghesia*.° Most of the fiction in this first book lies heavily under the influence of Svevo. Three of the stories center around the same Svevesque character: Adolfo Marsanich, a prefecture employee in a provincial city that is obviously Trieste although it is never named. The events and objects of these stories are almost entirely things that Vittorini had read about rather than known at first hand. He had spent some time in the Venezia Giulia as a bridge-worker, but he had never lived in Trieste and there was nothing in his experience—except his reading of Svevo—to give him any special knowledge of what went on in a provincial bureaucracy. These three stories ("Quindici minuti di ritardo," "Educazione di Adolfo," and "Raffiche in Prefettura")† are antibourgeois satires of a considerable cleverness, detached in manner and told with a certain hard and ironic precision. But there is nothing in them to suggest the highly personal style of Vittorini that was to emerge shortly. Like Proust's *Pastiches et mélanges*, they are imitations of a literary influence that serve simultaneously as a means of assimilating the influence and a declaration of independence from it. The effect of this encounter with Svevo is scarcely detectable in Vittorini's later work.

"La signora della stazione"‡ is more promising. The style is still realistic in the nineteenth-century manner and there is little of Vittorini's personal flavor in it, but for the first time the theme is one that lies at the heart of Vittorini's work: north and south, city vs Sicilian primitivism. The autobiographical element is rather elaborately disguised; the protagonist is a woman and not a man, she is of a different social class from Vittorini, and she goes from Trieste to Sicily instead of from Sicily to Udine. But her experience is essentially a discovery of Sicily that is also the discovery of sexual maturity and sensualism, a kind of concealed allegory of Vittorini's own youth. Norma, the young Triestine signora of the story, marries a railway official who is transferred to a station in a remote Sicilian village. For her husband, the *capostazione* Sebastiano, she feels a vague and confused affection but little real passion. The deeper urge of her nature is a nostalgia for the make-believe world of the past, the exotic and improbable realm of her childhood reading. "From those far-off times memories that were somehow tropical

° Roughly "Lower Middle Class"; equivalent to the French *petite bourgeoisie*.

† "Fifteen Minutes Late," "Education of Adolf," and "Squalls in the Prefecture."

‡ "The Lady of the Station."

came to her and she imagined that she had really lived, there by the fountain of life, among green birds and fabulous plants, in some America, on some Malayan isle or in the idyll of Paul and Virginia."[7] And a little later: "The station with the desert all around it, the gleaming rails, the long endless line of prickly-pears beside which a man walked blinded by the sun, carrying his coat and a spade on his back, sometimes provoked in her suddenly the perplexity of a child and she understood that in just such a moment that other sun of her childhood had struck her. Perhaps this Sicilian sun too, by the railroad track, would remain in her memory."[8] The elements of Vittorini's own experience are here: Sicily is connected with childhood, with the sun, but also with the exoticism of Robinson Crusoe, an evocation of a literary experience as much as a real one. Why should Norma imagine that the Sicilian sun "would remain in her memory?" Her hypothetical projection into the future is Vittorini's own projection backwards. In Sicily as a boy he read *Robinson Crusoe;* in the north he remembered the sun. And his attempt to recover Sicily, as he expresses it later in *Conversazione in Sicilia,* is simultaneously a geographical journey and a literary pilgrimage to the reading of his youth. Norma imagines "running away to a desert island" with the servant Lauretta. There they would live on figs and parrots and, accompanied by the phonograph they would bring along, sing "like real Negroes" a song full of the simplicity and poetry of America— "I can't give you anything but love."[9] In the end she goes off with Lauretta to gather snails.

In the light of Vittorini's later work the most significant of these *Piccola borghesia* pieces is the tale "La mia guerra."* Again there is the distortion of autobiography characteristic of both Pavese and Vittorini before they arrive at a frank expression of their personal dramas. The story is set in Gorizia, which Vittorini knew well from his bridge-building days, but it takes place in 1915-16 before he had left Sicily. It is the first of his stories to be narrated in the first person, but instead of the "confession" style of Svevo's Zeno the tone is that of the nostalgic recollection of childhood by an adult narrator. This narrator is a persona of the author—who was twenty-three when the story was published—and his account begins when he was seven, exactly Vittorini's age at the outbreak of the war. In other words "La mia guerra" is a kind of conjecture of what might have happened if Vittorini had gone north at seven instead of at seventeen. When the narrator-as-child is taken to live with his merchant grandfather and uncles in Gorizia (his father is a railroad employee

* "My War."

"obliged to live in certain little country stations in Calabria or Sicily or I don't know where"[10]) he is cut off by the war and obliged to stay until the city is liberated the following year.

Outwardly this is all that happens in the story. But the narration is not consecutive or sequential in any ordinary way. The method is impressionistic: the child sees the events of the war as a confused and diverting kaleidoscope, and this is the way they are presented to the reader. The first sentence conveys his bafflement, even years later, over his recollection of the events: "Seven years old: why in the world wasn't I going to school?"[11] In the confusion, the danger, the anxiety of the siege of Gorizia by the Italian army the children are left to their own devices. To them the cataclysm around them is merely a new game—"the game of war"—a phrase that would serve as a good title for a translation of the story. When the child is carried onto the balcony to see the cannons, the hillside swarming with men, he is afraid "for a whole evening." But quickly his fear is gone; in the dark and cavernous storeroom of his grandfather's shop he is soon playing cowboys and Indians with his cousins. It is in these passages of childish make-believe that Vittorini breaks out for the first time into something like his mature style, the style of *Conversazione in Sicilia.*

> Will I ever forget that long vaulted chamber, that smelled of stable and jungle and echoed with hoofbeats, with pirate boardings, with little cries of apes and parrots? With chicken-feathers in our hair cousin Boris and I quickly declared overselves enemies. Emilietta would be our prize; and was; we took turns at kidnapping and made her stay hidden, sometimes, in a packing-box for long pretended ambushes; hailing her queen of the Far West, queen of the Mato Grosso, the realms where Boris twirled the lasso and I waited at the pass to shoot with my Winchester the tiger with the eagle-beak and the rattle-snake-tail.[12]

This passage is closer to poetry than to conventional prose fiction. The punctuation is crucial: the comma after "chamber," the semicolon instead of a period after "was," do not correspond to any conventional idea of phrasing in either Italian or English. The effect is that of a kind of breathless childish rush; the narrator mentions the chamber, then after a faint pause (the comma) remembers its odor. "Emilietta would be our prize"—again there is a pause marked by the semicolon, and he seems to think of something to add, a detail —"and was." Was it Far West or Mato Grosso? The memories are jumbled together in a sequence that follows the narrator's associations rather than the chronology of events. And finally the ending, rising to a somewhat too tremoring climax, like an operatic aria: Vittorini had not yet perceived the analogy, but it was to provide the aesthetics of *Conversazione in Sicilia* a decade later.

*Viaggio in Sardegna** was written in about a month toward the end of 1932, "with a vivid pleasure in the writing, that is with perfect abandon to do the things to be said,"[13] but published in volume form only in 1936. The actual visit to Sardinia reported in the book evidently took place only slightly before the writing. This travel book, ostensibly factual, is actually a logical step in the coalescing of Vittorini's fiction technique. Regarded as a verbal construction with certain aesthetic aims, it is artistically organized to a much higher degree than most of the stories in *Piccola borghesia*. There is a striking parallel to another travel book Vittorini may have known: D. H. Lawrence's *Sea and Sardinia* (1921). In each case the visit to Sardinia is the stuff out of which the book is made, but it is not the real subject of the book. For Lawrence the real subject is a cult of elementalism that is fundamentally sexual: the blood in rebellion against the intellect. The chief difference between the two books is that these sexual implications are lacking in Vittorini. The reason for this is undoubtedly that for Vittorini Sardinia is the recovery of childhood, the discovery of self in childhood, and childhood is a time in which sexual experience is very largely submerged or unconscious. The discovery of self in childhood is at the same time the rediscovery of the primitive and genuine, the reconciliation with the earth. To whom does this happen exactly? One of the ways in which *Viaggio in Sardegna* anticipates *Conversazione in Sicilia* is that the narrator has a voice but no real identity. We never learn his name, his profession, the color of his eyes or hair. His reactions are so subjective, so intimately personal, that he gives the impression of speaking to himself. For this reason we are obliged to *become* the narrator in a highly empathetic way in order to make our way through the book. What happens to him happens to us. He is simply "I," "myself," author-persona and reader simultaneously. From the upper citadel of Cagliari he looks down on the streets of the city.

> At this hour they are deserted. The sun has slid behind a cloud and doesn't come out, because the cloud is stuck on a mountain. But the sky is still clear, in a kind of damp way, as on certain days when it is raining in the distance. I have the feeling of being alone, for the moment, in the whole Castello. From the city below rise the bleats of automobiles and the hum of the

* "A Trip to Sardinia."

crowd and more than ever, in my distance from the world, I have the feeling of being alone, in this necropolis.[14]

The delicately balanced punctuation of "La mia guerra" is here, and the essentially poetic and fantastic imagination (the "cloud stuck on a mountain"). In addition Vittorini uses for the first time another device of his mature style: the repetition or echoing of a phrase, sometimes with slight variations. Again it is a usage that any conventional writing teacher would correct; "I have the feeling of being alone" ("Mi sembra di essere solo") is repeated twice in successive sentences. This kind of echoing occurs in private thoughts but not in formal speech, at least not in the kind of ordered dialogue found in old-fashioned novels. In all of Vittorini's mature work the language is inward, subjective, rather than outward and logical. The echoing also resembles the repetition of motif in music, another anticipation of the "operatic novel" *Conversazione in Sicilia*. Giovanni Cecchetti calls this "the style of repetition and rebound" and connects it to Vittorini's American influences.[15] But the device is actually part of a quite personal rhetoric that Vittorini was working out for himself somewhat before his encounter with the Americans. There is no doubt that in the mid-Thirties he was powerfully impressed with American fiction and especially with Steinbeck and Saroyan. But he probably did not encounter either of these writers until around 1935, while *Viaggio in Sardegna* was conceived and written in 1932. If it is necessary to find an "American" book in Vittorini's work a better case can be made for *Uomini e no* (1945), which shows evidence of a strong Hemingway influence.

Viaggio in Sardegna gives the impression of going out of its way to avoid being specific, to avoid being a travel book. The effect is heightened by the altered title Vittorini provided for the new edition in 1952: *Sardegna come un'infanzia*, Sardinia regarded not geographically or touristically but quite subjectively "as a childhood." There is not very much information about how Sardinians make their living or what their colorful costumes are like, and when the narrator goes into a museum it is only to remark that he is not an archeologist and has no comment to make on the contents. The mysterious prehistoric *nuraghi* that every tourist inspects are to him only heaps of stones, interesting perhaps if they evoke certain emotions of the primitive. For the ordinary tourist the impressions of travel impinge superficially on the consciousness and then immediately reemerge in the form of trite comments on people, customs, and manners. For Vittorini, or for his narrator, the impressions penetrate inward and stay there, to provoke quite private reactions.

Instead of facts and steamer schedules the book begins with a kind of lyric poem that, arranged in lines, would look something like Montale. "I know what it means to be happy in life—it's the gift of existence, the taste of the passing hour and the things around you, sitting quietly, the gift of loving them, these things, and smoking, and a woman among them."[16] The entire book is written in the reflexive that makes it so easy to blur the line between the personal and the general in Italian. "Si va in giro per le vie disabitate"—but who wanders through the deserted streets? the narrator? "one?" the reader? or is this merely *what happens* in Sardinia, the Sardinian way of experience? The sensations are simply left hanging in the air. When human beings appear they are almost as depersonalized as the narrator himself: they are "someone," a line of women, a man in a doorway. Sometimes they are disembodied to the point of invisibility, their existence indicated only by the sound of an axe from a forest. The Sardinians have no faces; they consist of temperaments, emotions, modes of behavior. In the town of Tempio "one eats" in a tavern with "people of the place" who offer hospitality to the strangers and refuse to let them pay for anything. And Tempio in some mysterious way passes the word to Castelsardo, and Castelsardo to Sassari, and Sassari to Macomer, so that the guests are passed along through an invisible machinery of which they are hardly aware. This provokes a generalization about the primitive character. "Like all people who remain primitive at heart the Sardinians cherish this cult: a man cannot go about freely in their land without their finding out about it and making him an object of hospitality to be passed from hand to hand."[17] There is no mention in the book of another well-known Sardinian "cult": that of vendetta. Even thirty years later, in the countryside around Orgosola, the practice of family revenge, the ritual murder that provokes other murders in return, was deeply rooted in spite of everything the carabinieri and the provincial government could do to eradicate it. But Vittorini does not venture into this darker side of the primitive. He has not yet made, and in fact never makes, Pavese's discovery that the elementalism of the countryside is fatally attached to cruelty.

It hardly follows from this that Pavese's view is sounder, or that Vittorini is failing in some way to take account of the facts. Neither Pavese nor Vittorini is an anthropologist; their reactions are totally subjective and for them the "facts" are only starting points for emotions. For Pavese the country represented earth, blood, a mysterious primitive energy that led inexorably to violence. For Vittorini it represented the innocence of his childhood. Like all childhoods this

"Sardinia come un'infanzia" was not entirely blissful in its innocence, and it was essentially egotistical: inward-feeling rather than reaching outward to others. But it was a state in which the touch with primary things—sea, sun, food, the intimacy of one's own body—had not yet been blurred by the contact with civilization. In Cagliari the crowd in a piazza is "absolutely directionless, nervous, irrational, exclamatory; almost infantile."[18] But it is a crowd "nervously" in contact with its immediate sensory impressions, drawn this way and that by streetlights, intimate with the stone walls, excited by the darkness. And the naiveté, even the infantilism, of the impressions corresponds to the deliberate and highly poetic "naiveté" of the style. "And I understand this," the last chapter concludes, "that Sardinia for me is ended, that I will never possess it again, that it has passed forever into the time of my existence. If I happen to think of it now it is like an experience already distant, a kind of war inside me, or a love, that can never be repeated."[19] For Vittorini the artist this experience was part of the formation that led, not only to the themes, but to the style and poetic mode of *Conversazione in Sicilia.*

Vittorini's first novel *Il garofano rosso** has a somewhat complicated publication history. He began writing it in Florence in 1932, in his *Solaria* period and roughly about the same time as the composition of *Viaggio in Sardegna.* The first installment of the novel appeared in the *Solaria* issue of February 1933. By the time this issue actually appeared, in March, Vittorini was away on a trip to Milan. It was evidently not his first visit to the city that later became his home, but it was one that made a powerful and in fact a permanent impression on him.

> If I ever write my autobiography I will explain what a great importance this trip to Milan had for me. I came back enamored of places and names, of the world itself, as I had never been before except in my childhood. This state of mind had not come of itself; I had sought it out. Yet it came in an extraordinary way, after a period of five or six years during which it seemed to me that not since I was a child had I had spontaneous relations with the maternal things of the earth. It came at a time when I looked only to the past, when I wrote with my eyes to the rear.[20]

This passage is from the preface that Vittorini provided for *Il garofano rosso* when it finally appeared in volume form in 1948. The

---

* *The Red Carnation* (New Directions, 1952).

preface is a document of considerable importance, not only as a source of facts about the origin of the novel but as a guide to Vittorini's whole development in the period between *Il garofano rosso* and *Conversazione in Sicilia*. When he came back from Milan "enamored of places and names" *Il garofano rosso* was about half finished. Committed to *Solaria* for the remaining installments, he went on writing it. But he now found it difficult to take up "the things, the people, that had slipped away from me, in which I no longer believed."[21] Some kind of artistic reorientation or conversion had taken place in his attitude toward his writing. Meanwhile the serialization of the novel in *Solaria* was causing trouble with the censors; the third installment resulted in the seizure of the issue. The remaining installments were eventually published in *Solaria,* but the results were satisfactory to nobody. The censors were displeased with the novel for one reason and Vittorini for another, and the public received it profoundly mutilated by censorship. In the case of both Vittorini and the censors the dissatisfaction lay not with the heart of the book but with its superficial narrative surface: the characters, social milieu, and setting. The censors were "annoyed" (their own term; the book was officially judged *noioso alla censura*) because it dealt with the youth of the early fascist period and portrayed them in a manner other than the regime wanted Italian youth to be portrayed. Vittorini was dissatisfied first of all because, after the final installment appeared in *Solaria,* he had gone to work and removed the "annoying" parts in the hope of getting the novel published in volume form. This hope was futile; it was four years before the manuscript returned from Rome, and then it came back definitely rejected. But there were other and deeper reasons for Vittorini's dissatisfaction. On the surface at least the novel is about *liceo* students in a seaside city resembling Viareggio or Genoa. The milieu is upper middle class, the talk is of books and professors, the theme of sexual initiation is complicated by intellectual factors. None of this corresponded to Vittorini's own experience. This "falsity" would not be a matter of importance unless the writer considered it to be a matter of importance, but Vittorini did consider it so.

> I was twenty-five when I wrote it, or rather when I began it. I was still fond of shuffling the cards around and playing games on the reader. So, under the pretext of artistic invention, I tried to draw a "myself" that did not correspond to my actual self and a story that did not correspond to my story. There is no harm in this in itself; there is nothing wrong with presenting a

set of observed or imagined incidents in autobiographical form. But, in portraying myself as a *liceo* student, when I had actually gone to a technical school, and attributing bourgeois origins to myself whereas the relatives I had to make do with were actually poor devils of workers, peasants, or minor employees, I mixed up the characteristics of one environment with those of another, the mentality of one environment with that of another, the mood of one environment with that of another: and if the reader is going to consider the book as a document he needs to know this in order to draw the proper conclusions.[22]

This gets exactly at the heart of the difficulty. Not only the setting of this novel but the ambience and style of most of the *Piccola borghesia* stories were distractions in the main line of his development, attempts to be "literary" in a way that, for a time, he imagined fiction ought to be literary. In the middle of *Il garofano rosso* the Milan trip had reminded him that good writing, his writing, ought to be about "maternal things of the earth," matters that concerned him at the deepest level of his own nature. Furthermore in Vittorini's fiction the style is always a reflection of the initial impetus that led to the writing. In *Viaggio in Sardegna* and in one story of *Piccola borghesia*, "La mia guerra," the impetus was the nostalgia for his childhood and the effort to recover the spiritual state of this childhood, and the style corresponded. In the preface to *Il garofano rosso* he spoke of the pleasure he had taken in writing *Viaggio in Sardegna*, a pleasure connected to the "very narrow limits of the little thing I had inside me then."[23] This problem of "taking pleasure in writing," the belief that only material written with pleasure is a valid and genuine expression of one's self, is fundamental to Vittorini's aesthetic and one of the concepts he shares with Moravia and Pavese. The trouble with *Il garofano rosso* was exactly that it cost him cold sweat and was "marred by the nonpleasure of writing it."[24] This nonpleasure was connected to the style, and the style in turn was connected to the narrative matter of the book, the bourgeois and *liceo* setting. It was for this reason, as he explained in 1948, that no amount of revision or tinkering with technical details could get at the basic difficulty of the novel.

In its final form, as published in volume in 1948, *Il garofano rosso* is a realistic-psychological novel more or less in the tradition of the *Bildungsroman;* in such matters as its treatment of the theme of sacred and profane love it resembles typical examples of the genre like Hesse's *Demian*. It shows no visible mark of Svevo or any of the American influences in Vittorini's formation. Technically it is a kind of distillation or lowest common denominator of the European psychological novel: Proust, Lawrence, Maupassant, Hesse, Alain Fournier, Dostoevski. The protagonist Alessio Mainardi can only very generally be connected to any identity of the author. His generality, in fact, is the chief quality of his character; he simply represents youth, an abstract personification of youth, superficially installed in an upper middle-class Italian setting. The plot turns around four characters arranged in a highly symmetrical way. The *liceo* student Mainardi has an adolescent infatuation for Giovanna, the daughter of a colonel. He confesses this love to his friend Tarquinio, who is older than he is and a bad student in school, and Tarquinio in turn tells Mainardi about his encounter with the somewhat mysterious courtesan Zobeida (Vittorini in his preface calls her "the lady of easy virtue but not exactly a prostitute"[25]). This quadrilateral arrangement of lovers might serve as a framework for a Boiardo or Ariosto, for a piece of elegant Baroque tinsel. It is in the working-out of the plot that the modern psychologism comes in. As the novel proceeds a switching of the two couples takes place: Tarquinio seduces Giovanna and callously shows his friend the stained handkerchief of his achievement, and Mainardi meanwhile drifts into an obsessive relationship with Zobeida. Tarquinio obviously represents the grosser and more physical part of a single identity of which Mainardi is the other and more spiritual half. In the same way the two women of the novel are aspects of a single feminine principle. Tarquinio himself explains the symmetry to Mainardi in a letter that might be a passage from Hesse.

> You say you don't want me to speak to you of Zobeida? Curious! Perhaps you're afraid that your father might read my letters? Or does it make you angry and jealous that the possibility of a Zobeida exists for me? In that case, do you know what you are? You're a terrible egotist. You have Giovanna with everything that Giovanna signifies for you and you want Zobeida as well. Or perhaps you separate the two things in your mind and imagine it's natural to need a Zobeida too. But if I were you I wouldn't divide the two things. I would think of Giovanna as I now think of Zobeida, expecting from her what I expect from Zobeida.[26]

"Don't be horrified," he adds. But it is exactly this horror that lurks in the path of youth, the revulsion against merging profane and sacred love into one. This part of the novel is precise if not very original. The imagery or symbolic apparatus that supports this conflict is even more conventional. The flower of the title, a carnation that Giovanna gives to Mainardi, recalls Dumas' *La dame aux camélias;* it falls into the hands of Zobeida, she refuses to give it back and in this way "captures" that part of Mainardi's inner life he was cherishing in tribute to Giovanna, and so on. At the end of the novel the stained handkerchief is a second "flower" that stands in apposition to the carnation: just as Giovanna's innocence is appropriated by Zobeida, Zobeida's sensuality is imposed on the girl who is her symmetric opposite. Zobeida is exalted and "purified" through her possession of the symbolic flower, and Giovanna is degraded through Tarquinio's possession of the handkerchief. And just as both males are made complete by this double encounter, both women are made complete females, combining in their natures the spiritual and the sensual.

Underlying this romantic-psychological plot is a political theme, or the suggestion of one. The *liceo* professors are liberals, their students fascists. There are allusions to Rosa Luxemburg, to Liebknecht, to the murder of the Socialist deputy Matteotti in 1924 by the fascists. One of the more ingenious or original aspects of the novel is the effort to connect this theme to the sexual. Wearing Giovanna's carnation in his buttonhole, Mainardi is jokingly accused by Tarquinio of having joined the liberal Sword of Justice movement. Turning "red with anger," Mainardi tells him, "I wish you were another Matteotti and I'd make you understand."[27] But Tarquinio is right; Mainardi is at the bottom a "romantic avenger," and his sexual frustrations are connected to the violence of his politics. Repressed, bottled-up, falsified by bourgeois values, the sexuality of Mainardi's generation is translated to dreams of violence. Fascism has killed Matteotti, that is fascism has killed *someone,* and it is in the hope of sharing in this virility that Mainardi takes to the streets in a demonstration and finds himself smashing away at a crowd of middle-aged people with his fists. Then all at once he has the feeling that everything is "spoiled, pointless," and goes with Tarquinio into a cinema that offers "a more convincing whiff of death and ferocity."[28] The attempt to arrive at maturity through violence, through a sexually flavored sadism, has ended in a regression into childhood.

This incident is related in a diary that carries the story forward intermittently in the manner of Gide. Another long chapter consists of letters from Tarquinio to Mainardi, an attempt to solve the technical problem of conveying Tarquinio's thoughts in a narrative related quite subjectively by Mainardi. A similar function is performed by Giovanna's friend, called *la levatrice* or the midwife, who serves as a kind of messenger or emissary of Giovanna in a way something like that of the neoclassic drama (it is necessary for Giovanna herself to be kept in the background for technical reasons, in order for a suitable awe to be generated). These devices are brought up, used as needed, and then retired from the novel, sometimes rather awkwardly. The novel gives the impression of being threatened by a chronic crisis of point of view: will Mainardi be able to tell the story himself, with the aid of diaries, letters, and the midwife, or will the apparatus break down? It never does quite break down, and sometimes Mainardi, forgetting that he is a character in a novel, tells his story with a considerable eloquence. He is particularly good on his relations with his family. The father is a minor capitalist who owns a brick factory, and when Mainardi goes home on his vacation there is an interlude that is a kind of premonition of the homecoming in *Conversazione in Sicilia*. Even though the industrialist father and the middle-class mother are not Vittorini's parents, parents are parents and the emotions are fundamentally the same. Independence strives with the filial instinct, affection with rebellion. Confined to his room without supper because he has failed his exams, Mainardi hears the same noise of plates and spoons that had "taken his breath away"[29] when he was sick as a child. This return to childhood is suggested also in his attitude toward his father's workmen. The father's own attitude toward the workmen is fairly clearly indicated when he threatens to make the boy work in the kilns if he does not do better in his studies. The brick factory is a kind of penitentiary; why, then, are some men condemned to it permanently? Mainardi questions his father about this quite naively, and is surprised to learn that the father was once a socialist.

> "What!" I said. "You were a socialist and you aren't any more?"
>
> "My boy," said my father without looking at me because he knew certainly that his glance would have established between us the permanent gulf of a reproach, "socialism is an idea and anyone can have his ideas. In fact it's a generous idea and anyone in my situation can very well have been generous on occasion. But, in the end, everyone has to save himself in life."
>
> "Oh!" I exclaimed, "then you save yourself . . . at the expense of others who are lost?"
>
> I hardly knew what I meant, in my confusion, but my child's logic had come spontaneously to me, the logic I felt fluttering inside me like a creature with wings, and which I trembled for in the fear it might be forbidden.

My father continued not to look at me. He was in one of his indulgent moments and my logic was nestling there inside me, half reassured.

"Good heavens! They're not entirely lost . . ." my father said.[30]

This "child's logic," with its fluttering wings, suggests a tentative metaphor for the "abstract furies" of *Conversazione in Sicilia*. Passages like this, that seem to transcend the superficial setting and move toward the center of Vittorini's own private conscience, are the best part of *Il garofano rosso*. The difficulties, apart from the basically unsatisfactory nature of the setting, are structural: the crisis of point of view, the creaking narrative apparatus, the fear that the story will die if not kept going in some way by piling document on document. But these are the problems always facing the writer who moves from the story form to the novel, and in coming to grips with them for the first time Vittorini had at least taken a large step toward solving them. His own critical view of the novel, in the 1948 preface, is in part unjustified. Certain themes—not the banal device of sacred and profane love, but the narrator's mixture of curiosity and sympathy for the workmen, for example, and the sexual undertones in the "emotion" of fascism—are presented with a considerable subtlety. And for the serious student of Vittorini's development the novel is of interest as a kind of workbook or anthology of technical exercises, an attempt to master the superficial form of the novel before going on to *Conversazione in Sicilia*. In this way, questions of quality aside, it performs a function similar to Joyce's *Portrait of the Artist* in preparing the way for *Ulysses*. Finally, the very mistakes of this novel, and Vittorini's attempts to grapple with the mistakes, give us an invaluable insight into his development as an artist. He himself described *Il garofano rosso* as "constructed to be lived in, and by all the rules."[31] But after this first novel lay behind him he began to grasp that the rules for a work of art must come from inside the artist, and not from outside in something he has read.

A Marxist Fairy Tale

The unfinished novel fragment *Erica e i suoi fratelli*,* like much of Vittorini's fiction, has a rather complicated publication history. It was written in the early part of 1936, shortly before he turned to the

* Published in English as *Erica* in the volume *The Dark and the Light* (New Directions, 1960). In this usage *fratelli*, like the English "siblings," includes both brothers and sisters.

more important *Conversazione in Sicilia.* A fragment was published in 1938 by Pratolini in his *Campo di Marte,* and a somewhat longer excerpt in a literary almanac edited by Giansiro Ferrata in 1939. The complete text appeared only in 1954, in Moravia and Carocci's *Nuovi Argomenti,* and was published by Bompiani two years later in volume with the short novel *La Garibaldina.* According to Vittorini's account it was the outbreak of the Spanish War in July 1936 that brought the work on *Erica* to a standstill. But in later years he also recognized that this personal and political crisis was also involved with a crisis of novelistic technique. When the definitive version of *Erica* was finally published in *Nuovi Argomenti* he explained, "The way I am accustomed to narrating, from *Conversazione* on, is not exactly the same way in which this story is told. Today I am accustomed to conveying the feelings and thoughts of characters solely through their external manifestations. It isn't natural any more for me to write that so-and-so 'felt' a certain thing or 'thought' a certain thing. It seems artificial to me. Whereas in writing this book it was still natural (as it was in *Piccola borghesia,* in *Sardegna,* in *Il garofano rosso*) to say directly what a character felt and thought. As a result the book is a network of 'she feels' and 'she thinks,' of 'she felt' and 'she thought.' "[32]

Like many of Vittorini's theoretical comments on his work, this is a somewhat oversimplified view of a rather complicated technical problem. *Erica* is not really as conventional as his comment implies; in some respects it is a unique experiment, not only in Vittorini's work but in the whole of modern Italian fiction. It somewhat resembles certain of the persecuted-child stories of Katherine Mansfield, the ones in which English girls are sent to work as governesses in terrible German families. But the difficulty is precisely that Vittorini is not Katherine Mansfield, that the character of Erica is too far from his own temperament and emotions. By 1936 he had begun to regard the novel as a basically autobiographical vehicle, one in which the total personality and emotional experience of the maker were expressed. This is the reason for his dissatisfaction with "she thought" and "she felt"; what was important to Vittorini by 1936 was a total identification and merging of the reader's consciousness with the character's, and this could be achieved only through a technique of the utmost purity, one in which the author offers no comment or explanation on the unrolling of the action. If the protagonist or author-persona is to have emotions these must be externalized in the form of peripheral objects or characters, as they are in *Conversazione in Sicilia.* In Vittorini's later fiction the protagonist virtually disappears as a concrete and visible character; he is refined away until he becomes simply the consciousness of author and reader, a network of receptivities.

It is in this sense that *Erica*, in contrast to *Conversazione in Sicilia*, is relatively conventional. The central character is a girl of fourteen and the story is seen entirely from her viewpoint, although it is told grammatically in the third person. The unnamed city of the action is evidently Milan. Erica lives in a squalid working-class flat with her mother, her father who is an ironworker, and a brother and sister. Once again Vittorini returns to the nostalgia for childhood that preoccupies him from the time of the *Piccola borghesia* stories. The world Erica imagines in her private reveries is a kind of quasi-Sicilian Eden: "Often she dreamed of grapes, grapes of a delicate color, yellow frosted with cold, and grapes not to eat but to live in. There were fair woods with invisible birds singing, and globes of fruit that you could enter into and become happy. She was alone in a globe, but she knew that it was the same for everybody, and she felt a melodious certainty of company."[33] This passage from the first page of the novel is somewhat more significant, or more imagistically economical, than it seems on first reading. The word "company," for example, is to become one of the pivotal images of the novel and is here introduced for the first time. Erica's deepest longing is for *compagnia*, for a kinship, an understanding a communication with others. Earlier, as a young child, she has found this in her family. But the family disintegrates, the father loses his job and goes away to the mountains to work, the mother follows him, and Erica is left alone with her sister and brother. The *compagnia* becomes the house which is now her own, and the neighbors and shopkeepers who at first seem friendly to her. But these too betray her as her mother has; her cornmeal is stolen, the butcher and the baker refuse to give her credit. Her last *compagnia* is that of sex; at the end of the novel, or of the fragment as Vittorini left it, she has fallen passively and almost somnambulistically into prostitution. Insofar as the reasons for this are economic, the novel is a classic Marxist presentation of "vice." Her parents abandon her because poverty overcomes their natural instincts, because the father has been driven to the wall by capitalistic factory owners. The natural compassion of the neighbors and shopkeepers is submerged by their avarice. Erica sells herself not out of vanity or sensuality but simply in order to avoid starving to death; she is so far from taking pleasure in her profession that it seems to her "the repeated wounding of a wound that could never . . . come together and heal itself."[34] Yet when she buys a can of sardines with her meager coins she tells the shopkeeper, not without pride, "It's money that I've earned."[35]

But underneath this Marxist pseudo-structure, a parable of economic determinism that might have been invented by Zola, is another and somewhat more subtle structure. In the early scenes of the novel, when Erica is still seven or eight, her mother reads fairy tales to her. Soon she begins to understand that she has poor parents, exactly like the children in some of these stories. "And she began observing her mother and father with suspicion, she began to fear that they would become evil. From the stories she knew that poor parents do become evil, and carry off their children into the woods and abandon them there. And she began listening to what they talked about."[36] When this thematic thread is traced out the whole novel becomes a kind of retelling of *Hansel and Gretel*. But it is a fairy tale in which the wickedness of the parents is not simply a fixed premise that must be accepted, a *donnée;* it is a fairy tale in which the wickedness of the parents is explained and even in a certain sense justified in economic terms. The characterization of the mother, although it is sketched in the simplest of lines, is remarkably intricate. She feels a kind of instinctive animal maternalism toward her children, but resents this feeling in herself and reserves her overt affections chiefly for her husband; Erica notices that she laughs and is animated only when the father comes home. When the wages are reduced, when the father loses his job, when there is nothing to eat in the house, Erica hears her lamenting, "If only we didn't have these children."[37] Hunger hangs over the house like a nightmare. But even in hunger, Erica reflects, there can be *compagnia;* hunger is nothing to that other horror of being abandoned in the woods for the wolves to eat. *Homo homini lupus:* the wolves are the respectable petty bourgeois neighbors of the quarter. These include the minor tax official and his wife for whom the mother works at washing dishes before she abandons her family: a husband with an eggplant-colored hat, the wife "a kind of big-bellied child in a flowered robe, who sat on the sofa and sang soft words from *Traviata,* accompanying herself on the mandolin."[38] (*Traviata,* it should be noted, is an opera that romanticizes prostitution.) Vittorini's politics fluctuate over the course of his long career, but he is always solidly antibourgeois. As soon as these people realize that Erica is helpless they turn and rend her limb from limb, or try to; and yet they do so in the name of charity. Even when they steal her cornmeal they manage in some way to make it seem like kindness. They are the witches of the fairy tale, the ones who set a child to spinning a whole room full of wool in a day or be eaten alive, and yet at the same time they insist on their moral superiority.

If one of the big-bellied women, for example, had made her spin so much wool in a day it would not have been wickedness. For one of them, one of the "ladies" of the husbands with eggplant-colored hats, or one of the other women, it would never be wicked to give a child a mountain of wool to spin, or something like it, or worse. It would have been a kindness on their part. They would have said, "Do you see how kind we are to give you all this wool to spin?" And the whole world would have thought: "How kind they are to that child!" And when, in the evening, she hadn't been able to spin even a tenth of so much wool they would have said, "Oh, child, you don't deserve our kindness!" and all the others would have thought she didn't deserve this kindness. And Erica absolutely did not want to deserve their kindness. Instead she would rather take a chance of having her throat cut.[39]

So much for middle-class philanthropy. After the hypocrisy of these people the prostitution of Erica seems innocuous, the instinctive reflex of a starving child.

In actual fact the big-bellied women, in their secret minds, are morbidly obsessed with Erica's imminent fall, her virginity that totters precariously on the edge of a cliff. What will she do now? they keep asking themselves. When her coal is gone, when her cornmeal is gone, what will she do then? She does what she must; and one of the fine and precise points of her characterization is that, in spite of her vagueness about precise details of sexual relations, she understands the matter perfectly in its general outlines, as any child must who grows up in a single shabby room with its parents. Rejecting the wool-spinning offered her by the "ladies" (they are anxious to have her come and wash dishes for them for a lire or so a day), she instead quite deliberately and consciously exposes herself to the "throat-cutting" of defloration. This part of the novel is well done. Vittorini only rarely deals with erotic materials, but when he does so he treats them with precision and yet with great tact.

> All the time she had thought in the dark: but what's he doing to me? But what's he doing to me? And she had wept the physical tears of a creature being cut, trembling, shaking at the thought of the knife. This was all she had felt: a knife-pain, a dark cutting thing that opened a hole in her. Why like this? she had thought. But from the very pain she felt a confirmation that what she had set out to do, or let be done, was a way of

> earning a living. And she had swallowed her tears with a kind
> of proud exultation, for the spontaneous material proof they
> offered of the pain she had received and the living earned, the
> pain an absolute and unmistakable proof that she was earning
> a living.[40]

Erica's act is simultaneously a defeat of her physical body and
a victory over her enemies. Here the intricate relation between the
personal and economic threads of the novel becomes apparent.
Viewed in personal terms the story of Erica is that of a fall, a journey
from the innocence of childhood to the evil and pain of maturity:
the archetypal theme of initiation. But in social terms the novel is a
kind of fairy tale in which the child outwits the witches and escapes.
At the end of the novel, buying a can of sardines with her handful of
coins, Erica is happy for almost the first time in her life. The clerk
even calls her *signorina,* and the employees of the shop "salute her
entrance into the peaceful world of groceries."[41] She has finally
found the *compagnia* she sought. Although she does not realize it,
what she is entering is only the middle class populated by her
hypocritical enemies. But this is only natural and logical, since the
trade she has chosen, in the Marxist view, is a middle-class phenomenon created and sustained by the inequities of the capitalistic
system. In its treatment of sexual matters the novel is practical and
solidly antiromantic. Although in some ways it superficially resembles
Moravia's *La romana,* there are fundamental differences between
Erica and Moravia's heroine. Adriana begins her métier, or is led
into it by her mother, out of economic motives. But once established
in it she continues chiefly out of kindness of heart, feminine passivity, or simple weakness of character rather than out of avarice.
She is a kind of proletarian Violetta, essentially a romantic figure.
Erica is incapable of this sentimentalism. She is a real poor girl, one
created by an author who has been poor, even though she is also a
character in a fairy tale. To the big-bellied ladies with their mando-
lins the novel says: prostitution isn't fun, even though in your secret
thoughts you envy your fallen sisters. But at least it is an honest
way of earning a living, more honest than exploiting factory workers
or setting children to spin mountains of wool. If he had finished the
novel, Vittorini explained in his 1954 preface, he would have gone
on to show Erica progressing through other travails to other satisfactions and fulfillments: pleasure, friendship, love. What he seems
to have had in mind was a kind of *Bildungsroman* reflecting his own
view of the developing experience of life, which was by no means a
pessimistic one. He described the theme of the book as "the basic

happiness of life which, in spite of everything, can be gained precisely by starting from absolute disaster."[42] For Erica the disaster was her fall, the "knife-blade in the dark"; for Vittorini it was the whole malfunctioning social system, fascism, the Spanish War. But is it possible to build happiness out of an absolute disaster of any kind? It was because this question itself remained unresolved that the novel was never finished. As he himself admitted, ". . . the outbreak of the Civil War in Spain, in July 1936, rendered me suddenly indifferent to the development of the story I had labored over for six months on end."[43] Instead he turned, in his next and most important novel, to dealing with the "absolute disaster" in more direct terms.

The Operatic Novel

In the 1948 preface to *Il garofano rosso,* that key document for any serious student of his development, Vittorini describes his emotions on seeing his first opera, a performance of *Traviata* at La Scala probably in the fall of 1936. The Spanish Civil War had begun a few months before.

> In those days there was a special way of going to the opera, with your heart full of anxiety for the news from Spain, much as I imagine Verdi's contemporaries were full of the Risorgimento as they listened to his music, and as Verdi himself must have felt as he composed it. But the opera itself, along with the modern conditions under which I saw and heard it, had the effect of making me realize that the musical drama has the power, *denied to the novel,* of expressing through its complexity some splendid general emotion, indefinable by nature and independent of the action, the characters, and the emotions portrayed by the characters.
>
> Is it the music that does this? Music is for the opera what *something* should be for the novel. Why should the novel be denied what the opera has in music?[44]

In a completely fresh way, bypassing the history of literature he had never been taught, Vittorini had arrived at a personally useful insight about the origin of the novel. The discovery had been made by others before him, but for him personally it was an important one, and it was important that he worked it out for himself. For Homer narrative and poetry had been one; likewise with Virgil, Dante, and Milton. Then came the "separation of styles," approximately in the seventeenth century. The novel, an outgrowth of biography and letter writing, headed off in one direction and poetry continued in another. The novel became vernacular, bourgeois, factual; poetry moved increasingly toward the subjective and esoteric.

> The opera began in pure music just as the novel began in pure poetry. The opera has taken on, in its formation, a something else that is not music, just as the novel has taken on something that is not poetry. But the opera has remained music, while the novel has not remained essentially poetry. The opera has assimilated and reabsorbed into music, then reexpressed in music, all its originally nonmusical elements; the novel has not done the same for its nonpoetical elements. The opera has knitted together and the novel has split apart.

And he concludes, "To me, it is not that the novel enriched and magnified poetry by adding something to it, but that prose (the classic prose of antiquity) was more or less enriched by the poetry. So the novel marked the birth of a new kind of prose rather than a new kind of poetry."[45]

This is Vittorini's version of the "crisis in the modern novel." Naturally he was not the only one to object to the prosiness and flat factualism of modern fiction; the whole tendency of experimentalism in modern narrative, from Joyce and Proust to Pavese, can be regarded as an effort to "put the poetry back in the novel." Vittorini's particular contribution was to attack the problem with the freshness of an autodidact, and to apply to it a particular framework of rhetoric: that of the opera. When he speaks of opera it is Italian opera that is meant, and particularly Verdi. The chief impression made by operas of this kind on a person lacking in musical sensibility (e.g., Tolstoi) is the imbecility of the plot and the completely unnatural behavior of the singers on the stage. A chorus lingers singing "Andiamo, andiamo!" over and over instead of simply leaving for the place it is so imperative to go to. Violetta, dying of consumption at the end of *Traviata,* moves every heart with her superb aria before she collapses. In *Rigoletto* the murdered Gilda emerges from a sack and sings a duet with her father as she dies. But Tolstoi misses the point that the opera is *freed from the necessity* of realism through the effect of the music. When the "something" provided by music is added to the libretto the result is the total technical effect that Vittorini calls *linguaggio:* ". . . that which results from the action and the music together, as the unified language of the composer."[46] It was a "something" comparable to music that he sought to add to prose fiction. His new concept of the novel, at the point where the partly unsatisfactory *Il garofano rosso* and the unfinished *Erica* lay behind him, was a form that achieved its effects through pattern and rhythm, emotion-provoking in the diffuse and unspecific way that opera provokes emotion, "poetic" without being bound by the conventions and limitations of verse.

By 1938, when the manuscript of *Il garofano rosso* came back from the censors definitely rejected, he was in the middle of *Conversazione in Sicilia.** He was almost literally *nel mezzo del cammin di nostra vita;* he was thirty as he began the book, three books lay behind him, and three more plus some fragments were to be published after this central work. Silvestro, the narrator of the novel, hints at the presence of Dante and then rejects him, preferring to conduct his pilgrimage alone and on his own terms: "Every man is sick once, in the middle of his life, and knows that stranger his own sickness inside him, his helplessness against this stranger; and so understands his fellowman."[47] Like Dante's poem Vittorini's novel is the story of a journey, and the "abstract furies" that beset him as he starts out correspond to the darkling wood and the beasts. The reason why Silvestro needs no Virgil, or is denied one, is suggested by the key phrase "and so understands his fellowman." Silvestro's sickness, rather than a Christian sin or fall from grace, is that peculiar condition that moderns have come to call alienation: cut off from God, from man, even from the simplicities of concrete existence, he recognizes in his very isolation the element of humanity that links him to other men. In actual fact Silvestro has not one Virgil but many. The guides of his pilgrimage are the various characters he encounters on the journey and in the Sicilian village, his own mother, and finally the ghost of his brother. Each of these, by imperceptible stages, helps him to free himself from the furies that have followed him from the north. His manner of telling this story balances two more or less antithetic elements: on one hand its generality, the Dantesque element of allegory, and on the other hand the quite specific circumstances of his life. He is a typographer by trade and lives in Milan even though he is Sicilian by origin, he has a "girl or a wife" who waits for him at home, the massacres of the Spanish War shrill at him from the headlines. The opening paragraph is a stylistic model or matrix of the whole novel. Beginning with the word "I," it is simultaneously vernacular and rhythmic, even more intricate than it appears. As in a musical composition certain motifs or images are introduced, set aside for the moment, and then repeated with variations; in the first paragraph *furies, abstract, rain, water, shoes,* recur in an intermittent refrain. The paragraph ends with "a mute dream, hopelessness, quietude." The following passage, like an aria con-

* *In Sicily* (New Directions, 1949); also *Conversation in Sicily* (Penguin, 1961).

tinued by another singer, takes up these images from where the first
has left off ("This was the worst: the quietude of hopelessness")
and continues with other images which it adds in turn: blood, wine,
bread, Sicilian figs and sulphur, the "lost human race." This catalogue of concrete objects is an important clue to the nature, or more
precisely the effect, of the abstract furies. "It meant nothing to me
that my girl was waiting for me; go to her or not, or thumb through
a dictionary, was the same for me; and to go out and see friends,
other people, or stay at home was the same for me." The numbness
of alienation extends from words (thumbing through a dictionary)
to sexual experience and even to simple acts like drinking coffee and
eating bread— "as though," he concludes, "I had never struck anybody, or believed this possible"—the first suggestion of a political
theme, of the idea that one's relations with others can take the form
of antagonism as well as friendship. This opening chapter—the novel
is divided into sections averaging two or three pages each—ends
with a banal and almost Chaplinesque detail, the water leaking into
the narrator's broken shoes.

Like Dante's despair in the darkling wood, the spell of his
isolation is broken by a message: a letter from his father. Silvestro's
relations with his family correspond exactly to Vittorini's. At fifteen
he has run away, at thirty he returns. His father is a minor railway
employee who plays Macbeth in amateur theatricals—the role is a
particular irony, since ambition is exactly what he is lacking in.
Now he has left his wife—according to his own statement in order
to run away with another woman—and asks Silvestro to keep the
mother company in the Sicilian village on her name day (which
happens to be the eighth of December, the Feast of the Immaculate
Conception, the first clue that her name is Concezione). Silvestro
writes a conventional greeting card to his mother, takes it to the station to mail, and instead impulsively boards a train to deliver it
himself. He makes the long journey to Sicily, meeting on his way
various sympathetic and antipathetic people, and is reunited with
his mother in a scene dominated by sensory reawakening (cactus,
wood fires, the smell of a roasting herring). Quite literally his homecoming involves the ascent of a Purgatory; his mother lives at the
top of a hill and he has to climb a stairway to reach her.

> There were bundles of firewood on the stairs, in front of some
> houses, and I climbed, and now and then there was a patch of
> snow, and in the cold, in the morning sun, almost noon now, I
> arrived finally at the top overlooking the immense country of
> mountains and valleys spotted with snow. There was no one to

be seen, only barefooted children with feet ulcerated by chil-
blains and I made my way through the houses around the large
Mother-Church that I also recognized as something out of my
forgotten memories.[48]

The sensory and the Divine unite. Even earlier his reconciliation
with other men has begun. On the train ferry from the mainland to
Messina he tries to make friends with the Sicilians who are traveling
third-class—workers, laborers in the orange groves, railwaymen.
"There's no cheese like our own,"[49] he tells them, munching away at
the Sicilian cheese that tastes of goats and wormwood. But they are
wary, taking him for a northerner even though he speaks dialect.
One Sicilian, the smallest and darkest of the lot, stares hungrily at
the cheese and offers an orange to his child-wife, but she refuses.
"A Sicilian never eats in the morning,"[50] he tells Silvestro a little
defiantly. He offers Silvestro no oranges and Silvestro offers him no
cheese; they are unable to communicate as equals. The Sicilian decides Silvestro is an "Americano," i.e., an emigrated Italian, and
Silvestro complies by supplying fantastic details of an imaginary
New York. Although he would willingly have given cheese to the
Sicilian he is obliged, significantly, to *buy* oranges from him; even
though he is a worker in Milan his very possession of money marks
him as an alien and "capitalist" here. Yet a certain kind of understanding passes between the two before they separate. Discussing
unemployment in New York, the Sicilian contends that unemployment itself is not the root of the problem. He himself is not unemployed; like the other Sicilians he works all day long in the orchards.
The real "trouble" (*danno*) is hinted at as the rather intricate dialogue proceeds. He takes out the orange and offers it to his wife
again, but again she refuses it: "A Sicilian never eats in the morning."
He would like to eat, and he is not unemployed, but something un-
mentioned in the air is starving him to death. The "earth is offended"
—one of the recurring images of the novel is *il mondo offeso*. And
along with the offended earth goes the doomed humanity of the
opening chapter. "I have to say the furies were abstract, not alive;
furies connected in some way with the lost human race."[51] This
"doom" is in one sense political, but the political is connected to
everything else. Is it because of fascism that man can no longer
enjoy bread and friendship, or is it because he has forgotten how to
enjoy bread and friendship that fascism has so easily enslaved him?

The political thread of the narrative comes to the surface, somewhat more overtly this time, in the following passage dealing with
the train journey from Messina to Siracusa. Taking his seat in a

compartment, Silvestro hears two "baritones" speaking in dialect in the corridor outside. These voices belong to Coi Baffi and Senza Baffi (Mustache and No Mustache), two fascist agents who conduct a kind of duet in which they complain to each other of the "lack of respect and consideration" of people in general, and especially those they are obliged to arrest. "In Lodi, my barber." "My landlord, in Bologna." "They have no respect." "They have no consideration." The words *police* and *fascist* never break through to the surface, and this is not only because the novel was published under censorship. The passage deals with an immediate and local political phenomenon, and yet in another sense its implications are general or universal. The effect achieved is something like that of the Expressionistic drama: character is depersonalized and turned to type while at the same time retaining enough surface detail to lend an impression of concretion. Coi Baffi and Senza Baffi are a piece of local color, "two Sicilians of the carter variety," but they are also all men who become policemen, sergeants, jailers because they like to bully others. Naturally the threat of censorship that loomed over the book is an important factor in setting the tone of this passage and others. The effect of censorship was precisely to encourage a style of ambiguity, a style which is vague on the surface but speaks quite precisely to those who possess the key. This tendency to abstraction, to a style of suggestion rather than overt statement, is evident in a number of other writers who developed under fascism, from Moravia to critics like Alberto Carocci. Like the argot of prisoners, it is a language that proceeds on two levels, an overt surface and a concealed or semi-concealed code. This "duplicity" or tendency to say two things at once, it should be noted, is also characteristic of poetry itself.

On a simple level this technique is demonstrated by the passengers in Silvestro's compartment, who begin discussing the two fascists outside in veiled terms: "Don't you notice the smell?" "The smell? What smell?" "What? Don't you notice it? I mean that smell out there." The passengers really have no ideological objection to dictatorship in principle; their politics is simply a hatred of the police, which they connect, quite soundly, to the hunger that drives them to eat sour oranges. Coi Baffi and Senza Baffi understand this even though they are not very bright, and recognize their fellow Sicilians as their enemies precisely because they are hungry.

"Every starving man is a dangerous man," said Senza Baffi.
"How could he not be? capable of anything," said Coi Baffi.
"Of robbing," said Senza Baffi.
"That goes without saying," said Coi Baffi.

"Stabbing."

"Undoubtedly," said Coi Baffi.

"And of lending himself also to political crimes," said Senza Baffi.[52]

This might be a duet of two pompous courtiers in Verdi, for example from *Rigoletto*. In actual fact *Rigoletto* was censored because the Austrian regime suspected, probably correctly, that it contained a political message in code. In Vittorini's novel the political implications remain, for the most part, at this "operatic" level, a level that is emotional and aesthetic rather than ideological in any overt sense. In the train scene Coi Baffi and Senza Baffi are balanced off by the Gran Lombardo, another abstracted or semidepersonalized character who shares some of their physical qualities: " . . . a Sicilian, large, a Lombard or Norman possibly from Nicosia, a carter type like the voices out in the corridor, but authentic, forthright, and tall, with blue eyes."[53] He is one of the several Virgils of the novel, an encourager and guide to the uncertain traveler Silvestro. He ingenuously tells everything about himself: he is a landowner from Leonforte in the Val Demone, he has "three beautiful female daughters," and when he rides his horse about his estate he feels like a king. But he does not feel at peace with other men. "We are a sad people, we others."[54] The English translator Wilfrid David renders *noi* here as "we Sicilians"—but is it not as well all who suffer under tyranny, all the disenfranchised of the earth? The Gran Lombardo goes on to explain, or merely to remark calmly, that he believes man is ripe for new duties—not merely to rob and kill (the Abyssinian War?), not even to be a good citizen (conformity in a fascist state), but to do something "for the sake of our conscience in a new sense."[55] A naive passenger asks him, "Are you a professor?" and this provokes general laughter. But if he is not a teacher, or a prophet, what is he? He is a man, but he is "more a man," *más hombre, più uomo*. This is another of the key phrases of the novel, and in order to define the exact implications of it it is necessary to go back again to Vittorini's account of the writing of *Conversazione in Sicilia*.

> My thoughts came out of my needs, as my needs came out of the life I was living then, and the good will I felt toward the things of the earth and toward men. *Más hombre*, I thought. I believed I had caught these two Spanish words out of what was for me the Spanish War: the nights of listening to Radio Madrid, Radio Valencia, Radio Barcelona with my fellow workers; my thought was nothing more than *más hombre*, nothing more specific or rational. What does *más hombre* mean?

> "More a man," I suppose; this is what it meant to me as I wrote the book that was to be *Conversazione*, and my way of thinking about the novel I sketched above is a way that now, at last, I can explain—now that I have written other books and gone on seizing every chance I could get of seeing a good classic opera.[56]

It is useful to be aware of this passage in order to grasp that, when the expression *più uomo* recurs in *Conversazione in Sicilia*, there is a connection in Vittorini's mind to the Spanish War and all its political implications. The phrase is not very clearly defined either as a literary image or as a political concept: it is deliberately left diffuse. But the implication is clear that fascism is man-destroying—that Coi Baffi and Senza Baffi have become dehumanized puppets, whereas the Gran Lombardo and the others of the novel who "feel the need of doing something for the sake of conscience" are reinforced and enhanced in their humanity. This is connected to Silvestro's own inability, in the early part of the novel, to feel or love anything in the world around him; fascism anesthetizes the feeling and desiring part of man, leaving him in the "quietude of hopelessness."

This metaphorical framework of the Gran Lombardo and *più uomo* recurs frequently in the remainder of the novel. Somewhat later Silvestro, in a conversation with his mother, inquires whether his grandfather was a Gran Lombardo. When the mother asks what a Gran Lombardo is, he merely replies, "A man." This leads to a kind of repetitive litany that continues for several pages: Silvestro cites one quality after another of the Gran Lombardo (large stature, hairy body, blue eyes), the mother denies in turn that the grandfather had any of these qualities, and Silvestro insists that he was nevertheless a Gran Lombardo. The repetition is not syntactically rigid; there are backings and turnings, divagations in which the mother remarks that in Nicosia they make bread with hazelnuts on top or that she once had a pitcher from Aidone. But in its singsong return to the same refrain the passage is as invariable and monotonous as a children's chant. It arrives finally at the question for which all the other questions have been only preparation: "Didn't he say that our present duties are obsolete? That they are rotten, dead, and there's no satisfaction in performing them? . . . Didn't he say there was a need for other duties? New duties, not the ordinary ones? Didn't he say that?"[57] The mother doesn't remember whether he said this or not. But she does remember that "basically" he wasn't content with the world, but was content with himself. Clearly the grandfather was *più uomo*, a giant who spoke straight and saw clearly, a Gran Lombardo.

Technically this scene is an ingenious piece of indirection; the innuendo of the dialogue is always present under the surface but never emerges, or emerges only in cryptic form in the reference to "new duties." The logic it follows is that of a submerged track of emotion, Silvestro's gradual realization that there are other men who share his state of mind and are capable of taking action against the "furies." In this process of awakening the mother herself performs an important function, although she herself is unaware of it. In the quasi-religious pattern of allegory underlying the novel she represents charity, the Latin *caritas*. This has nothing to do with philanthropy either organized or unorganized; it is simply the state of mind of selfless love. It is the mother, first of all, who reintroduces Silvestro to the lost sensory world of his boyhood: lentils, dried tomatoes, rosemary, wine, melons, herring. Her *caritas* begins with acceptance of the world, of the hard and vivid sensations of existence. Together she and Silvestro recall a playful ritual that she and the children used to repeat. She would hide the melons in a place they could never find for all their searching ("It was as though you were hiding them inside yourself"[58]), then every so often, on Sunday, she would produce one as if by magic. It was for this that they called her Mamma Melon. The melon and the fish, along with her name Concezione, are three of the four motifs that define the mother. The fourth is her function as a village nurse: she goes daily on her rounds from one house to another giving injections to the sick. The untrained or half-trained *infermiera* who lives by giving injections is an Italian institution, but in the pattern of the novel the mother is something a little more complicated. In his manner of portraying her going from house to house injecting health into the sick, encouraging them to eat, bringing always light and warmth with her since a fire must be made to sterilize her instrument, there is no doubt that Vittorini intended her as a quasi-religious figure. She even announces as she enters each house, "I have my son with me," and the reaction of the villages is one of a dignified and suitable respect ("You've made him big like yourself").[59] The women who sit around the bed of the sick man are "like nuns," and the darkness of their huts is the mysterious darkness of the church. There is no inconsistency here with Vittorini's leftism and anticlericalism, or if there is a contradiction it is only superficial. The mother herself explains this point in speaking of the grandfather, who was "a great socialist, a great hunter, and great on horseback when he rode in the procession of Saint Joseph." When Silvestro asks how he could be a socialist and yet believe in Saint Joseph, she tells him scornfully, "He had enough brains to do a thousand things at once. He was a socialist because he understood politics. . . . But he could believe in Saint Joseph." But, Silvestro objects, wasn't the procession a thing of the priests? "You're an ignoramus! The procession was horses and men on horseback. It was a cavalcade."[60] The men rode on horseback and honored the saint precisely because they were men and not because the priests told them to; in the same way the mother gives injections out of humanity and not for the few pennies that, for the most part, she does not even receive. Her *caritas* is a quality of character, and consistent with, or even connected to, her quite human fallibility. (She contradicts herself frequently, saying at one time that it is worse if the man is sick and at another time it is worse if the wife is sick, and she even confesses to Silvestro a marital infidelity.) The mother personifies a concept basic to the novel: that the religious impulse may exist outside the organized Church, and even, under conditions like those of fascism, in opposition to the organized Church.

These injection-rounds of the mother play an important part in the change going on inside Silvestro himself, a change that it would not be inappropriate to call a "conversion." The theme of the rediscovery of sensory experience assumes slightly comic overtones when the mother insists that he witness the injection of a shapely widow to "see how well-made she is." Silvestro is embarrassed, the widow struggles, and the mother finally unveils her perfections; in the end all three are flushed and pleased. The innocent eroticism of this scene is a pendant to the opening passage of the novel, in which Silvestro explains that going to bed with his girl or thumbing a dictionary is all the same for him. Furthermore this rediscovery of the sensory involves a rediscovery of the poor, of the emotional ambience of poverty. The twenty-sixth chapter is a curious soliloquy, somewhat inconsistent in style with the rest of the novel, beginning, "I had been very sick, for months, some time before,"[61] and going on to portray the sensations of hunger and the despair of poverty. Almost immediately the chapter shifts from the first person to an impersonal "one does," "this is the way it is," and then to the third person represented by a hypothetical family. This turns into a kind of miniature narrative, a bare and abstract account of "the way it is" to be poor in Sicily. The husband and wife quarrel, the children out of hunger "devour chair legs, and would like to devour their father and mother."[62] The gas man has cut off the gas, the light man has cut off the lights. Finally comes the landlord, to suggest that it is "too extravagant" for the "sick gentlemen" to lie in bed and pay no rent, and that he should send his wife to wash the landlord's dishes. Poverty (economic oppression) leads to slavery (political oppression). The chapter ends as the invalid's wife, returning home, despairingly casts armloads of grass, flowers, and pine cuttings at him, bursting out, "Vegetables!"[63] None of these characters has names; they are rather sarcastic animated puppets. This exercise in abstraction or depersonalization, while interesting in a technical sense, is not one of the more successful passages of the novel. In fact its qualities and difficulties illustrate a tendency in Vittorini that is only latent in *Conversazione in Sicilia* but becomes dominant in his later work: the "collectivization" of character to the point where individual personality is submerged.

Here the technique is dropped after the brief experiment, but it leads to a somewhat more effective chapter on the subject of the humanness of humanity. The motif of *più uomo* is reiterated and reinforced, and the "operatic" repetition of motif reaches back even farther to the opening of the novel. The abstract furies are not specifically mentioned, but their attendant images—rain, broken shoes, the massacres in the headlines—come to the surface again.

> But perhaps every man is not a man; and the whole human race is not human. This is a doubt that comes, in the rain, when you have broken shoes, water in your broken shoes, and nobody in particular your heart is concerned with, no particular private life, nothing done and nothing to do, nothing to fear, nothing to lose, and you see, over there outside yourself, the massacres of the world. One man laughs and another man weeps. They're both men; the one who laughs has been sick too, he is sick; but he laughs *because* the other weeps. He can massacre, persecute, and if you, in your despair, see him laughing over the newspapers and the headlines, you don't go over to him but instead you weep, in your quietude, with the other who weeps. Not every man is a man, then. One persecutes and the other is persecuted; and the whole human race is not human, but only that part that is persecuted.[64]

This passage combines the operatic style (the repetition of the first sentence, the recurrence of laughing, weeping, water, broken shoes) with a technique something like that of the Elizabethan soliloquy, the essence of which is that the mind is seen in the *process* of working out its thoughts rather than presenting the thoughts in their final form. Beginning with the hypothesis that "perhaps" every man is not a man, the passage goes on to speak of doubts, of persecution, of laughing and weeping, and comes finally to the working out of its logic: "Not every man is a man, then." All this is provoked in Silvestro's mind by the shabby and obscure sufferings of the poor, while the mother, that imperfect Madonna, injects them with healing medicines. When he asks his mother what she thinks of these people her reply is characteristic: "I think that perhaps they won't pay me."[65]

This whole development of political and religious emotion comes to a climax in Silvestro's encounter with the knife grinder Calogero, a scarecrow-like figure who is half chimney sweep out of Dickens and half a crazy kind of saint. He meets the knife grinder immediately after another soliloquy in which the "offended world," impiety, slavery, and injustice are mentioned again. Chapter thirty-three, Silvestro's first dialogue with Calogero, is perhaps the most striking passage in the novel. Physical impressions of the knife grinder (the blackness of his face and clothes, the light that gleams "from various parts of his person and his cart") are alternated with an "operatic" dialogue par excellence. "Sharpen, sharpen!" the knife grinder repeats. "Haven't you got anything to sharpen?" For a time Silvestro fails to grasp what the conversation is about, exactly as he did earlier in the talk about the "smell" in the train compartment. Don't the people hereabouts give him anything to sharpen, he asks the knife grinder? "Nothing much worth while. Nothing much worth the trouble. Nothing much that gives pleasure." But surely the people in the countryside have knives, scissors? The knife grinder denies this. Then what do they give him to sharpen? "That's what I ask them" he cries back. "What will you give me to sharpen? Will you give me a sword? Will you give me a cannon? And I look them in the face, in the eyes, and I see that what they've got can't even be called a nail." Silvestro, and the reader, are drawn gradually into the innuendo. Skirting cautiously, the knife grinder comes finally to his conclusion as Silvestro, in his soliloquies, comes to the working out of his own thought. "Sometimes I think it would be enough for everybody to have their teeth and nails sharpened. I'd sharpen them into viper's teeth and leopard claws. . . ."[66] They wink, speak secretly into each other's ears, and cry "Ah!" What they say to each other Silvestro does not reveal, just as Dante is taciturn over his conversation with the five great poets in Limbo: "Then we moved on toward the light, speaking of things of which to remain silent is well here, just as it was well to speak of them there." In this chapter the problem of the specific and the general is solved to perfection. The knife grinder is a vivid concretion; the reader sees his "gleaming person" and hears his speech. But the political implications *remain* implications, remain abstract, and this lends them a universality that extends beyond the local and temporary problem of fascism. It is for this reason that *Conversazione in Sicilia,* while a "revolutionary" novel in a general and ethical sense, manages to transcend the limitations of a political tract, even so skilled a one as Malraux's *L'espoir.* It manages to do this because Vittorini, for all his concern with politics, is primarily an artist and relates to the writing of his novel primarily in artistic rather than politic terms. The concept of the autonomy of art recurs frequently in his *Diario in pubblico;* like Moravia he rejects the Marxist concept of art as a "superstructure" explainable in terms of the economic and political conditions that produce it. We are no longer involved in Homeric politics in any direct way, in other words it does not really matter to us who wins the Trojan War, and yet we still read the *Iliad* with pleasure. This can only be because Homer, beginning from certain specific political events, has managed to generalize his narrative to the point where anyone who has ever experienced human emotions can associate himself with it.

Vittorini's problem is not precisely parallel to Homer's. For one thing several centuries intervened between the events of the Trojan War and the final form of the poem as we have it, and a number of different hands modified the poem in this long process of universalization. The Greeks of the Pisistratan period were hardly more involved in Homeric politics than we are. But Vittorini was involved in fascist politics; fascism interfered with his artistic development and had the power to deprive him at any time of his freedom or even his life. There is therefore a control, an irony, in his half-veiled allusions to political conditions, but there is no Homeric serenity. It is this pressure under the surface, in fact, that produces the characteristic and strangely powerful effect of the novel. As it progresses and passes its point of climax—the dialogue with the knife grinder— the narrative becomes successively more personal; Silvestro develops from a passive narrator into the central figure of his own story. He gives a little penknife to Calogero to sharpen, and it is this negligible weapon that establishes a bond between them. Except for the train journey itself this is, significantly, his first overt action. For the rest of the novel pointed objects are equivalent to antifascist possibilities. Furthermore there is the unspoken implication that the novel itself —not only the novel as a form but the very novel we are reading— can be one of these "pointed objects."

This rather important connection is first suggested in the following scene in which Calogero and Silvestro go to visit the harness maker Ezechiele, "someone who owns an awl,"[67] as Calogero describes him. Ezechiele asks Calogero whether, by chance, he has come to borrow the awl. But Calogero replies that there will be no need of it this evening, since he has found a friend who has a blade. The harness maker comments that he is glad to hear this, and adds, "The world is offended, but not yet in here."[68] This somewhat mysterious phrase identifies him as one of the secret order of men of good will—an order that includes Silvestro himself, the little Sicilian on the train, the Gran Lombardo, and now the new friends who gather in the harness-maker's shop. Ezechiele—who has a prophet's name—is another in the succession of guides who help to free Silvestro from the abstract furies. "The world is big and beautiful," he tells Silvestro, "but it has been much offended. Everyone suffers for himself, but not for the offended world, and so the world goes on being offended."[69] There is no doubt that in the figure of Ezechiele the "possibility" of antifascism is specifically connected to writing, to the literary vocation. He has a "kind of notebook" on a little table, along with a pen and ink, and with these he "spends his days like an ancient hermit"[70] writing the history of the offended world. If any further testimony is needed that a pen can be a blade, the knife grinder immediately shouts, "Knives, scissors, pikes."[71] It is obvious that Vittorini has projected himself into Silvestro the linotype operator, whose job it is to put letters together and who suffers from abstract furies. But it is obvious as well that the abstract concept of Writer, or artist-as-revolutionary, is connected to this Ezechiele who records the history of the offended world, and who greets Silvestro in some mysterious way as a brother.

After their polyphonic conversation about knives, suffering, and the offended world, the friends add to their number a clothier named Porfirio, who possesses "half a pair of scissors," and then go to drink wine in a tavern. This second scene with Calogero and his friends suffers somewhat from redundancy: the religious images are reiterated, the tavern keeper Colombo is "a great Saint Bernard with a generous glance," Porfirio, whose name suggests the purple of vestments, speaks of cleansing water. "Ecco il vino,"[72] says Colombo, and he hardly needs to add that it is the body and blood of all men. Calogero, somewhat exalted, launches into a cryptic catalogue of sensations mingled with abstract images: earth, woods, women, trees and fresh figs, hearts in honored breasts, beer and incense, free race and free struggle. There follow some Pan-like cries. But this tavern scene is only an alcoholic hallucination, a Magic Theatre without substance, and Silvestro knows this even before the drinking ends. Recognizing Porfirio as the old Father Noah of the wine, he reminds himself, "it was not in this that I wanted to believe."[73] It is not through wine, or tavern camaraderie, that abstract furies are to be exorcised; this is too facile an escape.

Instead, returning to his mother's house, Silvestro encounters the last of the prophetic figures of the novel: the ghost of his brother Liborio, who has evidently been killed in the war. The dialogue tone, wry and ironic in the earlier encounters, now becomes genuinely tragic. "Do you suffer much?" "Millions of times . . . For every printed word, for every spoken word, for every millimeter of erected bronze."[74] Silvestro is a typographer; in the air is the unspoken implication that it is he who prints the words, who aids those who erect the bronze. Like Aeneus trying three times to embrace Creusa only to have his arms close on empty air, he tries three times unsuccessfully to offer the ghost a cigarette, and finally shouts, "Take it, then," into the night. In this final episode the motif of personal involvement or commitment emerges unmistakably as the dominant note, one that, like the theme of an operatic finale, gathers and assimilates the earlier motifs of the work. In this involvement Silvestro, the author, and the reader are merged into a single consciousness, a consciousness that becomes "more man" in its recognition of the frailty and guilt of common humanity. There is no mistaking the skill with which this is done. The conventional apparatus of the scene—the dream, the ghost, the banal religious symbolism—is no more damaging to Vittorini's final effect than similar conventions are to Verdi's. The narrative has been freed from the banality of its events and devices by "something which does for the novel what music does for the opera." The encounter with Liborio is a moving, strange, and original scene; there are few passages to match it in Italian literature or the whole of modern writing. It is followed by a kind of epilogue in which the mother washes the feet of a stranger who turns out to be the father: a prodigal father greeted by a forgiving son. But even this rather banal piece of allegory is saved by the oblique and poetic manner of its presentation.

Persons and Nonpersons

Conversazione in Sicilia is clearly Vittorini's central work. In perspective it becomes evident that everything before this novel, almost precisely in the middle of his career, is preparation for it, and everything that comes after is relatively anticlimactic. Moravia has no central work in this sense; some of his novels are more successful and some less, but they are the fairly even work of a writer who approaches technical problems with a consistent technical competence. If there is a single novel of this importance in Pavese's work it is *La luna e i falò,* and it comes exactly at the end of his career. In fact his suicide may be viewed, at least in part, as an effort to escape the consequences of the anticlimax that then confronted him. That he was aware of this problem is clear from the letter to Aldo Camerino quoted earlier: ". . . for a while—perhaps forever—I won't do anything else." In Vittorini the problem of anticlimax is evident in his subsequent work, but there are complicating factors. In the years immediately following *Conversazione in Sicilia* he was preoccupied with the war (his apartment was destroyed by bombing in August 1943 and most of his books were lost), with clandestine antifascist activity, and with politics. In 1945 he founded the independent-Marxist review *Il Politecnico*, and during much of the postwar period he worked for Einaudi as editor of the *Gettoni* series of novels by younger Italian writers. This activity was perhaps not inconsistent with fiction-writing, but undoubtedly it interfered with it. Two short novels came out of the period 1945-47, and they share certain characteristics: stylistically they lie heavily under the shadow of *Conversazione in Sicilia,* so much that they may almost be considered imitations, and ideologically they are influenced by the political tumult that was taking place inside Vittorini in the war years and after. The first of these is *Uomini e no,* a novel about the Resistance in Milan in 1944. It was conceived only very shortly after the events it relates, and published immediately after the Liberation in 1945. The title, literally "Men and Not," was influenced by Steinbeck's *Of Mice and Men* (*Uomini e topi* in Italian) and also reflects the special terminology of *più uomo* that Vittorini had invented for *Conversazione in Sicilia.* Technically this is an extremely peculiar novel; there is nothing like it in the rest of Vittorini's work or, for that matter, anywhere in modern literature. The skeleton of the plot is that of a conventional underground thriller. The protagonist, Enne 2 or N-2, is the leader of a clandestine antifascist band recruited mainly from Milan workers. He is involved with a woman named Berta, but there is a conflict in his mind between his love for her and his commitment to the Resistance cause. The group takes part in the assassination of some German officers, there are reprisals, and another attack is planned on the fascist tribunal which is to select a hundred or more hostages for execution. This attack goes badly, several comrades are killed, and in the end N-2 waits in a dingy apartment for the militia who are closing in on him.

But such a bare summary gives only an inadequate idea of the novel, or no idea at all. In the first place its style, or *linguaggio,* is an even more radical extension of the technique developed earlier for *Conversazione in Sicilia.* The texture of the novel is built around a half-dozen key images or concepts, some of them already used in *Conversazione in Sicilia:* passivity, broken shoes, the offended world, happiness (*essere felice*), duty, the idea of manness or *più uomo.* The device of repetition or echolalia is extended and used frequently now as a polyphony involving several voices. Sometimes, as in the scene in which the antifascist workers discuss whether it is right for someone involved in the Resistance to have a *compagna* or common-law wife, the technique becomes a kind of phrasebook style in which endless grammatical variations on the same phrase are presented in turn.

"You know that many of us have this. Many of us have a *compagna*, many of us have a family . . ."

"I have a *compagna* too," said a fourth, suddenly.

"You see?" said Mambrino. "Even Pico Studente has a *compagna*. Many of us have a *compagna*."

"And maybe even the captain has a *compagna*," Pico Studente went on.

"Do you hear what Pico Studente says? said Mambrino. "Maybe even the captain has a *compagna*."

"Maybe so," Pico Studente said. "Who can judge whether he has? We know nothing about the captain. What do we know about the captain? He's the oldest of all of us, and he may even have three or four children, he may even have a large family."

"You hear?" said Mambrino. "All of us have a *compagna*. All of us have a family. But nobody stays with his family. You tell us, Barca Tartaro. Do you stay with your family?"[75]

And so on; this is by no means the end of the discussion about families, *compagne*, and the difficulty of having a family when one is in the Resistance. Another striking passage involving only two voices is N-2's dialogue with Berta about the mountains: "You can almost see the mountains." "Can you see the mountains from Milan?" "Don't you see them? You can see them."[76] This sounds like an echo from "Hills Like White Elephants," and in fact *Uomini e no* is the most Hemingwayesque of Vittorini's novels, both in its style and in its conventionally romantic plot. There is no question that Vittorini was intimately familiar with Hemingway's work in this period and somewhat earlier. In 1941, in the suppressed *Americana* prefaces, he wrote, "Symbols are born in Hemingway without uterine labor; through elision, suggestion, and repetition of images: as Minerva was born from the brow of Jove."[77] In addition to this stylistic influence it is likely that the plot of *For Whom the Bell Tolls* lay in the back of Vittorini's mind as he wrote *Uomini e no*. There is a great deal of talk in Hemingway's novel about men and nonmen; the old Anselmo is afraid he will not have the courage to kill the bridge sentry, Pablo becomes a nonman through his cowardice and then partially regains his manhood at the end of the novel, and so on. Hemingway's novel is structured economically around the personal sacrifice of Robert Jordan as Vittorini's is structured around N-2;

both plots cover only a few days and observe a relative unity of action. There is a young woman-old woman relation in both (Maria and Pilar, Berta and the older Selva who advises her), and both plots involve a conventional apparatus of sacrifice, betrayal, and futile heroism. The endings in particular are parallel: the wounded Jordan lies waiting to ambush the fascists, the surrounded N-2 waits in his room for the militia. Hemingway's concept of manhood, of heroism, turns around the Spanish word "rare"; *es un hombre muy raro* is the partisans' praise for the brave and capable. Vittorini continues to use the concept *più uomo* of *Conversazione in Sicilia,* and adds another pivotal phrase, *essere in gamba,* "to be in good shape," to be capable, vigorous, literally to be on one's feet. This dictionary meaning, however, is modified in the course of the novel into a quite private talisman or password of the antifascist underground. The brave of the novel are *in gamba,* the fascists and those who passively accept fascism are not. At the same time this rather rudimentary terminology, in both Hemingway and Vittorini, implies an ethic that is fairly complex and sophisticated. Vittorini's concept of "more man" stands in opposition to the fake manliness of the fascists, their rhetoric, their cult of youth, their bemedaled chests. Essentially it is a humanism of an activistic and committed type, but by no means entirely political; it involves a warmth of feeling, a capacity for quite personal sensory enjoyment not ordinarily associated with the underground partisan. Just as Pilar in *For Whom the Bell Tolls* continually reminds Robert and Maria how important it is to love when one is young, Vittorini's novel insists on the "humanness" and therefore the validity of wine, food, love, sunshine, the simplest of physiological pleasures. It is because the underground workers feel and want these things that they are not fascists, that they are superior to the fascists.

But Gide has reminded us that it is out of fine sentiments that bad novels are made. The basic difficulty with *Uomini e no* is that Vittorini's commitment to the novel, to its framework of ethical polarity, is so highly personal that he loses artistic control. Like most fiction written during or immediately after a powerful experience, it is emotionally too close to its subject. It is hard to take exception to Vittorini's dislike of fascists, or to his horror at the Nazi reprisals against Milan civilians (a man is torn to pieces by a dog, women and children are shot and left in the streets). These things happened; no feeling person can fail to be shocked by them, and they are perfectly fitting subjects for fiction or other artistic expression. But when they are dealt with in the heat of immediate emotion the result is melodrama or facile propaganda. The very sanctity of the cause, the absolute ethical polarity it implies, is Vittorini's chief obstacle in his effort to make out of these things a valid work of art. The novel almost surmounts this difficulty through its technical originality, the style that Vittorini invented for *Conversazione in Sicilia* and uses again here with only slight modifications. But *Conversazione in Sicilia* has at least a certain number of simply but powerfully sketched characters (the mother, the knife grinder Calogero, the little Sicilian with the oranges); *Uomini e no* has only puppets. N-2, with a label instead of a name, like a character in an Expressionistic drama, fails to come alive and remains faceless and anonymous. If he is compared with another antifascist hero who goes about in disguise, the Pietro Spina of Silone's *Pane e vino* and *Il seme sotto la neve*, his thinness and total lack of reality are evident. The technique of deliberate "depersonalization" which was fairly effective in *Conversazione in Sicilia* has here degenerated into automatism, the facelessness of pulp fiction. Sometimes the political polarity of the novel is embarrassing; when a fascist militiaman dies screaming "*Mamma mia!*" the unseen narrator comments, "Even a son of a bitch can say mamma."[78] In fact the intrusion of this narrator, who appears only infrequently, is one indication of the technical difficulty of the novel. He is not N-2—Vittorini wishes to keep us at an aesthetic distance from him and thus does not tell the story from his point of view—and he is not quite Vittorini himself. He is a faceless voice, a kind of loudspeaker brought up on occasion to make comments that none of the characters can make, and the fact that he exists at all shows Vittorini's uncertainty over the narrative apparatus of the novel.

It is when this problem of point of view is solved that the novel comes up, occasionally, to a level something like that of *Conversazione in Sicilia*. Much of *Uomini e no* is pure dialogue relieved only with bare stage directions. These passages (conversations among the workers, dialogues between Berta and Selva, some of the love scenes) are relatively successful. In one scene the bodies of civilian hostages lie in the street while the rather stupid militiamen keeping watch over them chew sandwiches. Two young men who are obviously antifascists begin conducting a conversation with them, ostensibly about the sandwiches.

> "Good, eh?" said one.
> "Not bad at all," one of the men answered.
> "What do they have in them? Meat?"
> "Oh, yes. Meat, and other things."
> "Bones too?"
> "Bones? What do you mean, bones?"[79]

This leads by subtle steps to a discussion of cannibalism at which the militiamen finally take offense; the technique is exactly that of the conversation about the "smell" in the train corridor in *Conversazione in Sicilia*. Language that says one thing while seeming to say another is useful for prisoners and for the populations of occupied countries; ambiguity in identity, in action, in speech, is the essence of the clandestine. These double entendres—there are several more such passages—are the most obvious technical successes of *Uomini e no*. One of the curious qualities of the novel is that these all take place when N-2 is absent. There is something about his presence, his "sanctity," that discourages these ingenuities of double language. It is perhaps because a double entendre, even as grim as the one about the sandwiches, is a kind of joke, and the passages dealing with N-2 are rigidly serious; they resemble hagiography more than the technique of ordinary fiction. It is a temptation to conclude that the novel would be better with N-2 removed. But without N-2 there would be no center to the novel and no novel at all.

In Vittorini's next novel *Il Sempione strizza l'occhio al Fréjus* (1947)* these technical problems are dealt with in a somewhat more satisfactory way. The hovering narrator is gone, and the story is told in the first person by a member of the family it describes. This short novel is relatively plotless and consists of no more than a setting, a half dozen or so characters, and a series of conversations. Vittorini is thus freed from the difficulty he has in *Uomini e no* of surmounting a rather banal adventure-thriller plot. The structure returns to the simple network of dialogues that was so effective in *Conversazione in Sicilia,* although the motif of travel, of the seeking wanderer, is missing. This simplicity allows Vittorini to concentrate on the matters of cadence, of flat but deftly sketched character, of poetic ambience, where his touch is sure. The result is a minor but charming and relatively successful piece of fiction.

"In our family we are a houseful of people. . . ."[80] There is the mother, a brother who works, his girl Anna, a sister Elvira, and the "mother's husband" and the narrator, both of them unemployed. Finally there is grandfather, white-haired, deaf, infirm, but still a giant of a man with muscles like tree knots, the elephant of the English title. The setting, like those of *Conversazione in Sicilia* and *Uomini e no,* is geographically quite specific: a house near the Lambrate woods on the outskirts of Milan. Even though the story is narrated by the unemployed brother, it turns around the grandfather

* Literally "The Simplon Winks at the Fréjus"; translated as *The Twilight of the Elephant* (New Directions, 1951).

as a wheel turns about the axle. The attitude of the rest of the family toward him is somewhat ambivalent. They respect him and even fear him a little, they object because he eats more bread than the rest of them put together, but at the bottom they recognize him as a kind of patriarch in the Biblical sense, a fierce, mysterious, silent force that holds the family together. In his youth he was a construction worker, and his chief claim to distinction is that he helped to drive the Fréjus Tunnel through the Alps. But the mother, who defends him and interprets him for the others, contends that he built practically every other monument of the history of civilization as well: the Milan cathedral, the Colosseum, the Great Wall of China, the Pyramids. This theme of universality escapes pompousness simply through the ironic and half-playful way it is presented. The children are skeptical; the mother is firm in her faith.

> She may mean more than we think she means. She's not stupid. She certainly doesn't mean anybody except grandfather, that great seated bulk, but if she wanted to indicate his whole race and ours she could only point to him. It's only he that she refers to as "your grandfather," "our grandfather." But there is no reason why she shouldn't use the name of "grandfather" for all those in the world who are like him.[81]

"Those who are like him" include his fellow workers on the Fréjus, those who built the Duomo, the Colosseum, the Chinese Wall, the Pyramids. And who else? The reader who sets out here like Dante in his letter to Can Grande della Scala to find allegorical levels will have practically no place to stop. First of all the grandfather is a real grandfather, a "naturalistic" character whose background and temperament can be accepted quite literally. Second, he can be identified with Vittorini's own youthful experience as a construction worker; the grandfather personifies a nostalgia for hard work, common action, exposure to the elements, the solving of physical problems through determination and ingenuity. As a kind of part-time Marxist Vittorini regards the real advances of civilization as material, technological, rather than intellectual, and while the grandfather is not exactly anti-intellectual he is hardly a scholar or abstract thinker. At the next level down there is a somewhat ironic religious implication: the grandfather as Jahveh. Finally, the grandfather with his roots three generations back in Italian history represents the nineteenth century, the Risorgimento, the heroic epoch in Italian destiny: ". . . his eyes for us, in spite of their mildness, are the eyes of names learned in school, of Mazzini, of Garibaldi, as well as his own. It is for this now that we stop and look. Could we lack in respect for another century?"[82]

And yet when the novel is weighed as a whole, in its final aesthetic effect, it is possible to ignore all these complicated hints and regard the grandfather simply as a kind of tough nexus of humanity, "more a man" than the others. In Vittorini's frame of values the workers, those who make things with their hands, those who are in contact with basic physical realities, are admirable; bureaucrats, exploiters, and policemen are not. Those who suffer are *più uomo;* those who make suffer are less, or not man at all. Like the Gran Lombardo in *Conversazione in Sicilia,* the grandfather is *più uomo* as well in his patriarchal virility. Contrasted to him in this whimsical Holy Family, the mother's husband (he is given no other name) plays a kind of semicomic Joseph. Joseph may be a saint, but what a pitiful figure he cuts next to Jahveh! For all his "human" weakness he is not even related to the Son of Man. Blond, cheerful, compliant, the mother's husband meekly bows his head before the elephant-grandfather. The mother's scorn for him, as she compares him to the grandfather, reaches sarcastic heights.

> "Have you ever looked at him, blond man?" she says. "Have you ever measured your little finger next to his thumb? Or your knee next to his wrist? Come on, now, blond man," she cries.
>
> My mother's husband has let go of her waist, and pulls in his head, muttering that now my mother will ask him if he's ever measured his fist against my grandfather's ballocks.
>
> "Sure I can ask you," my mother cries. "Or have you ever measured yourself, all of you, against his member? That's what I ask you, little blond man. Have you ever considered the figure you cut, all there is of you, next to his member?"[83]

To this the mother's husband only turns red and mutters, "Madonna! O Madonna." Like Tennyson's Ulysses he might lament, "We are not now that strength which in old days / Moved heaven and earth." Except that he cannot add, "that which we are, we are," since he meekly accepts the mother's view of him as not much of anything. His unemployment—the economic equivalent of his impotence—is only a detail of his whole spiritual anemia, along with his blondness. In actual fact the family lives on the money the brother makes by repairing bicycles: trivial adjustments of minor units in the industrial system.

If the novel has any plot at all it depends on the intrusion of an outsider into the family: the highway worker called Smoke-Face who is laying asphalt on the road outside the house. First he waves as his machine goes by, then he stops to talk, finally he comes into the house and becomes something like a member of the family. In appearance, with his black face and white teeth, he resembles the knife grinder of *Conversazione in Sicilia;* he has the same abrupt youthfulness, the same laughing and yet suggestive manner. His is another of Vittorini's "prophets," an Ezekiel or Isaiah who wanders into the novel with his face covered with soot. (Silone's Pietro Spina also stains his face; in a nation controlled by criminals the honest man must go about in disguise). Smoke-Face smiles and likes everybody, but his immediate affinity is for the grandfather. It is the invention of this character that saves the novel from a rather pointless dialogue, taking place entirely within the family, without beginning or an end. With a gesture "like a caress" the grandfather reaches out to see whether Smoke-Face's soot will come off or whether he is a Negro. It will come off with vaseline, he is informed, and this makes him laugh for the first time in several months, "a sound like a stream flowing inside him."[84] The grandfather represents the past, Mazzini and Garibaldi, Vittorini's own youth; Smoke-Face represents the possibility that something like the grandfather can be reborn in the present. This is the possibility—to put it in political terms—that a modern proletariat can recapture something of the energy and idealism of the Risorgimento. At the religious level of the novel Smoke-Face represents the rebirth of the God, and so on. The pattern of the novel is meaningful no matter which of the various frameworks is applied to it, or even if no particular framework is applied to it, if it is taken quite simply as the story of a family and an outsider who makes friends with it. Smoke-Face at least is not bourgeois, that much is clear. His blackness, the result of his trade, is a kind of negritude, marking him as one of the excluded and disenfranchised of the earth. But in the middle of the black face are the white teeth of his laugh; his cheerfulness stands in marked contrast to the wooden seriousness of the hero of *Uomini e no.* N-2 may be "more man" in a figurative sense, but he fails to coalesce as a concrete or believable person, and this is fatal to the novel. Smoke-Face surmounts this difficulty and manages to be perfectly human and yet emblematic, metaphorically significant, at the same time.

A similar but somewhat more playful complexity of meaning is attached to the meal which Smoke-Face shares with the family, the central event and in fact the only real event of the novel. It is a kind of Last Supper: Black-Face shares the bread of the family, predicts certain sufferings and transcendences, and offers them a salted anchovy (the fish is a paleo-Christian symbol) which only the elephant-grandfather is allowed to touch. The others sniff its odor, and put its salt on their bread. But the meal is more meaningful and a good deal more ingenious as an "economic satire" in the manner of Swift. Except for their weekly quota of bread, most of which is eaten by the elephant, the family lives on chicory which they gather along the roads. Boiling this in a huge pot, they ladle it into bowls and eat it for their one meal of the day. But in this manner, the mother fears, the children will grow up not knowing how to eat soup or cut up chicken. So at every meal there is an elaborate pantomine in which they pretend to eat other things, and always with the proper table manners: antipasto, fried potatoes, meat, fruit, and wine sipped from empty glasses. The meal in which Smoke-Face joins them is a particularly elaborate one, with an oil-cruet, fruit bowls, and even triple silverware added to the ordinary settings. With tears of hunger streaming down their cheeks the children go through the motions of eating. The meal is a parody of polite bourgeois etiquette; the "modest proposal" is that children, while starving to death, should nevertheless learn good table manners by pretending to eat air. This forestalls in advance the bourgeois criticism that the lower classes are uncouth and would not appreciate the better things in life if they were given to them. Smoke-Face here serves the function of the outside observer, always a useful device in fiction where a customary situation or procedure must be explained to the reader. He comments that he too would like to take part in the charade and learn how to eat chicken. "Never had a chance to learn,"[85] he says, laughing. But this joke is not his real response to the ritual of the meal. In the mock-religious framework of the novel his responding act is to offer them the fish which is both spirit (the odor which is all the children get) and flesh (the meat eaten by the elephant). The family grumbles at this, as humans frequently grumble when God gets the best of things and they are left with the smoke.

Smoke-Face finally digs into his pocket and pays for a real meal, including wine, chestnuts, and more anchovies. In the course of this meal the adults at least are considerably cheered by the wine, and Smoke-Face produces a reed fife (*piffero,* a rather funny word in Italian) and plays on it. He has learned this skill, he explains, because ever since childhood it has been his dream to be a sorcerer. This idea echoes back and forth in an "operatic" conversation that dominates most of a chapter. Why does he wish to be a sorcerer and play the fife? Why does he search for the one theme that is exactly suited to his purposes?

The man takes his full glass in his hand. He laughs and empties it. He has already said that he didn't know why he was looking for his theme. Now he answers my mother: "But yes, lady. It's for enchanting elephants."[86]

"Elephant" in this sense is simply physical humanity, the warmth of companion flesh. Smoke-Face goes on to explain that he had never understood why he liked to sit next to a working companion or a traveler on a train, and then realized that he "liked to be near an elephant." At this point elephants, fifes, and sorcery begin to emerge as another metaphor for the personal and technical problem Vittorini discussed in the preface to *Il garofano rosso:* how to express a highly personal emotion through the outworn and banal apparatus of fiction? how to communicate realities and yet transcend conventional realism? In both *Conversazione in Sicilia* and *Il Sempione strizza l'occhio al Fréjus* the answer is conveyed in musical terms: the "something which does for the novel what music does for the opera," the fife that "enchants elephants." In the later novel the metaphor first emerges in the pantomine dinner. The *linguaggio* or style (metaphorically the fife-playing) makes even this improbable scene seem acceptable. But here the technique seems to turn inward on itself in the Gidean manner. The meal is made "real" in two ways: the reader accepts the improbability because of the whole style and treatment of the chapter, and inside the framework of the novel the family accepts the food as real through the "enchantment" of their own way of talking about it. Through language the meal becomes a ritual, and the fact that the food is unreal no more interferes with the validity of the ritual than the invisibility of the Divine interferes with the validity of the Mass. "Music does something," and this music is externalized both by the poetic and echoing quality of the dialogue and by Smoke-Face's piping. Thus Smoke-Face, in addition to prophet and revolutionist, is also the artist.

Before he leaves the family Smoke-Face offers a final and cryptic piece of wisdom: he explains how elephants die. Never in all of Africa is a dead elephant seen in the jungle. Instead, when their last hours come upon them, they make their way to "secret cemeteries, unknown even to them while they're alive."[87] There they simply stretch out and die, a burden on no one. (The word *peso*, burden, weight, is one of the recurring motifs of the novel.) After offering this zoological information, Smoke-Face winks, makes "a farewell sign," and takes his departure. Several days later the family learns of his death. Meanwhile the grandfather is pondering the matter of the death of elephants. In the final chapter he puts his coat and hat on, takes his stick, and without a word wanders off toward the woods. The mother refuses to let the children go after him, commenting,

"We too are elephants."[88] But the ending of the chapter is ambiguous, in the whimsical and antitragical way that dominates the whole tone of the novel. "It's not the beginning of night, it's the end," the mother tells them. And she explains that the workmen who are going to their jobs will find the grandfather and bring him home again. "Meanwhile let him get disenchanted," she advises. (*"Ma si sbizzarrisca,"* literally "Let him get rid of his bizarreries.) The bizarreries are, perhaps, the sentimental romanticism of the Risorgimento, but they are also the enchantments of the novel itself, the fife-playing. Is it really possible to get rid of these? The tension between enchantment and reality is the essence of Vittorini's method. In the end it is not really certain whether the grandfather will come home. Is it possible to count on the working men? The novel ends just before we find how it will all turn out.

The Collective Novel

In the period 1945-49 Vittorini's thought was very largely pre-occupied with politics. During much of this time, as editor of *Politecnico,* he served as a kind of focus of an independent-revolutionary movement among Italian intellectuals that gradually drifted away, if not from Marxism, at least from the wartime alliance with the Communist Party. In Vittorini himself the climax of this process is marked by his 1947 open letter to Togliatti, in which he reproaches Party communism for having lost its revolutionary impetus and declined into a dogmatic bureaucracy not fundamentally different from that of the capitalist state. Above all, in this letter, he is concerned with the effects of Marxism on intellectual life and the creative artist.

> Committed to the struggle for the conquest of a classless society, Marxism has not yet developed very much in the direction of its intrinsic significance. Neither has it discovered a means or method of preventing various kinds of decline into cultural automatism, into political automatism of one sort or another—of keeping alive in man that spirit of ascent which at one time, under the name of Protestantism, represented the ascending spirit of the bourgeoisie. A society, even a classless one, in which man lacks this spirit . . . will be a society in which no new Marx, no new philosopher, no new poet, no new political man will have a reason for living.[89]

It was also in this period that Vittorini produced his longest and most complicated novel, *Le donne di Messina* * The political roots of

* "The Women of Messina."

the novel are clearly visible: the Vittorini who wrote it is still a revolutionary, believing in the "spirit of ascent" and even in the classless
society, in economic communism, but at the same time committed
to a concept of personal individualism that would allow each human
being, including the artist, a free expression of his identity. If this is
politically inconsistent—and it is in many respects—the inconsistency
is reflected in the somewhat confused and unresolved pattern of
conflict in the novel. Vittorini struggled over this book for many
years. It is clear that he intended it as the climactic work of his
career, a vast and complex "epic of modern Italy" that would finally
fulfill the promise of *Conversazione in Sicilia.* The earlier novel, he
came to believe in the postwar years, was marred by the censorship
under which it was written, and also suffered somewhat from the
"birth pangs" of the technique he had worked out in the very process
of writing it. *Le donne di Messina,* freed from these disadvantages,
was to be the complete expression of his technical development as a
novelist.

He evidently began it as early as 1945; the first fragments of
the narrative appeared in *Rassegna d'Italia* in 1947, the year of the
Togliatti letter. In 1949 the first of two versions of the complete
novel was published by Bompiani. In this form it was generally
judged, by Vittorini himself as well as by its critics, to be somewhat
unsatisfactory. At Vittorini's request the edition was not reprinted
and soon became a rare item. Meanwhile, beginning in 1952, he took
up the narrative again and began rewriting it. In 1964 a second and
final version appeared. Shortly after it was published Vittorini, in a
statement in *La Fiera Letteraria,* called the earlier version "old-
fashioned, and here and there false," and spoke of his dissatisfaction
with the plot, especially "certain authoritarian structures of the nineteenth-century novel."[90] All this throws some light, although perhaps
not enough, on the state of the final version of the novel and the
various difficulties that are apparent in it, as well as on its obvious
merits.

First of all, the final version gives the impression that the
mechanisms or points of view of three different novels have been
combined in a rather unsatisfactory way and never thoroughly
assimilated to each other. The structure of the novel as originally
conceived, to judge from the *Rassegna d'Italia* fragments, was the
train journey of the narrator's Uncle Agrippa through the confusion
and dislocation of postwar Italy. This original plan was picaresque:
Uncle Agrippa's search for his lost daughter Siracusa leads him from
place to place and from person to person until a kind of cross-section
of the nation—or at least its poor and disenfranchised—is established. The second apparatus is that of an "I" narrator who expands,

from his identity as Uncle Agrippa's nephew, to a kind of national consciousness, the archetype of the postwar wanderer: "I am Apulian and haven't been able to rest until I have begun this coming and going between Molfetta and Milan that at every station shakes me from my torpor of a man hanging to the baggage rack . . . Or I am Milanese and yet I haven't been able to stay in my plain of a thousand trades, I too have wanted to try dealing in lemons. . . ."[91] In the 1964 version of the novel these two structures recur only intermittently and are submerged in a third apparatus: the story of a group of refugees and houseless persons who build a new community in a mountain valley south of Bologna. This last structure is "collective" both in ideology and in narrative technique, and it is the most original part of *Le donne di Messina* even though it is, in some respects, the least successful. In theme it is a kind of Marxist *Robinson Crusoe;* Vittorini had finally rewritten the book that fascinated him from the time of his childhood. The refugees begin from zero, with nothing but some mine-sown land and the rubble of a few buildings shattered by the war, and gradually build a kind of microcosm or model of an ideal society. This community—at least as the refugees plan it—is collective in the economic and political sense, resembling the classless society of Marxist theory, and yet allows for a certain minimum of individuality. "A man wants a life for himself," the hovering narrator comments, "and says he wants 'a room.' And there is no doubt he was born *also* to have a life for himself, not only a life with others. He has the right to have 'a room.' "[92] In that *also* lies the fundamental question of the novel, a conflict, not entirely resolved either in Vittorini's mind or in the work itself. Is man born to be a collective animal or an individual? Is it possible to create, to make love, to have a decent minimum of privacy, in a collective society? In this novel Vittorini anticipates the problem of the relation of individualism to socialism that only a little later is to preoccupy Pasternak, Djilas, and Yevtushenko.

In narrative technique the novel makes some remarkable attempts to present this theme in an appropriate "collective" manner. A good part of the narrative is presented through a *Registro* or journal kept by an anonymous scribe as a sort of semi-official record of the community. Here outward progress is recorded—the transition from wheelbarrows to a mule-drawn cart, and from the cart to a truck—and comments are also made on personal matters such as the various relations of loyalty and authority in the community. In these chapters there are at least three levels in the transmission of the narrative material. The refugees themselves do things, relate to each other, and conduct conversations. These are recorded by the *Registro,* and finally the hovering narrator reports bits and fragments of the *Registro*, comments on it, and sometimes expresses his incomprehension of certain entries or speculates on what they might mean. This puts the reader at a considerable distance from the actual events; it insulates him from the story to the point where, in the end, a good deal of it fails to come to life. The technique is somewhat different from Pavese's, for example, in *La luna e i falò*, or Conrad's in the novels related by Marlow. Through their narrators Pavese and Conrad maintain an initial distance from the events, but at a certain point the narrating intelligence plunges inward and shares the most vivid emotions of the central characters. The execution of Santina in *La luna e i falò*, Jim's death in *Lord Jim*, are seen with a direct and excruciating precision, even though in a technical sense they are related at second hand by persons who never saw them. This is a kind of subterfuge, a poetic license conceded by tacit agreement between the author and the reader. But Vittorini doggedly clings to the letter of his apparatus; we know *only* what the hovering narrator knows, and where he is not present (and he is really present nowhere) we see things only darkly through a mirror of rumor. Occasionally this narrator speaks in his own voice and is revealed as a persona of the author: the owner of the voice mentions that he too, at the age of thirteen, wandered about Italy on trains, that he had a Sicilian mother, a brother called Rosario (the dead soldier-brother in *Conversazione in Sicilia* is named Liborio), a boyhood where "the sun is the mummy of eighty centuries of sun."[93] In these passages the novel reads like a kind of curious sequel or appendix to *Conversazione in Sicilia*.

The *Registro* is only one of several "collective" techniques in the novel. In another the narrator is somewhat less conspicuous, withdrawing until he is almost invisible. Shortly before the middle of the novel a long passage (four chapters) is devoted to comments by various members of the community speaking in their own voices. This covers chiefly the period of the first winter of the community, from February to May: ". . . things told by the inhabitants themselves, in the nights of the following summer, to refresh their memories, or to inform, one to another, a friend or a new acquaintance who asked them about something."[94] Then follows a quasi-epic "They tell," and the passages labeled with the names of the speakers. The voices—resigned, stoic, precise in a laconic kind of way—resemble those in *Spoon River Anthology*; there is something unreal and sybilline in their intuition, as though it were coming from beyond the tomb. "For us there are no Sundays," said Pompeo Manera the peasant.

There are no hours, from March to November, when we don't work. We have the winter to rest in. The earth is asleep, it isn't

> to be disturbed, and we shut ourselves in the stable with a little
> fire, a little wine, a few chestnuts, and take our pleasure for the
> whole year.[95]

The others, the town-bred and the workers, counter this with a
defense of their own way of life, their Sundays, and the dialogue
continues: a kind of archetypal debate of the social classes. In contrast to the sparseness of the *Registro* these passages are essentially
lyrical. They convey little information about the characters or their
actions; their function is to communicate the mentality and emotional
state of the speakers, and their social classes, rather than to advance
the narrative. A second round of these Spoon River voices in the
1949 version of the novel was deleted in the final edition.

A considerable attempt has obviously been made to draw all
these materials into an integrated whole. The original frame-story
(Uncle Agrippa's search for his daughter) is linked to the story of
the mountain community through a subplot: the love of the young
man Ventura and a girl who is finally revealed as the daughter Siracusa herself. This device of the long-lost child, with its somewhat
implausible coincidence, is rescued from banality by the obliqueness
of its presentation. Like the conventional adventure-story plot of
Uomini e no, it is hinted at or impressionistically sketched rather
than recounted directly; if the reader is aware of the conventional
device at all it is merely as a skeleton that serves to support a highly
lyrical surface. There is a second connection between Uncle Agrippa
and the communal village: in the train scenes in the early part of the
novel he has long conversations with a character called Carlo il Calvo
(Carlo the Bald), who seems to have his own mysterious reasons for
traveling about Italy and asking question of people. Carlo gradually
emerges as some kind of spy for the authorities, the agent of an
Establishment determined to prevent spontaneous communal efforts
from succeeding. He returns frequently to the village and makes
vague threats to the refugees, pointing out to them that they have no
proper deeds to their land and are not paying taxes on their harvests.
But in time his cryptic antagonism comes to focus on a single member of the community: Ventura. It is evident that an invisible connection links these two men, making them enemies and yet in some
mysterious way blood brothers.

The last third of the novel, the part Vittorini rewrote the most
radically in the 1964 version, is dominated by the conflict between
Carlo and Ventura. It is the most successful part of the novel and
also the most conventional; there is a direct simplicity of narrative
line and two fairly solid characters emerge at last from the fuzziness

of the "collective" technique. Both Ventura and Carlo are former fascists; it transpires even that they were officers together in Salò militia that committed so many atrocities against the rural population in the last months of the war. Now the Referendum of June 1946 is over and Italy is a republic; the self-serving Carlo has become a spy for the new government. At the end of the war Ventura was safe in an Allied prison camp, but escaped and has joined his cause to that of the villagers. In the village, even though he is withdrawn and diffident, he becomes a kind of spiritual center of the effort to create the new community. In the allegorical sense Italy's effort to rebuild itself both economically and psychologically begins with a recognition of the nation's part in the guilt of the past. This existentialist responsibility is what the fascist-turned-democrat Carlo refuses to accept. His real motive in harassing the villagers, as he admits to Uncle Agrippa, is not to drive them from the land but to drive Ventura from their midst. "It wasn't enough for him to become a fugitive, an outlaw, and he committed the even graver foolishness of joining a bunch of desperados who are quite different from him, of embracing a cause that was exactly the contrary of his own, so that he has kept all his old enemies and lost those who used to be his friends."[96] Carlo knows that without Ventura the communal effort will come to nothing. In the climactic scene of the novel he sends to the village a group of young "hunters," actually former partisans, in the hope of scaring Ventura away. At this point all the elements of postwar Italy have been brought into the allegory. There are two kinds of former fascists: those who have managed to insinuate themselves into the new government, and those who face up honestly to their responsibility for the past. The former partisans have been captured by the Establishment as part of an apparatus of official patriotism. The Italian people (the villagers) muddle along in their own way trying to wrest a living from the earth: beginning with their hands, then with wheelbarrows, then with a cart, then with a truck, they painstakingly recapitulate the history of civilization from stone age to the twentieth century. Are they moving toward Marxism, toward a truly collective society? So they believe; and so, evidently, Vittorini himself believed in the period when he first conceived *Le donne de Messina* around 1946.

The outcome of this question hinges not so much on Carlo or Ventura as on what the partisans will do when they reach the village; that is, when they encounter the real economic and human problems of postwar Italy. Protected and solaced by Siracusa, Ventura goes into hiding from them. But in spite of their red kerchiefs and Sten guns, the threat of the partisans is an empty one.

Instead of searching for Ventura (rooting out the last vestiges of fascism) they sit in the shade telling stories about their wartime exploits, complaining because there is no Coca-Cola in the village and the beer is warm. They are impatient to get back to Modena, where people live like civilized human beings, with refrigerators, and every café has a jukebox. The Italian youth of 1944 was unexpectedly and incredibly heroic; the youth of 1946 is already corrupted by the gradual advance of materialism. When the "hunters" leave the village two of the most loyal of the community, Fazzoletto Rosso and Toma, go with them.

In an epilogue added to the final version of the novel the fortunes of the village are followed into the Sixties, the period of neocapitalistic prosperity. Uncle Agrippa is still traveling around Italy on trains; he has turned into a kind of Italian version of the Wandering Jew, condemned to homelessness, to perpetual motion. Carlo is still a spy for the authorities, although there is not much to spy out in a time when the proletariat has been pacified with refrigerators and motor scooters. The village is unrecognizable; gradually it has turned into a shoddy collection of neon signs and jukeboxes identical to every other town in Italy. The communal ideal is forgotten, unless it is now represented by the priest who teaches the children their catechism. As for Ventura, he has lost his identity and is simply "the husband of Teresa," as Siracusa is now called. In twenty years he has progressed from fascist to penitent to a revolutionary who became old-fashioned even before he had time to apply his revolutionary ideals to reality. The goal he worked for—the abolition of poverty through the sharing of goods in common—has been made obsolete by the Economic Miracle. It is Carlo who explains all this, talking finally to himself and to the reader more than to Uncle Agrippa. At the end of the novel he is by no means an unsympathetic character; he is a spokesman for capitalism and private property with many cunning arguments to present, even if he is portrayed somewhat ironically. If he seems to break in half as a character—if the novel itself seems to break in half or into several pieces, so that it gives the impression of a kind of crazy-quilt of incompletely assimilated styles—this only reflects Vittorini's vision of what happened to his country between 1944 and 1964. It is possible in this way for a novel to be a relative failure technically and at the same time a document of considerable interest—not so much for the light it throws on Italy and Italian social and political processes in the period involved, but for the insight it gives of the relation between these processes and Vittorini's rather complex and troubled aesthetic development.

A Final Conversation

Vittorini's last complete work of fiction, the short novel *La Garibaldina,** was written in 1949-50 and first appeared in the Florentine review *Il Ponte* in the spring of 1950. In structure it almost exactly resembles *Conversazione in Sicilia:* a train journey ends in a town where multiple voices speak to the hero, where he arrives at some kind of reconciliation with the alien world and with his unquiet self. The technical differences are slight but important. There are two central characters instead of one, and the narrative is told in the third person; the whole tone is less subjective. The autobiographical typographer has been converted to a Sicilian soldier going home on leave, and the mother of *Conversazione in Sicilia* has been rolled together with the Gran Lombardo, the knife grinder, and the other fantastic-prophetic characters to form the Garibaldina, a figure more mythical than realistic. Where *Conversazione in Sicilia* consists of a series of conversations, *La Garibaldina* is really built around a single dialogue, that between the soldier and the old lady. There is a greater unity in this final novel, if there is less poetic intensity and a little less stylistic inventiveness.

By 1950 it is clear that the train journey is a kind of personal myth for Vittorini. His whole subdued nostalgia for his childhood, an emotion that remains half-concealed in his fiction and is only rarely expressed in overt form, is bound up with it. And in his later writing the train journey is always backwards: where the Sicilian boy set out with a pass in his pocket to explore Italy and the wider world, the mature writer returns to Sicily in search of his childhood. But why is the protagonist of *La Garibaldina* portrayed as a soldier, a figure very different in background and temperament from Vittorini? Specifically he is a *bersagliere,* a sharpshooter of the elite corps connected in the Italian mind with the struggle for national freedom, the Risorgimento, the heroism of the 1915 Alpine campaign. This particular soldier happens to be named Innocenzo; he is a kind of Candide or Simplicissimus, quite unaware that he stands for anything except a soldier trying to get home on a three-day pass. His leitmotif is the song of the migratory harvesters chant at him from another train, reminding him of his rather humble social status: *"Il soldato va alla guerra, mangia male, dorme in terra."*† It is true that the old lady, when she meets him on the train stalled

* Included with *Erica* in *The Dark and the Light* (New Directions, 1960). The title is also that of a popular song of the Risorgimento.
† "The soldier goes to war, eats badly, sleeps on the ground."

in a tunnel, calls him "an angel in the heart of the mountain,"[97] but
he regards this merely as an example of her whimsical eroticism.
Yet in spite of his innocence he is condemned to play his part; he
cannot shed the heritage of history behind him any more than he
can shed his uniform. As for the old lady she has her historical role
too; according to her own account she was a kind of camp follower
of the Risorgimento. It is true that she would have to be almost a
hundred years old to have done everything she says; but she is less
a real old lady than a kind of walking embodiment of history. In
order to free the story from any rigid restriction in time and space
the first sentence of the novel indicates the date vaguely as "June
19**." If *Le donne di Messina* is an attempt at a national epic this is
something on a smaller scale, a national fable. The best analogy in
American literature would be something like Benét's story "The
Devil and Daniel Webster."

The soldier, like any soldier, has no particular desire to take
part in an allegory. He is deliberately traveling light; he sets out on
his journey without anything in his hands, without even a lunch to
eat on the train, literally and symbolically without baggage. But
before he gets home, through a series of petty but inexorable con-
cessions, he ends up carrying the old lady's baggage, even though
she has promised him a carriage which does not materialize. Soldiers
are used to broken promises from their elders, and he is cheerful.
"I didn't want to carry even a parcel." And he laughs: "I wanted to
go the road with my hands in my pockets."[98] But this is exactly what
he cannot do; Italians are Italians, Jews are Jews, Tibetans are
Tibetans, and each is obliged to carry the baggage of his history.
Who obliges him to carry it? The force of history, personified as a
kind of Vestal of the national myth. The Garibaldina calls him her
"orderly." When she is absent he grumbles and tries to give the
baggage to others, but when she returns (on horseback!) he obedi-
ently picks up the bags and follows her. By this time she has re-
christened him "Fortunato," and in spite of everything he feels
fortunate indeed to be carrying her burdens. "He saw her there, in
her gray veil, and she was as exciting as a young girl. And exactly
because of her ancientness, not because there was something young
in her."[99]

The merit of the novel lies in the skill with which this rather
playful allegory is combined with the more personal theme of the
train journey. The final effect of the narrative is anything but "allegorical"; it is rich in the most vivid and precise kind of physical
detail. At night in a remote Sicilian station the train begins to move:
"There was a hoarse blast of a horn, then the jerk of the couplings

from car to car, a jerk of the wheels, then an opaque glimmer from a passing open door, then the black station gone by, the black tower of the watertank gone by, Comiso was gone now in the black night of prickly pears that passed on the left and the right."[100] Or the arrival at Gela: "The train slowed, there was the reflection of a street lamp approaching on a yellow wall, the whiteness of a side-walk passed under the already opened door, two trainmen jumping down one after the other, the screech of the wheels stopping as the brakes gripped them."[101] This insistence on the phenomenology of physical experience approaches that of Robbe-Grillet and the *nouveau roman*. But where Robbe-Grillet's magnification of detail is on the one hand objective and on the other hand obsessive, almost neurotic in its concentration, Vittorini's detail is highly personal and emotional and at the same time serene, nostalgic. These powerful memories of his boyhood wanderings, the train sounds and flashes of light, lend the novel a power of reality as great as anything in Vittorini's work.

Ostensibly these experiences of the train journey happen to the soldier, but they also "happen" to the voice that tells the story; the author-persona and the reader participate in the sensations through an obvious bond of empathy. The soldier and the Garibaldina are symmetrical and more or less equally important characters. But the Garibaldina is seen only at second hand, and that part of the novel that deals with her lacks this sensory immediacy. Furthermore she and the soldier, in a certain sense, are an ill-sorted pair. The soldier is essentially a realistic character drawn from real life, even though he is grudgingly made to carry a certain burden of allegory. The old lady is sheer fable, a kind of Rabelaisian fairy godmother. She her-self hints broadly and candidly at her mythical nature. "You've heard of Cornelia the mother of the Gracchi. You've heard of Lucretia. . . Don't you recognize me?"[102] Vittorini might have made her, at least on the surface, typical of the provincial Sicilian aristocracy, but he did not choose to do so. The old prince in Tomasi di Lampedusa's *Il gattopardo* is a historical archetype; the Gari-baldina is fantasy. There is no reason why a character in fiction should not be fantastic. The difficulty is that the soldier and the old lady do not seem to belong in the same novel. He talks like a soldier; she speaks with the improbably grandeur of a puppet queen. He has a realistic surface; she has none, or rather she has several realistic surfaces which melt away when any attempt is made to examine them. Like a character in a drama of Strindberg, she seems to change form, name, identity at will. Is she or is she not a baroness? "That's a title that people without fantasy stick on me. . . . But it's

my daughter who married a baron, not me. Because I stayed repub-
lican even after the meeting of Garibaldi with Savoy."[103] These
sibylline utterances are comprehensible only if she is understood not
as a human being but as a myth, a personification of the brief
moment in Italian history when nationalism and liberalism, the
freedom of the human spirit, were one. The Garibaldina has the
same degree of reality as John Bull or the Statue of Liberty. If she
expresses herself with wit and eloquence it is only because rhetoric,
l'arte di ben parlare, is an Italian national tradition.

Toward the end of the novel the Garibaldina, for a while,
disappears. The soldier is left standing in a street with her suitcases
while certain disembodied voices—the tutelary spirits of the town,
of Sicily itself—speak to him out of the darkened houses. The voices
comment on the Garibaldina, offer impractical advice to the soldier,
quarrel among themselves. "*Che pazza, eh?* She's a real madwoman.
She has more energy in her body than we need in a town [*paese,*
also country] like ours. . . What trick has she played on you?"[104]
This device of the antiphonal voices that at the same time seem to
share a single personality is one of the most successful inventions of
the novel. Vittorini manages to make a whole people speak more
effectively than he does either in *Conversazione in Sicilia* or in the
self-consciously "collective" technique of *Le donne di Messina.* Like
a Greek chorus, the voices are basically right-minded but conventional, timid, suspicious of extraordinary personality. They waste
their time turning over nuances and discussing rumors while the
real course of history is being prepared by others, while Clytem-
nestra is sharpening her axe. They accuse the Garibaldina of various
obscure sins, of being the kind of woman who follows the regiments
and gives birth in guardrooms, of having become Garibaldi's mistress shortly after her First Communion ("very fond, in his old age,
of little girls."[105]) The Garibaldina reappears and disappears again,
leaving him more confused than before. Finally he is menaced by a
crowd of migratory harvesters, the same who jeered at him earlier
from the train. They accuse him now of some vague crime, perhaps
toadying to the aristocracy, because he carries the Garibaldina's
bags. They suggest instead that he should carry their knapsacks,
and offer to salt his private parts if he refuses. The proletariat is not
presented very endearingly in this last novel of Vittorini. Where is
the soldier's duty? In carrying the burdens of a disenfranchised
poor, or the burdens of a national myth? The dilemma is reduced
by the arrival of the Garibaldina herself, on a spirited black-and-
white horse. With a certain sarcasm she points out to the harvesters
that the sun is up and they have not come to work on time; after a

typical Sicilian argument they meekly agree to work the day for a lira instead of twenty-two soldi. "Eh, Fortunato," she cries to the soldier. "Now do you believe I have a carriage?" His opinion is that if she has a horse she probably has a carriage. "I promised I'd make your fortune and I will," she tells him.[106] The ending is strange. The soldier walks away, walks faster, as though he hopes to escape from her. He crosses a piazza, rounding a church where bells are summoning the faithful to mass. At every bell-stroke the doves fly out of the campanile, then settle back again, as though the doves themselves are making the bells ring with their circling. As he turns down the hill toward the sea the doves wheel gleaming in the sun, "with one old whore of a dove leading the flock of males and females." The soldier, Innocenzo or Fortunato as his name may be, is last seen singing the popular song of the *belle époque* that inspired the title: "You're the star of us soldiers . . . Biondina . . . Capricious Garibaldina . . ."[107]

It is fitting that Vittorini's fiction ends in this somewhat ambiguous scene, mingling religious and political symbolism with a highly poetic sensuality. The tension between politics and the personal vocation of poetry, of poetically expressed experience, dominates Vittorini's whole work. But since this "tension" is a highly fluid complex of emotions and nostalgias rather than an intellectual dualism, it is difficult to describe it with precision or to trace it out in the works more concretely than the works themselves express it. The term "politics" particularly is unsatisfactory. In the closing scene of *La Garibaldina* this end of the tension is expressed chiefly in the workers who surrender to the Garibaldina's demand for collective sacrifice, and in the image of the male and female doves led by "one old whore" who is patently also to be identified with the Garibaldina. Yet it is obvious that for a writer in a Catholic tradition the figure of the doves entering and leaving the companile has religious implications—oblique as they may be, and perhaps even only partly conscious on the part of the novelist. In Christian iconography the dove signifies the Holy Spirit. The doves leave the companile whenever the bells ring, i.e., whenever the Church makes an official noise, and return when it is silent. This might be taken as a fairly comprehensible and simple comment on the relation between spirit and ecclesiasticism, except that the chief dove of all is identified with the Garibaldina, who personifies the often anticlerical impetus of the Risorgimento. It is possible to argue that true spirit often stands opposed to ecclesiasticism, that the Risorgimento was more genuinely "religious" than the Church that opposed it, and so on. But this kind of attempt to clarify ambiguities, to resolve apparent contradictions, is exactly what Vittorini's work does not invite. His fiction deals with networks of emotions; these emotions, it is true, are instigated by concrete events of the real world, but it is a mistake to associate them too closely, or confine them too literally, to these concrete events. In this sense the kind of unfocussed and elusive emotion achieved at the end of *La Garibaldina* is typical of Vittorini's whole work.

In spite of the effectiveness of this scene it is quite evident that *La Garibaldina* is not Vittorini's most successful or important novel. Pavese's last novel, *La luna e i falò*, is the culmination of his career; it is his most complex work, the most ambitious, and the one in which the artistic problems of a lifetime are finally resolved. *L'attenzione* does not occupy quite this place in Moravia's work, but at least it is as intricate, and as competent, as anything that precedes it. But the careers of Moravia and Pavese are linear; with each succeeding novel their fiction becomes more complex, richer in texture, more competent. Vittorini's work, whether or not he intended it or was aware of it, is concentric: the novels before *Conversazione in Sicilia* are apprentice work, and the novels after it labor under an obvious burden of anticlimax. When his whole work is regarded in perspective the other novels are chiefly valuable in the light they throw on *Conversazione in Sicilia*. If this seems unfair to novels of the competence, the brilliant stylistic vividness, of *La Garibaldina*, this is simply a tribute to the power and originality of this single and central work. For *Conversazione in Sicilia* Vittorini invented a unique novelistic language, and he is perfectly correct in his assertion that this language adds something to conventional fiction comparable to what is added to the opera by music. The difficulty is that this language was invented for a particular novel, or more precisely for the particular, if unfocussed and ambiguous, set of emotions that preceded the writing of the novel. And the effort of creation necessary to invent this style permanently determined Vittorini's qualities as a stylist. Everything after *Conversazione in Sicilia* is told in this Vittorinian "language," even in instances where the language, it might be objected, is not entirely appropriate or effective. Pavese, toward the end of his life, argued for the absolute necessity of creating a new aesthetic for each new artistic work. This is precisely what Vittorini was unable to do. The language of *Conversazione in Sicilia* recurs, in what strikes the reader as diluted form, throughout the rest of his fiction.

If Vittorini has a limitation, then, it is that he succeeds totally only in a single novel. Yet there is a sense in which his achievement is more striking than that of Moravia or Pavese. The narrative texture he invented for *Conversazione in Sicilia*—with great pains, and working under considerable handicaps—is a more original literary instrument that anything in Moravia or Pavese, or for that matter anything in Italian fiction up to Vittorini's time. Its place in Italian literature is comparable to that of the Faulknerian rhetoric in American literature. Furthermore Vittorini shares with Moravia and Pavese certain qualities that bind the three together in spite of their superficial differences: a seriousness free of pomposity, a lack of sentimentalism, a genuine and total commitment to the craft of artist. There is no posturing or flashy rhetoric in their work, and, even in the case of Moravia, no cheap appeal to mass popularity. Their antisentimentalism and their economy of words lend their work a hardness of detail, a sensory precision that is the opposite of the romantic, in spite of the obvious emotion underlying the work of all three. Forged in censorship, their work is remarkable for its frankness. Influenced in all three cases by foreign models, it surmounts these influences and arrives at a totally original narrative technique that at the same time shows the evident strength of the lessons learned and assimilated. And the final quality they share is perhaps the most important one: they manage to create a fiction that, while objective and even ironic in its treatment of autobiographical material, is nevertheless a highly personal means of expression. On the one hand it achieves the detachment of traditional realism; on the other hand it communicates the intimacies of personal consciousness to a degree commonly associated with lyric poetry. The goal of all three is expressed in Pavese's comment that the reason for writing fiction is "the impulse to bring into focus the irrational and indistinct that lurks at the bottom of our experience."[108] This making distinct the indistinct, verbalizing the irrational, is perhaps the hardest task an artist can assume.

Notes

ALBERTO MORAVIA

1. Jean Starobinski, "Truth in Masquerade," in Victor Brombert, ed., *Stendhal* (Spectrum Books, 1962), 119.
2. *L'uomo come fine e altri saggi* (Bompiani, 1964), 62. Hereafter *OCF*.
3. Quoted in Oreste del Buono, ed., *Moravia* (Feltrinelli, series La Biblioteca Ideale #1, 1962), 72. Hereafter *DB/M*.
4. *OCF*, 212.
5. *OCF*, 159.
6. *Racconti* (Bompiani, 1952), 37. Hereafter *Ra*.
7. *Ra*, 49.
8. *Ra*, 49.
9. *Ra*, 44.
10. *Ra*, 46.
11. *Romanzi brevi* (Bompiani, 1964), 184f. Hereafter *RB*.
12. *RB*, 185.
13. *RB*, 232.
14. *RB*, 237.
15. *RB*, 252.
16. *RB*, 340.
17. *L'amore coniugale e altri racconti* (Bompiani, 1958), 32. Hereafter *AC*.
18. *AC*, 87.
19. *AC*, 151.
20. *AC*, 163.
21. *AC*, 278.
22. *AC*, 279.
23. *AC*, 284.
24. *AC*, 289.
25. *AC*, 293.

26. *L'automa* (Bompiani, 1963), 57.
27. *DB/M*, 11.
28. *DB/M*, 11.
29. *DB/M*, 65.
30. *Gli indifferenti* (Bompiani, 1956), 12. Hereafter *Gli I.*
31. *Gli I*, 27.
32. *Gli I*, 30.
33. *Gli I*, 350.
34. *Gli I*, 78.
35. *Gli I*, 342f.
36. *Gli I*, 205.
37. *Gli I*, 326.
38. Quoted in *DB/M*, 36.
39. *Le ambizioni sbagliate* (Mondadori, 1935), 325. Hereafter AS.
40. *AS*, 151.
41. *AS*, 391.
42. *RB*, 53.
43. In a letter to the writer, undated [1966].
44. *RB*, 45.
45. *RB*, 36.
46. *RB*, 141.
47. *La romana* (Bompiani, 1953), 168. Hereafter *Ro.*
48. *Ro*, 404.
49. *Ro*, 405.
50. *Ro*, 496.
51. *Ro*, 381.
52. *Ro*, 147.
53. *Ro*, 202f. My italics.
54. *Ro*, 190.
55. *Ro*, 212.
56. *Ro*, 213.
57. *Ro*, 214.
58. Malcolm Cowley, ed., *Writers at Work: The Paris Review Interviews* (Viking, 1960), 219.
59. *Il conformista* (Bompiani, 1951), 114. Hereafter *Con.*
60. *DB/M*, 60.
61. *Con*, 348.
62. *Con*, 385.
63. *Il disprezzo* (Bompiani, 1954), 41. Hereafter D.
64. *D*, 43.
65. *D*, 145.
66. *D*, 235f.
67. *D*, 249.
68. *D*, 259.
69. *DB/M*, 10.
70. *DB/M*, 61.

71. *La ciociara* (Bompiani, 1957), 15. Hereafter *Cio.*
72. *Cio,* 5.
73. *Cio,* 13.
74. *Cio,* 348f.
75. *Cio,* 15.
76. *Cio,* 11.
77. *Cio,* 10.
78. *Cio,* 164.
79. *Cio,* 167.
80. *Cio,* 159.
81. *Cio,* 312.
82. *Cio,* 414.
83. *La noia* (Bompiani, 1960), 7. Hereafter *N.*
84. *N,* 154.
85. "I pittori malati di Verona," *Corriere della Sera,* September 6, 1959; reprinted in *Saggi Italiani* (Bompiani, 1960), 44.
86. *N,* 101.
87. *N,* 134.
88. *N,* 315.
89. *N,* 344.
90. *N,* 184.
91. *L'attenzione* (Bompiani, 1965), 34. Hereafter *Att.*
92. *Att,* 265.
93. *Att,* 216f.
94. *Att,* 231.
95. *Att,* 52f.
96. *Att,* 348.

CESARE PAVESE

1. *La letteratura americana e altri saggi* (Einaudi, 1953), 193. Hereafter *LA.*
2. *Il mestiere di vivere: Diario 1935-1950* (Einaudi, 1955), 26. Hereafter *MV.*
3. This influence is analyzed at some length by Lorenzo Mondo, "Fra Gozzano e Whitman: Le origini di Pavese," *Sigma,* 3/4 (December, 1964), pp. 3ff.
4. *LA,* 293.
5. Notes to Pavese's *Poesie edite e inedite* (Einaudi, 1962), 222. Hereafter *PEI.*
6. *Lettere 1945-1950* (Einaudi, 1966), 532.
7. *PEI,* 11.
8. *PEI,* 13f.
9. Preface by Massimo Mila to Pavese's *Poesie* (Einaudi, 1962), vii. Hereafter *P.*
10. Erich Auerbach, *Mimesis* (Princeton, 1953), 3.

11. *LA*, 330.
12. *LA*, 249.
13. *LA*, 335.
14. *Racconti* (Einaudi, 1960), 9.
15. *Romanzi* (Einaudi, 1961, 2 vols.), I:36. Hereafter *Rom.*
16. *Rom*, I:65.
17. *Rom*, I:81.
18. *Rom*, I:59.
19. *Rom*, I:57.
20. "Semplicità," *PEI*, 128.
21. *LA*, 36.
22. *MV*, 166.
23. *MV*, 131.
24. *MV*, 133.
25. *MV*, 172.
26. *Rom*, I:125.
27. *Rom*, I:124.
28. *Rom*, I:135.
29. *Rom*, I:157.
30. *Rom*, I:168.
31. *Rom*, I:161.
32. *Rom*, I:172.
33. *MV*, 172.
34. *Rom*, I:187.
35. *Rom*, I:189f.
36. *Rom*, I:200.
37. *Rom*, I:200.
38. *Rom*, I:263.
39. *Lettere 1924-1944* (Einaudi, 1966), 490.
40. *MV*, 400.
41. *Rom*, II:315.
42. *Rom*, II:342.
43. *Rom*, II:379.
44. Quoted in Michele Tondo, *Itinerario de Cesare Pavese* (Padua: Liviana Editrice, 1965), 88.
45. *MV*, 187.
46. *Rom*, I:268.
47. *Rom*, I:302.
48. *Rom*, I:279.
49. *Rom*, I:291.
50. *Rom*, I:313.
51. *Rom*, I:323.
52. *Rom*, I:324.
53. *Rom*, I:325.
54. *Rom*, II:176.
55. *Rom*, II:179.

56. *Rom,* II:253.

57. *Rom,* II:260.

58. *Rom,* II:261.

59. Davide Lajolo, *Il "vizio assurdo"* (Milan: Il Saggiatore, 1960), 281. Hereafter *VA.*

60. *VA,* 288.

61. *Rom,* I:329.

62. *Rom,* II:10.

63. *Rom,* II:12.

64. *Rom,* II:17.

65. *Rom,* II:28.

66. *Rom,* II:123.

67. *Rom,* II:130. In the original "fascist" is *repubblichini,* referring to the conscripts of the Salò Republic.

68. *Rom,* II:131.

69. *Rom,* II:385.

70. *Rom,* II:394.

71. *Rom,* II:417f.

72. *Rom,* II:391.

73. *Rom,* II:391.

74. *Rom,* II:442.

75. *Rom,* II:450.

76. *LA,* 193. This article is translated in *Western Humanities Review* XI:3 (Summer 1957) and reprinted in the appendix of my *America in Modern Italian Literature* (Rutgers, 1964).

77. *Rom,* II:463.

78. *Rom,* II:394.

79. *Rom,* II:464.

80. *MV,* 302.

81. *Rom,* II:510.

82. *MV,* 303.

ELIO VITTORINI

1. *Diario in pubblico* (Bompiani, 1957), 173. Hereafter *DP.*

2. *DP,* 58.

3. *DP,* 198.

4. *Conversazione in Sicilia* (Bompiani, 1953), 8. Hereafter *CS.*

5. *CS,* 8.

6. *Sardegna come un'infanzia* (Mondadori, 1952), 9. Hereafter *S.*

7. *Piccola borghesia* (Mondadori, 1953), 122. Hereafter *PB.*

8. *PB,* 122f.

9. *PB,* 128.

10. *PB,* 9.

11. *PB,* 9.

12. *PB,* 20.

13. Preface to *Il garofano rosso* (Mondadori, 1948), 19. Hereafter *GR*.
14. *S*, 73.
15. Giovanni Cecchetti, "Elio Vittorini," *Italica*, 29:1 (March 1952), 8.
16. *S*, 9.
17. *S*, 30.
18. *S*, 71.
19. *S*, 101.
20. "Truth and Censorship: The Story of *The Red Carnation*," *The Western Humanities Review*, IX:3 (Summer 1955), 199. This American version of the preface to *Il garofano rosso* is based on a text revised by Vittorini himself for translation and differing in some respects from the original. Hereafter *GR* preface (*WHR*).
21. *GR* preface (*WHR*), 200.
22. Preface to *GR*, 34f.
23. Preface to *GR*, 29f.
24. Preface to *GR*, 29. This entire passage, including pages 29 and 30, was deleted in the revision Vittorini made for the *Western Humanities Review* translation.
25. Preface to *GR*, 34.
26. *GR*, 128f.
27. *GR*, 58.
28. *GR*, 78f.
29. *GR*, 104.
30. *GR*, 114f.
31. Preface to *GR*, 8.
32. *Erica e i suoi fratelli; La Garibaldina* (Bompiani, 1956), 285 (author's note). Hereafter *EG*.
33. *EG*, 7.
34. *EG*, 104.
35. *EG*, 107.
36. *EG*, 9.
37. *EG*, 11.
38. *EG*, 15.
39. *EG*, 87.
40. *EG*, 103.
41. *EG*, 106.
42. *EG*, 286 (author's note).
43. *EG*, 284 (author's note).
44. *GR* preface (*WHR*), 203. The italics of *"denied to the novel,"* and certain other modifications, were made by Vittorini in his 1954 revision for translation.
45. *GR* preface (*WHR*), 204f.
46. Preface to *GR*, 20f.
47. *CS*, 122.
48. *CS*, 51.
49. *CS*, 15.

50. *CS,* 17.
51. *CS,* 8.
52. *CS,* 24.
53. *CS,* 27.
54. *CS,* 29.
55. *CS,* 31.
56. Preface to *GR,* 27f. This passage has been newly translated from the revised version Vittorini made in 1954 for *The Western Humanities Review.*
57. *CS,* 85.
58. *CS,* 75.
59. *CS,* 107.
60. *CS,* 66.
61. *CS,* 119.
62. *CS,* 120.
63. *CS,* 121.
64. *CS,* 122.
65. *CS,* 123.
66. *CS,* 160-163.
67. *CS,* 167.
68. *CS,* 168.
69. *CS,* 172.
70. *CS,* 172.
71. *CS,* 172.
72. *CS,* 179.
73. *CS,* 186.
74. *CS,* 200.
75. *Uomini e no* (Bompiani, 1949), 48f. Hereafter *UN.*
76. *UN,* 127.
77. *DP,* 146.
78. *UN,* 82.
79. *UN,* 111.
80. *Il Sempione strizza l'occhio al Fréjus* (Bompiani, 1947), 5. Hereafter *SF.*
81. *SF,* 20f.
82. *SF,* 69.
83. *SF,* 30f. In the second sentence of this quotation Vittorini may have reversed thumb and little finger by mistake.
84. *SF,* 48.
85. *SF,* 58.
86. *SF,* 107.
87. *SF,* 125.
88. *SF,* 153.
89. "Lettera a Togliatti," *Politecnico,* 35 (January/March, 1947), reprinted in Marco Forti and Sergio Pautasso, eds., *Il Politecnico: Antologia Critica* (Milan, Lerici, 1960), 183.

90. *La Fiera Letteraria*, XL:6 (February 14, 1965), 10.

91. *Le donne di Messina* (Bompiani, 1964; the second and final version), 5f. Hereafter *DM-2*.

92. *DM-2*, 165.

93. *DM-2*, 140.

94. *DM-2*, 173.

95. *DM-2*, 175.

96. *DM-2*, 278.

97. *EG*, 131.

98. *EG*, 210.

99. *EG*, 277.

100. *EG*, 152.

101. *EG*, 188.

102. *EG*, 138.

103. *EG*, 138.

104. *EG*, 223.

105. *EG*, 240.

106. *EG*, 277f.

107. *EG*, 279.

108. *LA*, 335.

A Reader's Bibliography

This list includes selected materials useful to the reader who wishes to extend his knowledge of Moravia, Pavese, and Vittorini. In the case of the basic works of the three novelists, the dates of Italian versions are those of original publication in volume form; for English translations the date of the most conveniently available translation has been used.

MODERN ITALIAN FICTION: GENERAL

Fernandez, Dominique, *Le roman italien et la crise de la conscience moderne*. Paris: Grasset, 1958. Translated in Italian as *Il romanzo italiano e la crisi della coscienza moderna*. Milan: Lerici Editore, 1960.

Pacifici, Sergio, *A Guide to Contemporary Italian Literature*. New York and Cleveland: Meridian Books, 1962.

————, *The Modern Italian Novel from Manzoni to Svevo*. Carbondale, Ill.: Southern Illinois University Press, 1967.

Piccioni, Leone, *La narrativa italiana tra romanzo e racconti*. Milan: Mondadori, 1959.

Whitfield, John H., *A Short History of Italian Literature*. Penguin Books, 1960.

Wilkens, Ernest H., *A History of Italian Literature*. Cambridge, Mass.: Harvard University Press, 1964.

ALBERTO MORAVIA

Basic Works in Italian and English

Gli indifferenti. Milan: Editrice Alpes, 1928.

The Time of Indifference. New York: Farrar, Straus and Young, 1953.

La bella vita. Lanciano, Editore Carabba, 1935.

Le ambizione sbagliate. Milan: Mondadori, 1935.

Wheel of Fortune. New York: Viking, 1937. Also *Mistaken Ambitions*. New York: Signet, 1965.

I sogni del pigro. Milan: Mondadori, 1940.

La mascherata. Milan: Mondadori, 1941.

The Fancy Dress Party. New York: Farrar, Straus and Young, 1952.

L'amante infelice. Milan: Mondadori, 1943.

L'epidemia. Rome: Documento, 1944.

Due cortigiane. Rome: L'Acquario, 1945.

Agostino. Milan: Bompiani, 1945.

Two Adolescents. New York: Farrar, Straus, 1950. (Includes *La disubbidienza*).

La romana. Milan: Bompiani, 1947.

The Woman of Rome. New York: Farrar, Straus, 1949.

La disubbidienza. Milan: Bompiani, 1948.

Included as *Luca* in *Two Adolescents* (see above).

L'amore coniugale e altri racconti. Milan: Bompiani, 1949.

Conjugal Love. New York: Farrar, Straus and Young, 1951.

Il conformista. Milan: Bompiani, *Racconti*. Milan: Bompiani, 1951.

The Conformist. New York: Farrar, Straus and Young, 1951.

Il ˙disprezzo. Milan: Bompiani, 1954.

A Ghost at Noon. New York: Farrar, Straus and Young, 1955.

Racconti romani. Milan: Bompiani, 1954.

Roman Tales. New York: Farrar, Straus and Young, 1956.

La ciociara. Milan: Bompiani, 1957.

Two Women. New York: Farrar, Straus and Cudahy, 1958.

Nuovi racconti romani. Milan: Bompiani, 1959.

More Roman Tales. New York: Farrar, Straus, 1964.

La noia. Milan: Bompiani, 1960.

The Empty Canvas. New York: Farrar, Straus, 1961.

L'automa. Milan: Bompiani, 1963.

The Fetish and Other Stories. New York: Farrar, Straus & Giroux, 1964.

L'uomo come fine e altri saggi. Milan: Bompiani, 1964.

Man as an End. New York: Farrar, Straus & Giroux, 1965.

L'attenzione. Milan: Bompiani, 1965.

The Lie. New York: Farrar, Straus & Giroux, 1966.

Una cosa è una cosa. Milan: Bompiani, 1967.

Selected Criticism

Baldanza, Frank, "The Classicism of Alberto Moravia." *Modern Fiction Studies,* III (1958), 309ff.

Bergin, Thomas, "The Moravian Muse." *The Virginia Quarterly Review,* XXIX (1953), 215ff.

Cecchetti, Giovanni, "Alberto Moravia." *Italica,* XXX (Sept. 1953), 153ff.

Dego, Giuliano, *Moravia.* London: Oliver and Boyd, 1967.

Del Buono, Oreste, ed., *Moravia.* Milan: Feltrinelli Editore (series La Biblioteca Ideale No. 1), 1962.

Grisi, Francesco, *Incontri e occasioni.* Milan: Ceschina, 1965.

Heiney, Donald, "Moravia's America," in *America in Modern Italian Literature.* New Brunswick, N.J.: Rutgers University Press, 1964.

Lewis, R. W. B., "Eros and Existence," in *The Picaresque Saint.* New York: Lippincott, 1949.

Limentani, Alberto, *Alberto Moravia tra esistenza e realtà.* Venice: Neri Pozza Editore, 1962.

Pacifici, Sergio, "The Fiction of Alberto Moravia: Portrait of a Wasteland." *Modern Language Quarterly,* XVI (March 1955), 68ff.

————, "Alberto Moravia's L'Automa: A Study in Estrangement." *Symposium,* XVIII (1964), 357ff.

Sanguineti, Edoardo, *Alberto Moravia.* Milan: Mursia Editore, 1962.

Schettino, Franca, "Contemporary Italian Writers: Alberto Moravia, a Monographic Study." *Italian Quarterly VIII* (1964), 65ff.

CESARE PAVESE

Basic Works in Italian and English

Lavorare stanca. Florence: Solaria, 1936; Enlarged edition, Turin: Einaudi, 1943.

Paesi tuoi. Turin: Einaudi, 1941.

The Harvesters. London: Peter Owen, 1961.

La spiaggia. Rome: *Lettere D'oggi,* 1942.

The Beach. London: Peter Owen, 1963. (Includes *Fuoco grande*).

Feria d'agosto. Turin: Einaudi, 1946.

Il compagno. Milan: Einaudi, 1947.

The Comrade. London: Peter Owen, 1959.

Dialoghi con Leucò. Turin: Einaudi, 1947.

Dialogues with Leucò. Ann Arbor: University of Michigan Press, 1965.

Prima che il gallo canti. Turin: Einaudi, 1949. (Includes *Il carcere* and *La casa in collina*).

The Political Prisoner. London: Peter Owen, 1955. The House on the Hill. New York: Walker, 1961.

La bella estate. Turin: Einaudi, 1949. Includes title novel plus *Il diavolo sulle colline* and *Tra donne sole.*

The Beautiful Summer (with *The Political Prisoner*). London: Peter Owen, 1955. *The Devil in the Hills.* New York: Farrar, Straus, 1959. *Among Women Only.* New York: Farrar, Straus, 1959.

La luna e i falò. Turin: Einaudi, 1950.

The Moon and the Bonfires. New York: Farrar, Straus and Young, 1953.

Verrà la morte e avrà i tuoi occhi. Turin: Einaudi, 1951.

La letteratura americana e altri saggi. Turin: Einaudi, 1951.

Il mestiere di vivere (*Diario 1935-50*). Turin: Einaudi, 1952.

The Burning Brand: Diaries 1935-50. New York: Walker, 1961.

Notte di festa. Turin: Einaudi, 1952.

Fuoco grande (with Bianca Garufi). Turin: Einaudi, 1959.

Racconti. Turin: Einaudi, 1960.

Romanzi (2 volumes). Turin: Einaudi, 1961.

Poesie. Turin: Einaudi, 1961.

Poesie edite e inedite. Turin: Einaudi, 1962.

Lettere (2 volumes). Turin: Einaudi, 1966.

Included in *The Beach* (see above).

The Selected Works of Cesare Pavese, tr. and ed. by R. W. Flint. New York: Farrar, Straus and Giroux, 1968. Includes *The Beach, The House on the Hill, Among Women Only,* and *The Devil in the Hills.*

Selected Criticism

Baden, Hans Jürgen, *Literatur und Selbsmord.* Stuttgart: Ernest Klett Verlag, 1965.

Biasin, Gian-Paolo, "Il rapporto Io-Altri nei romanzi 'politici' di Cesare Pavese." *Italica,* XLIII (June 1966), 141ff.

———, "The Smile of the Gods." *Italian Quarterly,* X (1966), 3ff.

Calvino, Italo, "Pavese e i sacrifici umani." *Revue des Etudes Italiennes,* XII (1966), 107ff.

Chase, Richard H., "Cesare Pavese and the American Novel." *Studi Americani,* III (1957), 347ff.

Fernandez, Dominique, *L'échec de Pavese.* Paris: Grasset, 1968.

Fiedler, Leslie, "Introducing Cesare Pavese." *Kenyon Review,* XVI (1964), 536ff.

Freccero, John, "Mythos and Logos: The Moon and the Bonfires." *Italian Quarterly,* IV (1961), 3ff.

Guiducci, Armanda, *Il mito Pavese*. Florence: Vallecchi Editore, 1967.

Heiney, Donald, "The Moon and the Bonfires," in *America in Modern Italian Literature*. New Brunswick, N.J.: Rutgers University Press, 1964.

Hood, Stuart, "A Protestant Without God: On Cesare Pavese." *Encounter*, XXVI (1966), 41ff.

Lajolo, Davide, *Il "vizio assurdo."* Milan: Il Saggiatore, 1960.

Mollia, Franco, *Cesare Pavese*. Florence: La Nuova Italia Editrice, 1963.

Norton, Peter M., "Cesare Pavese and the American Nightmare." *Modern Language Notes*, 77 (1962), 24ff.

Rimanelli, Giose, "The Conception of Time and Language in the Poetry of Cesare Pavese." *Italian Quarterly*, VIII (1965), 14ff.

Tondo, Michele, *Itinerario di Cesare Pavese*. Padua: Liviana Editrice, 1965.

See also *Sigma* 3/4 (Silva Editore, Turin), a special number devoted to Pavese.

ELIO VITTORINI

Basic Works in Italian and English

Piccola borghesia. Florence: Solaria, 1931.

Viaggio in Sardegna. Florence: Parenti, 1936

Americana. Milan: Bompiani, 1940. (Vittorini edited only).

Il garofano rosso. Milan: Mondadori, 1948.

The Red Carnation. Norfolk, Conn.: New Directions, 1952.

Conversazione in Sicilia. Milan: Bompiani, 1941.

In Sicily. Norfolk, Conn.: New Directions, 1949. Also *Conversation in Sicily*. Penguin, 1961.

Uomini e no. Milan: Bompiani, 1945.

Il Sempione strizza l'occhio al Fréjus. Milan: Bompiani, 1947.

The Twilight of the Elephant. Norfolk, Conn.: New Directions, 1951.

Le donne di Messina. Milan: Bompiani, 1949. Revised version, 1964.

Erica e i suoi fratelli; La Garibaldina. Milan: Bompiani, 1956.

The Dark and the Light. Norfolk, Conn.: New Directions, 1960.

Diario in pubblico. Milan: Bompiani, 1957.

Le due tensioni: appunti per una ideologia della letteratura. Milan: Il Saggiatore, 1967.

Selected Criticism

Addamo, Sebastiano, *Vittorini e la narrativa siciliana contemporanea.* Caltanisetta: Sciascia Editore, 1962.

Bocelli, Arnaldo, "L'Arte di Vittorini." *Mondo,* XVIII (1966), 9ff.

Cambon, Glauco, "Elio Vittorini: Between Poverty and Wealth." *Wisconsin Studies in Contemporary Literature,* III (1962), 20ff.

De Tommaso, Piero, "Elio Vittorini." *Belfagor,* XX (1965), 552ff.

Ferretti, Giancarlo, "Una conversazione cominciata in Sicilia." *Rinascita,* XXIII (1966), 25ff.

Forti, Marco, "Vittorini e *Le donne di Messina.*" *Letteratura,* XXIX (1965), 70ff.

Heiney, Donald, "Vittorini, the Opera, and the Fifth Dimension." *College English,* XVII (1966), 135ff.

Lewis, R. W. B., "Elio Vittorini." *Italian Quarterly,* IV (1961), 55ff.

Pacifici, Sergio, "Understanding Vittorini 'Whole.'" *Italian Quarterly,* I (1958), 95ff.

Pampaloni, Geno, "I nomi e le lacrime di Elio Vittorini." *Il Ponte,* XI (1949), 2053ff.

Pautasso, Sergio, *Elio Vittorini.* Milan: Borla Editore, 1967.

Piccioni, Leone, "Coerenza di Vittorini," in *Sui contemporanei.* Rome: Fabbri Editore, 1953.

See also the special number of *Il menabò* (10, 1967) devoted to brief pieces by Vittorini and criticism of his work by others.

Index

Index